CW01123876

**Financial Times Pitman Publishing books**

We work with leading authors to develop the strongest ideas in business and finance, bringing cutting-edge thinking and best practice to a global market.

We craft high quality books which help readers to understand and apply their content, whether studying or at work

To find out more about Financial Times Pitman Publishing books, visit our website:

www.ftmanagement.com

# THE
# INFLUENTIAL
# STRATEGIST

Using the
power of paradox in
strategic thinking

Patrick J. Thurbin

**FINANCIAL TIMES**
PITMAN PUBLISHING

**FINANCIAL TIMES**
# MANAGEMENT
LONDON · SAN FRANCISCO
KUALA LUMPUR · JOHANNESBURG

*Financial Times Management delivers the knowledge, skills and understanding that enable students, managers and organisations to achieve their ambitions, whatever their needs, wherever they are.*

London Office:
128 Long Acre, London WC2E 9AN
Tel: +44 (0)171 447 2000
Fax: +44 (0)171 240 5771
Website: www.ftmanagement.com

*A Division of Financial Times Professional Limited*

First published in Great Britain in 1998

© Financial Times Professional Limited 1998

The right of Patrick J. Thurbin to be identified as Author of this Work has been asserted by him in accordance with the Copyright, Designs and Patents Act 1988.

ISBN 0 273 63097 0

*British Library Cataloguing in Publication Data*
A CIP catalogue record for this book can be obtained from the British Library.

All rights reserved; no part of this publication may be reproduced, stored in a retrieval system, or transmitted in any form or by any means, electronic, mechanical, photocopying, recording, or otherwise without either the prior written permission of the Publishers or a licence permitting restricted copying in the United Kingdom issued by the Copyright Licensing Agency Ltd, 90 Tottenham Court Road, London W1P 0LP. This book may not be lent, resold, hired out or otherwise disposed of by way of trade in any form of binding or cover other than that in which it is published, without the prior consent of the Publishers.

1 3 5 7 9 10 8 6 4 2

Typeset by M Rules
Printed and bound in Great Britain by
Biddles Ltd, Guildford and King's Lynn

*The Publishers' policy is to use paper manufactured from sustainable forests.*

## ABOUT THE AUTHOR

**Patrick J. Thurbin** is the Director of the Management and Business Development Research Unit and Principal Business Consultant at the Business School, Kingston University in the UK.

He combines a wide range of consulting assignments in national and multinational organizations with research and lecturing at the University. His academic activities provide an exposure to management thinking from many cultures. He is a Director of the well-established Open Learning MBA programme at the University, lecturing in strategy; a Visiting Professor in Management at Grand Valley State University in Michigan, USA; and lectures on innovation on the Open University MBA programme and in business strategy at the prestigious Academy of National Economy in Moscow, Russia.

His research on ways in which business growth can be supported by leveraging organizational knowledge is extensive. His book *Leveraging Knowledge* (also published by Financial Times Pitman Publishing) provides an international benchmark in this area. Consulting activities range over industries as diverse as aerospace, retail and distribution, software development and civil engineering where business growth is the main focus.

Before becoming an academic he spent some 20 years working in the UK, Europe and the USA, gaining practical management and business experience in production, research and systems development.

*This book is dedicated to my wife Daisy whose inspiration and support continues to make every day a pleasure.*

# CONTENTS

| | |
|---|---|
| Acknowledgements | x |
| Preface | xi |
| Introduction | xvi |

## Part I
## THE WORLD OF THE STRATEGIC THINKER

**1 Competitive advantage and growth**    3
- Thinking about and tackling the competition    5
- Conventional models used to guide thinking and analysis    11
- Competition viewed from various levels    19
- Innovation leads to sustainable competitive advantage    23
- Firms compete in national and global arenas    26

**2 Agreeing what counts**    29
- Identifying the owners    31
- Corporate level strategies and adding value    33
- Stakeholder analysis determines the pay-off    38
- Social consciousness through corporate strategy    40

**3 Forecasting the future**    43
- The global economic dimension    45
- Competing at international levels    48
- Forecasting the future or building scenarios    53
- Planning as thinking    56

**4 Chaos or control**    59
- Riding the waves or navigating the ship    61
- Logic is still a powerful tool    64
- Empowerment and control    66
- Innovation as a challenge to implementation    69

## 5 Myths and realities of strategic planning — 73
Planning as strategy — 75
The manager as a strategic thinker — 78
Making sense of a complex and dynamic organization — 81
Dialogue helps to create new knowledge — 83

# Part II
# STRATEGIC THINKING REVISITED

## 6 Understanding the organizational mind — 89
The truly dynamic organization — 91
The transition from evolution to revolution — 96

## 7 Learning the business lexicon — 103
Language as organization — 105
The impact of language on strategic thinking — 114

## 8 Learning from the strategy gurus — 121
Simon on decision making and choice — 123
Ansoff on planning — 125
Porter on competitive positioning — 126
Mintzberg on emergent strategies — 127
Quinn on logical incrementalism — 127
Peters on chaos — 128
Hamel and Prahalad on competence — 129
Ohmae on critical issues — 131
Goold, Campbell and Alexander on corporate parenting — 132
Senge on learning organizations — 135
Heijden, Wack and De Geus on scenario planning — 137
Nonaka and Takeuchi on knowledge creation — 139

## Part III
## UNDERSTANDING THE POWER OF PARADOXICAL THINKING

**9 An introduction to the use of paradox** — 147
- The paradoxical statement — 150
- The use of tension — 153
- The use of premise — 158

**10 Constructing and deconstructing paradoxes** — 161
- Mastering the skills of organizational dialogue and debate — 164
- Using paradox in organizational settings: some guides and exercises — 208

## Part IV
## HARNESSING THE POWER OF PARADOXICAL THINKING

**11 Developing your power as a strategic thinker** — 219
- Identifying your top ten paradoxes — 225
- Underlying perspectives that drive the key paradoxes — 235

## Part V
## APPLYING PARADOXICAL THINKING IN YOUR ORGANIZATION

**12 Implementing a development programme** — 245
- An audit of organizational paradoxes — 248
- Workshop 1: Creating sustainable competitive advantage — 254
- Workshop 2: Implementation of strategies — 260
- Workshop 3: The scenario approach to creating new thinking — 267
- Summary — 273

Epilogue — 275

Index — 277

# ACKNOWLEDGEMENTS

I am indebted to Dean Miles and all my colleagues at Kingston University Business School who gave me the space to think and contributed to the ideas that resulted in this book. Also to my publisher Pradeep Jethi who provided both the creative tension and professional backup that underpinned the writing process. Acknowledgement is also due to the publishing team at Financial Times Management, Anne Hendrie Williams for editing the original manuscript and Linda Dhondy the project manager.

A book such as this must also acknowledge the many writers, researchers and practising managers whose thoughts have become embedded in my own. Many of these are referenced in the text and are so famous that to mention them here would be both redundant and pretentious. But I would particularly wish to acknowledge the impact that Gary Hamel, Keith Prahalad, Michael Porter, James Quinn and Henry Mintzberg have had on my efforts to progress the art of strategic thinking.

On a more personal level I would like to acknowledge the help of the many CEOs and individuals who have given their time to talk through the ideas contained in this book. Also particular thanks to my close colleagues John Cheetham, Derek Taylor, Ian Hinton and Ken Harry to whom I will be forever indebted.

# PREFACE

This book provides a breakthrough approach for the reader who seeks excellence and mastery in strategic thinking. The approach relies on gaining a deep understanding of how a paradoxical statement can be used to frame arguments, and then harnessing the tension that this represents in an organization. The power of the paradox is that it represents a statement containing contradictory and apparently mutually exclusive propositions that are promoted as able to operate at the same point in time. For example:

> *We need clear corporate policies and strong central control, while promoting entrepreneurial behaviour across all of our activities.*

Many of us will have heard this form of argument. But what we rarely do is see it as a source of tension that can be harnessed and used to promote new thinking. In this book we will show how such paradoxical statements can be constructed and deconstructed in order to create new strategic thinking.

Strategic thinking is about finding original ways of structuring and representing the complexity and mess that are at the root of modern organizational endeavour. In this book, the strategic thinker is cast as both a sense maker and a custodian of the organizational consciousness. The outcome of the thinker's efforts must be superior organizational performance. But the role is far less instrumental than that of the conventional strategic planner. These are fairly grand and sweeping generalizations to make about a subject that many managers describe as being a mixture of corporate planning fantasy and unsubstantiated exhortations aimed at keeping the management gurus wealthy. You may well be one of those managers. Someone who relies on pragmatism and healthy doses of cynicism to help deal with the ambiguities and uncertainties of organizational life. But in spite of this experience, everyone wants to believe in the power of strategic thinking.

Unfortunately once someone claims that they have found a winning approach then they are seen as crazy or at best naive. It comes as no surprise that everyone is seeking the 'magic bullet' that will bring order to unmanageable chaos. Contemporary pundits exhort 'living on the edge' and 'embracing chaos' as the way to create winning strategies. But the ease with which this is said belies the complexity and dangers that come with this approach. This book will show the reader how to move towards this 'edge' while maintaining the stability that is essential for sustained and profitable growth. Not a miracle cure, but a safe and well-considered approach that incorporates the best thinking and experiences of our time.

Experience tells a manager that reasoned argument and logic are the only real way to gain co-operation and support from others. The extensive use of approaches such as investment appraisal, forecasting and even business process re-engineering is a testimony to the comfort sought from certainty and order. The experts and influencers are able to convince others, through the use of strong argument often presented as a premise, that their way provides the greatest chance of success. In this book we will show that the complexity and dynamics of the modern environment now calls for a much more searching and open approach. The 'game' is too important to be handed over to the organization's orators. New strategic thinking is today's strategic imperative. Once again easy to say, but this book shows how to harness the best of the current thinking and theorizing around strategy making to a new approach that taps into the power of organizational paradoxes.

Strategic management is in many successful organizations an obvious and explicit process. In others it is hidden, intuitive and essentially tacit, the strategies often being driven by one or two power figures and shared only in terms of executive control. For some, hiding the thinking behind strategies is a deliberate political decision. It would be naive and unhelpful to deny that this was sometimes the reality. But the messages in this book can be applied to advantage in all of these cases. Thousands of companies, represented by many more thousands of managers, will ensure that strategic thinking and the more visible strategic management activity remains a complex and ever-changing art form. But within all of this there exists an underlying structure and force that drives this strategic thinking. It is these drivers and their representation through the use of argument, premise and paradox that provides the new ground that has to be tackled by the strategic thinker who wishes to excel. Identifying the ideas encapsulated in a universal set of organizational paradoxes creates the map that will lead the reader to a breakthrough in contemporary strategic thinking.

The effective strategic thinker lives in a world that thrives on arguing about trade-offs. You may reflect on how, when faced with a strategic issue, your own thinking proceeds. A general model could be as follows, albeit conducted in an intuitive flash:

- What is the key issue?
- What outcome is being sought?
- Who are the key players?
- How are the arguments being presented?
- What are my views concerning these arguments?
- Which extreme do I support?
- How can I best present my argument for one or other of the conflicting ideas?

Bring five managers together and present them with a strategic issue and you will get more than five suggestions on how to develop winning strategies. For example, when faced with a corporate turnaround situation where share prices are falling and the competition is rampant, the managers are likely to argue over trade-offs between:

- strengthening central control versus encouraging more local decision making;
- communicating a clear corporate business message on how to survive *versus* opening up the debate and seeking new ideas on survival;
- emphasizing the use of clear management processes *versus* encouraging on-the-spot decision making;
- encouraging competition between product managers and divisions *versus* seeking co-operation and the benefits from sharing resources and knowledge.

The strong arguments would rage on. The less extreme strategic situations are also likely to find managers polarized over trade-offs such as:

- the need to reduce the costs while producing a world-beating quality product;
- promoting a brand image while wanting to be recognized in the marketplace for innovations and breakthrough products;
- recognizing the need to develop core competencies while wanting to take advantage of outsourcing and strategic alliances.

The concerted drive or focus for managing these conflicting ideas is to achieve superior performance for the organization and a position of sustainable competitive advantage. This applies to both profit and not-for-profit organizations. In not-for-profit organizations the focus may be more on gaining resources and how to attract key staff than on profit and competitors, but it is still competition. The strategic thinker is thus charged with promoting superior organizational performance while managing and balancing the interests of a wide group of stakeholders, becoming in effect ultimately responsible for the health of the corporate body. To do this the strategic thinker has to be able to create a process that attracts support, leads to action and results in superior organizational performance. This represents a formidable but exciting challenge, perhaps the ultimate management challenge.

The key to achieving this is to be able to identify the way in which ideas, embedded in the use of paradoxical statements, are being used and to harness the resulting tension to good effect. This is a key skill that the strategic thinker has to develop, and the exercises provided in the book will make this possible. Through learning how to create and manage organizational dialogue, where the outcomes are less prescribed, the new strategic thinking that will distinguish the organization from its competitors, can be found. The reader will learn how to harness the tensions that are present in all organizations and use this to influence strategic actions and achieve breakthrough performance.

As with any activity that adds value, there is a need to challenge the existing organizational wisdom and contemporary views as to best practice. Historically, this has been the domain of the change agent or facilitator. In this book, you are invited to adopt a paradigm shift to this view. The change agent approach relies on someone determining what end goal or intermediary set of behaviours are required for success, and how best to get there. The paradox approach relies on harnessing the on-going and inherent tensions brought about by the collective thinking of the organization, tapping into the very essence that has created best practice and empowering the organizational knowledge base.

Best practice, captured in the organizational knowledge base and processes, represents the outcome of years of experience from managers, academics and the gurus. This knowledge must be utilized and leveraged to advantage. But it is vital that change for change's sake is not allowed to jeopardize that hard-won experience. Here the strategic thinker has to help identify where that very learning is being blocked by the closed arguments and one-sided debates that put the organization at risk. How to move from debate to dialogue is one of the key benefits to be gained from studying this book.

Aggressive competitor activities, trends and moves in stakeholder values, and the industry and global dynamics will increasingly call for new thinking around current and planned strategies. All our experiences and senses tell us that this cannot be managed by one person, no matter how charismatic or powerful that person may be. The strategic thinker thus has to be able to help other managers to see the anomalies in their business and organizational activities as a potential source of new learning, and then to be able to present these anomalies in a form that can exist alongside some deeply held values and beliefs. The strategic thinker has to learn how to challenge the very perspectives that they themselves hold and those of other managers and colleagues. The use of organizational paradoxes becomes the vehicle for influencing these mental models and perspectives. This book shows the reader how this can be tackled and applied to power figures, groups and colleagues in a way that makes change both sensible and reliable. Conventional strategic management approaches, including planning and control models are the means through which these changes will be processed, and the three outline workshop programmes in *Chapter 12* provide a guide on how to match conventional strategic management to this new approach.

Harnessing the power of paradox in strategic thinking thus becomes a priming agent or a front-end input for well-understood strategic management processes. The strength of the approach is that it does not challenge existing processes. It becomes a stimulant to enhance breakthrough strategic thinking that can then be integrated into the mainstream business thinking and action processes. If at times you have difficulty framing or reconciling the inherent contradictions that arise when formulating strategy or want to have a once-and-for-all understanding of the strategic thinking process, then this book is for you.

# INTRODUCTION

I have written this book for the manager and business owner who is interested in improving their skill as a strategic thinker. More importantly to provide an approach that will enable you to stimulate new strategic thinking in yourself and with colleagues that will translate into tangible benefits. There are three sources that we tap into in order to create new knowledge. We can:

- repackage the knowledge that we already have and use it in novel ways;
- seek new knowledge from outside of our experiences to date;
- engage in dialogue and conversation with colleagues that challenges our perceptions and mental models and leads to new thinking.

All three are powerful approaches, but it is the last that is the focus of this book.

Thinking about business and how to best develop organizational performance is something that managers pride themselves on being able to do well, although the myriad of texts, journals and management magazines, backed up with academic studies and executive courses, tell us that the 'truth' has yet to be discovered. Is strategic thinking a bit like seeking the alchemist's stone, the holy grail which all managers are inspired to seek? This book will help you to dispel some of the myths, confirm your own gut feel and experience and provide the means to become a master of strategic thinking.

The tradition in management and business is to support the notions of competition and win/lose. We are encouraged to find ways of getting the best deal, either for ourselves, or for the organization. Managers are constantly trying to find the ideal or at least the optimal approach to adopt, while the arguments and persuasive cases that are used are based on a storehouse of beliefs such as: whether to support central control or local autonomy, short-term profitability or long-term investment. We are taught to select and make choices that will ensure survival and eventually success. This creates a world in which the manager is surrounded by an apparently endless set of contradictory situations. It is this that creates the opportunity and the excitement for the strategic thinker.

## INTRODUCTION

This book represents a break with tradition. It provides a unique opportunity to gain the skills required to challenge the conventions that have enshrined management as the pursuit of opposites. The reader is encouraged to explore the complex phenomena found in organizational settings using the notion of the paradox. Fundamentally, a paradox embraces clashing ideas. When we present two apparently mutually exclusive but equally attractive ideas in a single statement we create a paradox. It is the skill of being able to function while holding these contradictions in our minds, the Janussian phenomenon, that will be developed by the reader. The power that resides in capturing these paradoxes is that they represent a metaphor for the organization. This is a serious book, in that I am inviting you to grapple with some difficult concepts and notions, but it is also practical. Managers are capable of thinking deeply about their world of work, but they also know that outcome and performance are the end-products towards which they must strive. This applies equally to a charity, a hospital or what some might see as hard-nosed business. The book provides the means of both gathering the understanding, practising the skills and applying the learning for the benefit of the stakeholders.

The pay-off from studying this book is to gain excellence in strategic thinking. I am deliberately presenting a view of strategy making, and subsequent implementation, that highlights the cognitive and sense-making aspects of the manager. The way in which sense or interpretations are made of complex situations is, I believe, the basis for subsequent action and continuous learning. The reader is therefore encouraged to use this book as a means of gaining a deeper insight into their personal sense-making approaches and those used by others with whom they work. The aim is to help the reader develop the skills required to recognize the mindsets, language, models and arguments being used by other managers involved in strategy making. A clear guide is presented on how to harness the power of the paradox as a metaphor for understanding organizational complexity. This approach will rapidly improve the quality of your strategic thinking.

Strategic management is in many organizations an obvious and explicit process. In others it is a more hidden, intuitive, tacit and taken-for-granted activity. Often the key strategies are created and driven by one or two power figures and shared with others only in terms of executive control. In some organizations the strategic process involves a high level of analytical work, but in others a sensing and more qualitative approach dominates. Both the quantitative and qualitative approaches to analysis find their supporters in organizations. There are exponents of strategies that stem from the discovery of hard and unambiguous data and those who value the softer signals. By harnessing the power of the paradox, the reader will discover how to polarize the ideas that are driven from a desire for order and the completion of the task with those that favour exploration. You will also be able to recognize and frame those ideas that derive from a deep attachment to the traditional management conventions and those that seek to embrace radical innovation and change. Polarizing these contrasting perspectives will reveal the structure on which the tensions in the organization have been built. Balancing these tensions in order to move the organizational thinking in ways that will result in superior performance will be the pay-off for this effort.

## A guide to the book

I am assuming that you are a busy and experienced manager, pragmatic in your approach and prepared to commit time to study as long as the benefits are able to outweigh the effort. This guide will help you to find your way to the areas that suit your critical thinking and quest for accelerated learning. You can use the guide shown opposite along with the text that follows.

The book is presented in five parts:

1. The world of the strategic thinker
2. Strategic thinking revisited
3. Understanding the power of strategic thinking
4. Harnessing the power of paradoxical thinking
5. Applying paradoxical thinking in your organization.

The structure of the book can be understood by reading the few italicized paragraphs that follow on page xx.

INTRODUCTION

# A GUIDE TO THE BOOK: THE POWER CYCLE

## Strategic thinking as a driver of business growth and sustainable competitive advantage

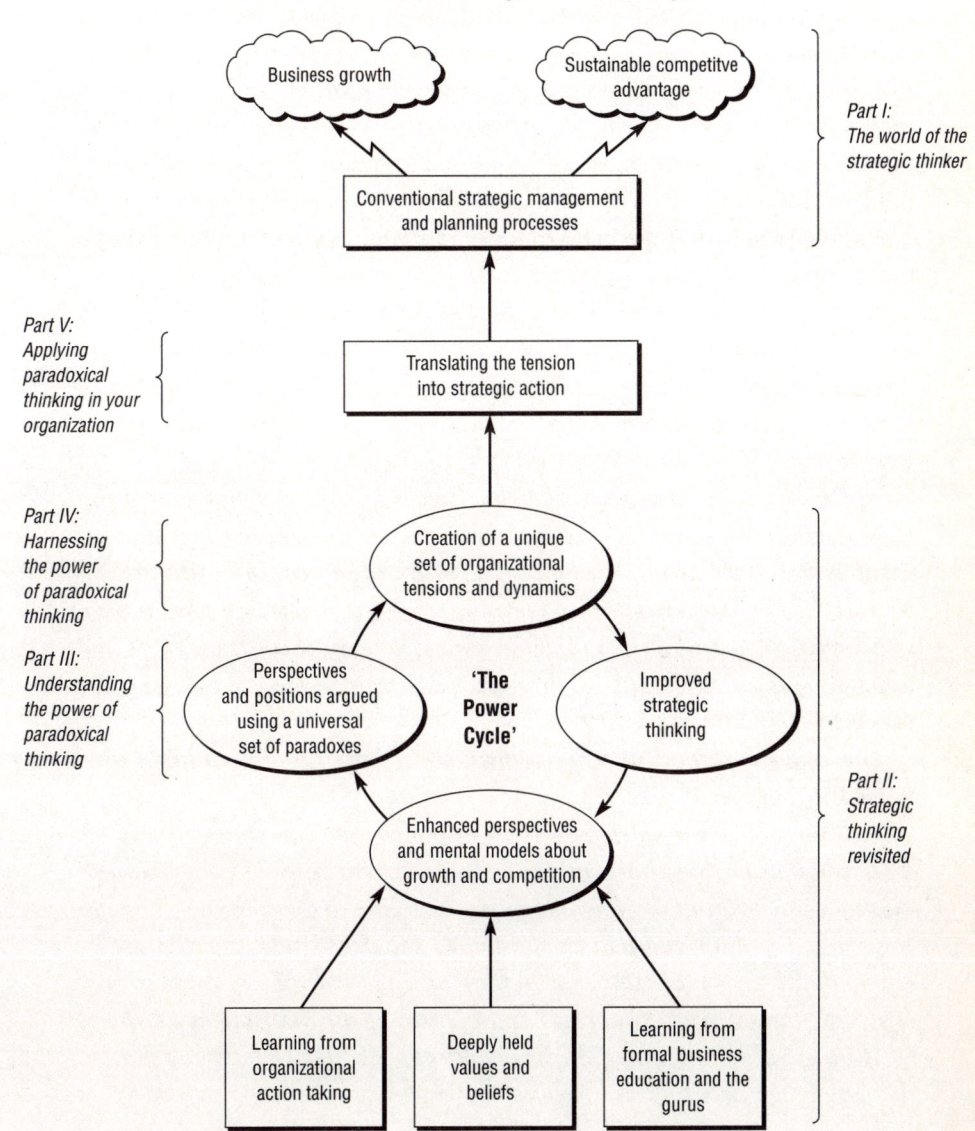

- Business growth
- Sustainable competitve advantage

Conventional strategic management and planning processes

*Part I: The world of the strategic thinker*

Translating the tension into strategic action

*Part V: Applying paradoxical thinking in your organization*

Creation of a unique set of organizational tensions and dynamics

*Part IV: Harnessing the power of paradoxical thinking*

Perspectives and positions argued using a universal set of paradoxes

'The Power Cycle'

Improved strategic thinking

*Part III: Understanding the power of paradoxical thinking*

Enhanced perspectives and mental models about growth and competition

- Learning from organizational action taking
- Deeply held values and beliefs
- Learning from formal business education and the gurus

*Part II: Strategic thinking revisited*

## INTRODUCTION

*Organizations use a variety of approaches to creating, developing and implementing strategies that they believe will ensure their survival and growth. Competition and gaining competitive advantage, in a marketplace or industry, are dominant features of the thinking behind the strategy-making process. The notions of satisfying stakeholders, corporate governance and demonstration of a social consciousness are used to temper the cut and thrust of competition. Proponents of a planned approach to securing the future clash with those that favour a more pragmatic and unstructured style. The middle ground is held by those supporting a more incremental or evolutionary approach. This is the conventional and well-documented world of the contemporary strategic thinker. But we need to look closer at some of the influences on the thinker.*

*The strategic thinker uses a set of mental models about how to grow an organization and promote superior performance. These models are underpinned with deeply held values and beliefs. The models will also have been influenced by exposure to formal business education and experience. Within an industry, and the organization itself, there exists a complex language and a set of behavioural norms that both help and hinder the development of new thinking. The dominant feature of argument and debate around how to grow the organization is the use of opposites. These are framed and presented as a collection of paradoxical statements. A paradoxical statement is where two contradictory and apparently mutually exclusive propositions are promoted as able to operate at the same point in time.*

*The skill of being able to recognize and frame these paradoxes provides the strategic thinker with a powerful tool. One that can be used to reveal the mindsets and perspectives of colleagues and other managers. The residual tension that surrounds these organizational conversations about opposites, can then be harnessed to create the new strategic thinking. This new thinking will be unique to the organization and must be translated into organizational action and pay-off. The conventional strategic management processes and the use of the instrumental aspects of strategic planning make this translation possible. The approach does not challenge or upset the experience organizations have gained from using conventional strategic management processes. Its purpose is to act as a front-end input or stimulator that promotes enhanced strategic performance. 'The Power Cycle' represents the generation of a unique set of tensions that stimulate and drive strategic action.*

That is the book's structure, and the salient features of each section are provided below to help you plan how to proceed.

**Part I** is aimed at the reader who wants to revisit some of the concepts and approaches that are used in strategy making. It provides a summary of how strategists and their organizations approach the task of gaining competitive advantage. Conventional and well-tested models used by strategy makers are presented to give both an overview and a comfort factor for the reader who is familiar with the topic. We also begin to explore how the use of particular models gives an indication of differences in style between strategic thinkers. For instance in the way that competition is approached. Competition suggests an ability to measure performance and this first section opens up the debate as to 'what really counts'. It highlights questions around:

- who are the owners and who do the managers represent?
- how important is it to consider all of the stakeholders?
- who manages the corporate consciousness?

Strategies are increasingly influenced by what has been called the 'global dimension.' We therefore highlight the features and models that influence thinking in this area to help the reader prepare for some of the more searching debates that will arise in later sections.

We conclude by presenting a head-on clash in how to approach strategy making between those who favour control and logic, and those who favour chaos. We begin to grasp the subtlety of language and see how the use of premise and rhetoric dominate the arena of strategy making. This is a key area for the reader to tackle, as the way that language is used to formulate and win arguments is a skill that has to be understood. Understanding and influencing our own mental models and those of colleagues is at the heart of the work of the contemporary strategic thinker. As we proceed to unravel the use of the paradox you will see how their origins can be found hiding in rhetorical or persuasive statements. This section provides an early insight into how this unravelling process can be tackled.

**Part II** explores the notion that an organization can be said to represent the collective minds of all the players and looks in greater depth at how the organizational language impacts on the strategic thinking of the managers. We begin to unravel the 'business lexicon' by looking at the expressions that have become the *lingua franca* of this world of strategy making. For example, we unpack some of the meanings behind popular expressions such as: core competencies, value chains, strategic intent, industry foresight and critical success factors. The argument presented is that language is the essence of an organization and that key paradoxical statements become the organizational metaphor. These paradoxes represent our collective meaning as to what drives the organizational mind.

This section also tackles the realism, or otherwise, of the existence of an organizational mind. If it is sensible to talk about a dynamic organization, then how is that dynamism created and used? If we are to tap into the tensions in an organization, then we need to have a view on the extent to which we can generalize from individual to collective mind sets. The section concludes by looking at the contribution that the management gurus can make to our quest to become masters of strategic thinking. We scan from Mintzberg to Hamel and Prahalad in our search for inspiration and enlightenment. Our purpose, in presenting these expert views, is to reveal the impact that they have on the basic thinking that managers use when approaching strategy making. Understanding the extent and subtlety of this influence becomes the starting point for the new learning that we are inviting you to tackle.

**Part III** takes us to the heart of the world of the paradox. We show how the paradoxes that exist naturally within organizations can be framed, and the tensions that they contain harnessed. Paradoxes represent opposites, and we take some time to explain how it is important to separate out the emotional tension from the creative tension. As someone once said, 'Conflict between ideas is good, conflict between people is bad.' Easier said than done, and the section gives guidance on how to challenge assumptions in a way that will promote this creative tension.

To become a master at anything is not easy: it involves lengthy practice and reflection. We therefore provide plenty of opportunities for deconstructing and constructing paradoxical statements. This is made possible by presenting a series of vignettes or short incidents where you are invited to test your abilities both as a strategic thinker and a master of the paradox. To help the reflective learning process, we have provided a series of summaries that will help you to review your analytical work. The section concludes by showing you how to deal with the paradox, once it has been framed and agreed. This raises your expertise in the use of the paradox to a new level. Providing guidance on how to accept, change the level of application or introduce a time dimension to leverage the power that results from your analytical work. We also provide guidance on how to begin using your new skills in both informal and structured settings.

**Part IV** is unashamedly aimed at developing and honing your skills. It introduces some new thinking about how anomalies arising from the normal organizational activity can be used to trigger the strategic-thinking process, and shows how this can create a new role and way of working for the strategic thinker who is using the power of the paradox. We then help you to identify your 'top ten' paradoxes that you will use in the development workshops that are presented in Part V. We also show how these key paradoxes can be grouped under two main categories, those that emphasize control and those that are about values. This leads to considering how the paradoxes represent multiple frameworks in the organization, and how utilizing the inherent tension provides a unique focus and organizational power.

**Part V** is aimed at helping the reader apply the skills that have been developed to the wider organization. It begins with an audit that can be used by your colleagues to assess their use of the ideas and the balance that they would strike in a series of paradoxes. We then present three distinctive workshops that use the outcomes from this audit as a base on which to develop the strategic-thinking expertise of the team. The first workshop adopts a conventional approach to strategy making. This provides a safe environment in which the team can explore the benefits to be gained from harnessing the power in the paradoxes that have been identified. The workshop objective is how to create sustainable competitive advantage for the organization. The second workshop focuses on the implementation of strategies. This is often the weakest link in the strategic management process, and creates a change of pace as the team now face some hard trade-offs. This workshop introduces a new approach, the 'CRASH test' and the more conventional McKinsey 7–S framework. The team are challenged in having to determine the implementation approaches to be used on the strategies that emerged from Workshop 1. But they are still using the power of the paradox approach and developing their strategic-thinking skills. The third workshop provides an opportunity for the team to stretch their abilities as strategic thinkers. It is based on the scenario approach, to thinking about the future, pioneered at Shell Oil and now used in major leading-edge companies. The workshop takes the team through each stage and here the power of the paradox in strategic thinking is finally tested and captured.

You will find that this book is a challenge in that it confronts many of the 'truths' that you have already discovered about strategic management. Mastery in strategic thinking starts with a confrontation of personal beliefs and the models and perspectives that you use. It then accelerates when you can carry out this confrontation process with colleagues. The pay-off is when it becomes an on-going and natural process for both yourself and the organization. The power of the paradox is central to the development of this mastery, and the outcome is sustainable organizational growth.

# Part I
# THE WORLD OF THE STRATEGIC THINKER

Chapter 1

# COMPETITIVE ADVANTAGE AND GROWTH

Thinking about and tackling the competition  *5*

Conventional models used to guide thinking and analysis  *11*

Competition viewed from various levels  *19*

Innovation leads to sustainable competitive advantage  *23*

Firms compete in national and global arenas  *26*

## THINKING ABOUT AND TACKLING THE COMPETITION

When thinking about competition, managers see rival firms fighting for a bigger market share. They also know that competition will always be a major concern if they are to survive and grow. Although this dominates the thinking of managers, they are often unable to quantify, with any certainty, what it is about the competition that really counts. This feeling of uncertainty and a level of ambiguity as to what counts compels them to focus on being more efficient and think of the things that they need to do to prepare themselves and their firms from some form of attack. Managers find this military metaphor frames their thinking and results in actions and behaviours that convince them that they are doing the right things. More advertising, getting the price right, improving the customer service, making sure that the product is available with the right features and that it is available where the customer can see the benefits.

Managers like to feel comfortable with their views on how best to compete. Straightforward unambiguous views are the ones that sit most easily with the hard-pressed manager. Getting people to standardize work routines and establish logical and measurable short-term objectives dominates everyday thinking. Control and order are favoured over chaos. Making the decisions to pursue the short-term actions that lead to measurable success are made very easily against this background of perceived certainty and order. Thinking and decision-making aimed at longer-term success is for most managers much more difficult. Short-term success predominates as a motivator for most middle managers. This may sound a bit cynical to readers who are perusing this book with a view to gaining a wider insight into how to improve their understanding of strategic thinking. But this view, that managers focus on the short-term, would have been totally accepted some 60 years ago, and the success that some organizations achieved with a totally inward-looking perspective was outstanding in terms of growth and profitability. The firm was seen as a collection of resources that had to be allocated and optimized in order to obtain success. Efficiency and originality in how these resources were acquired and used was a hallmark of the world-beating firm.

Some 30 years ago, the theorists managed to persuade managers and owners that events outside the firm did in fact have a major impact on what went on inside. Rational and logical thinking about how these outside forces impacted on the firm then became the predominant model that was used by managers to make sense of their experiences. Obviously there were many managers who questioned these mindsets or perspectives as their experiences indicated that things were not always so straightforward and deterministic. Unfortunately the swing, as in many enlightened theories, towards a more experiential or human side of how firms can best compete over both the short- and long-term went too far. Harnessing the creativity of everyone in an organization and learning how to effectively communicate at all levels was taken up by many of the gurus and consultants, and the old drive for efficiency and objectivity with the associated measurement and control was thrown out with the proverbial bath water. What has all this got to do with paradoxical thinking?

> **What is it about the competition that really counts?**

Managers have been brought up on a diet of problem identification and decision-making that encourages the cult of choice, or selecting the best among alternatives. We have been talking about choices between how best to view the organization, internal allocation of key resources or gauging the impact of external factors and adjusting to suit; about a perspective of organizational life that favours rationality and control and one that encourages experimentation and embracing elements of chaos; and about a view of organizations as staffed by people who follow orders and instructions according to a set of well-defined plans and those that encourage individuals to create flexible ways of thinking and working. If we asked a group of managers, today, where they stood on these apparently mutually exclusive issues we would find many who would have strong and clear arguments for one or the other and a group who would suggest that both can be seen to have their place according to circumstances.

What we have here is a classic case of managers being unhappy or at least unfamiliar with the way paradox is being used, in conversation and argument, to exert power over the thinking of others. This has important implications for the manager who is considering actions towards helping the firm to become more competitive. To explore this assertion a bit further, we need to have an initial look at this notion of paradox.

A paradox presents an apparent contradiction between equally credible assumptions about a set of issues or conclusions. When taken separately, the arguments supporting these paradoxical assumptions appear sound, but when considered together the arguments appear to be contradictory and mutually exclusive. That is it seems impossible, or at least impractical, that they can both exist at the same time or within the same perspective. Using this broad definition of paradox, it becomes obvious how the use of this notion can be seen as providing a powerful base for argument and persuasion. Once a paradox has been posed and accepted as representing mutually exclusive and contradictory positions, then the arguments and attempts at persuasion can begin.

If on the other hand, we accept that a paradox can exist, then we are starting to adopt a somewhat enlightened, but at the same time risky stance. We are acknowledging that inconsistencies can exist in the way that we make sense of the complexities of organizational life and the rivalry of firms. We are taking a stance that sees opposing views as being able to illuminate and inform the richness of each viewpoint as opposed to being mutually exclusive and requiring an adversarial stance. We are in fact encouraging tension between contrary positions and perspectives in order to enrich each perspective.

To give an example of how paradoxical thinking can add value to our views on organizational activity, we can look at the apparent paradox presented by the cost *versus* quality argument that has pervaded management thinking for generations. In many manufacturing environments, the quest for quality is paramount. The aim is to produce a product that is to specification and that will delight the customer. By this means, less time will be spent on rework and rejection of faulty output. Long production runs that optimize the utilization of machinery and people are the determining criteria for such an approach. However cost is also of paramount importance if the bottom line performance objectives are to be met and a competitive price can be offered in the marketplace. Long runs may lead to lower manufacturing costs, but they can also mean higher finished goods inventory costs, and a reluctance to incorporate changes in the product that might enhance product quality and function.

**A paradox captures the tension between ideas and people.**

The tensions created by holding quality and cost as mutually exclusive goals, a paradoxical situation, have given rise to breakthroughs in thinking about production operations management such as 'just in time.' Here, for example, the set-up costs are considered in relation to stock holding costs and relationships with suppliers negotiated such that the production process can be constantly improved and adapted to suit the efficiency of the operation without jeopardizing the quality of the delivery schedule and hence quality of the service. This approach, that leads to breakthroughs in thinking about manufacturing, relied on accepting the reality of the elements in the paradox, challenging the underlying assumptions and the result was a reconceptualization of the issues of manufacturing that encompassed all of the desired goals as opposed to an approach that sets out to win the argument for one or other of the goals. It is this very act of opening up the debate as opposed to holding on to a few well-tried sets of recipes that the use of paradoxical thinking encourages. The approach is to encourage you to reduce the use that you make of analogy as, although this is a useful way of communicating position and perspective, it is also limiting, as it reduces the set of solutions available to you.

This book will help you to adopt metaphors and handle paradox in ways that will enlighten and enrich the way that you make sense of strategic thinking and organizational complexity. In this section we are setting out to encourage you to challenge the way that you currently view approaches to competition and to rethink some of your accepted recipes.

One wonders what it is that academic study and the management gurus can add to the rich set of recipes for beating the competition that managers hold and use. Managers have experience on their side and apart from learning about currency fluctuations and the best way to set up an overseas trade deal, then things should go fairly smoothly and for most companies they do. The problem begins to show itself after time. Various firms, and their managers, begin to compete in the marketplace. After a while they all reach a plateau through a process of evolution and survival of the fittest and perhaps the luckiest. Those that get ahead, and stay ahead, have just got the edge that makes all the difference. Then firms, or their managers, begin to seek out more subtle winning ways. It is here that the management gurus and the academics begin to earn their place. They themselves are of course also competing and, although one expects a degree of unbiased advice and observation, it is not too difficult to see how persuasion becomes a key skill for the guru, consultant and academic, but hopefully from an ethical or at least professional base. So how do the gurus and management theorists begin to add to the efforts of the front line managers in the competing firms?

Academics like to contrast and compare. Strategy is presented in three ways:

- as being about choice that is based on rationality and a future that can be visualized and determined;
- as managing a series of evolving stages that require the setting up of interlinked processes;
- as a question of reacting to and taking advantage of events that happen outside the firm which are determined by the nature of the industry environment and the ways firms compete in that environment.

By presenting their arguments in this way, they are then able to develop and expand linked theories, knowing that they have already eliminated a whole range of counter arguments and challenges. In this way the territory is mapped out and charted for the intrepid voyager.

Most people would agree that the purpose of competition is to maximize the future share of profits from a particular marketplace. This can then be tackled by adopting a particular view about how best to proceed. The two conventional perspectives used are those adopting a market-based view and those supporting a resource-based view. The market-based view of strategy brings into play an identification of the forces in the marketplace, such as buyer power, supplier power and that the larger the market share, then the more powerful the firm can be. Gaining control or at least influencing those forces to the advantage of the firm are seen as the basis for good strategy making.

The resource-based view of the firm focuses on the way that a firm can acquire and allocate its resources in a way that will give competitive advantage. This brings into play notions of establishing core competencies and leveraging assets and knowledge in the various activities of the firm's operations. The resource-based view sees the firm as a collection of resources that include technical knowledge in the form of patents and licences plus access to finance and to the inherent knowledge and experience held by the incumbent managers and workers. The emphasis is less on gaining copious amounts of such resource, but more on how this resource is leveraged and deployed. The overall approach is to seek less

**Building core competencies appeals to the pioneering spirit.**

resource-intensive ways of achieving strategic objectives. The challenge is to turn intellectual leadership and thinking into market leadership and to do this ahead of the competitors. Although competition and the associated theories tend to take on a present time perspective, there is also a body of research that has argued that competing is more about preparing and managing the future than about dealing with the present.

Competition for the future is presented as taking place at various stages and levels. The stages can be described as:

- competition for intellectual leadership where knowledge and learning are seen as paramount
- competition that will lead to being able to identify and dominate the way in which the products, services and industry itself develops
- competition for a share of the market and for a dominant position in that market.

This approach suggests that firms must concentrate on identifying, developing and/or acquiring sets of core competencies that can be used as the basis from which to begin to shape and dominate the market. Here we see the link between resource-driven perspectives and those of the market perspective. The core competence school has attracted a lot of support with its appeal to the pioneering and value building that most managers like to engage in. This involves auditing the existing skills and competencies, and identifying where these are strengths. Then engaging in mental exercises to synthesize these skills and knowledge. This results in competition with other firms to maximize the share of the market. Sales of the core product is thus maximized by applying these competencies. Notions of expanding market share through promotion of a brand image, that can be marketed on a global basis, form the underpinning to this quest for a grand model or perspective on how to think about competing successfully.

There are obvious caveats to this persuasive model. For example, some firms may have reached an exclusive arrangement with an overseas government, such as Pepsi Cola in India, which gives them enormous advantages over the competition, others may be located where the sources of raw material are or where labour rates give unique advantages. Also firms are increasingly forming coalitions based on core competencies, and in effect forming virtual organizations. Decisions on what to outsource, and how far to downsize and in what areas are all concerns that influence the thinking of managers on how to compete. In all these areas, the academics, gurus and consultants have evidence, views and models that are based on a mixture of pure theory and empirical evidence based on observation, analysis and synthesis. In among all of this, we will continue to argue the presence and value of the power of paradoxical thinking. But first we need to take a more detailed look at how the theories and models are used to present the strategic thinking and competitive strategy arguments.

## CONVENTIONAL MODELS USED TO GUIDE THINKING AND ANALYSIS

Managers use models in order to analyze business situations. They seek hard or quantifiable data for use in the analysis process and add to their interpretations elements of soft data based on their experiences and perspectives. It would also be reasonable to assume that the very choice of which models to use and how to source and select hard data represents a held perspective or initial interpretation. Managers thrive on the use of intuition and soft data. Having to make decisions, select priorities and manage conflicting sets of information engenders this type of responsiveness based on intuition. The presence of paradox again becomes apparent where soft and hard data would at first sight appear to be mutually exclusive phenomena. Most managers would agree that the tensions created by these views have at times lead to a breakthrough in understanding a complex area under analysis. At other times it results in futile argument and unyielding opposition to agreeing a path of action. The myth of the cold-blooded analyst resisting the emotional efforts of the intuitive and synthesizing manager has been immortalized by sayings such as 'paralysis by analysis' and 'seat of the pants management'. We need to develop our views on models and analysis a bit further before we look at some of those used for strategy making and competitive positioning.

Management is sometimes referred to as the art of the generalist. If we have a simple easily definable situation, with interconnections that can readily be understood and agreed upon, and we have a language that is shared by the participants, it is not difficult to think of producing a model with quantifiable parameters. This model can then be used to predict valid outcomes consistently and in a representable way. The question we then have to address is how generalizable is the resulting model to other and perhaps increasingly complex situations? Also, how far can we rely on our intuition to validate these outcomes?

Perhaps our concerns should be centred on how potentially disastrous the outcomes of using pure analysis in a situation would be if a mistake occurred and what would happen if we were relying on intuition and the mistake occurred. Here we would be faced with a high level of uncertainty as to which approach to adopt. Our intuition would suggest that a combination of both approaches would be advisable, the balance depending on the complexity and dynamics of the situation. The analysis would be checked by intuition and then used to inform and enrich the analysis. We need to be cautious, and not to assume that intuition is the only path to creating new knowledge and understanding. This is an easy mistake to make as the experienced managers are those most likely to use intuition. Their limitations may arise from the development of tunnel vision and a reluctance to unlearn previous winning formula.

The analytical process, on the other hand, can be used by the experienced manager to counterbalance the use of intuition through having to make their assumptions explicit. In this way causing them to expose and negotiate the sub-models and the criteria that they are using in their sense-making processes. We are arguing here that the explicit models used by the analyst should be used primarily to inform perspectives on a particular set of features in a situation and not be seen as a superior way to arrive at a solution and a decision. Figure 1.1 illustrates this interplay of analysis and intuition.

> **The trick is fitting the approach to the context.**

An effective manager needs to be able to access and use these analytical tools and also to be capable of recognizing when a rapid response to a situation requires the use of intuition. It is not a question of making the right choice, but knowing which approach is appropriate to the situation in the context being faced. Use of specific models can in themselves be seen as a way to shift the mindsets of managers by making explicit statements about their values and assumptions. We need to look at some of the more popular models that are being used in organizations and at their underlying structures.

Models are often described as being 'at a meta level.' Analysts call

COMPETITIVE ADVANTAGE AND GROWTH

**Figure 1.1**
**STRATEGIC OPPORTUNISM USED BY MANAGERS**

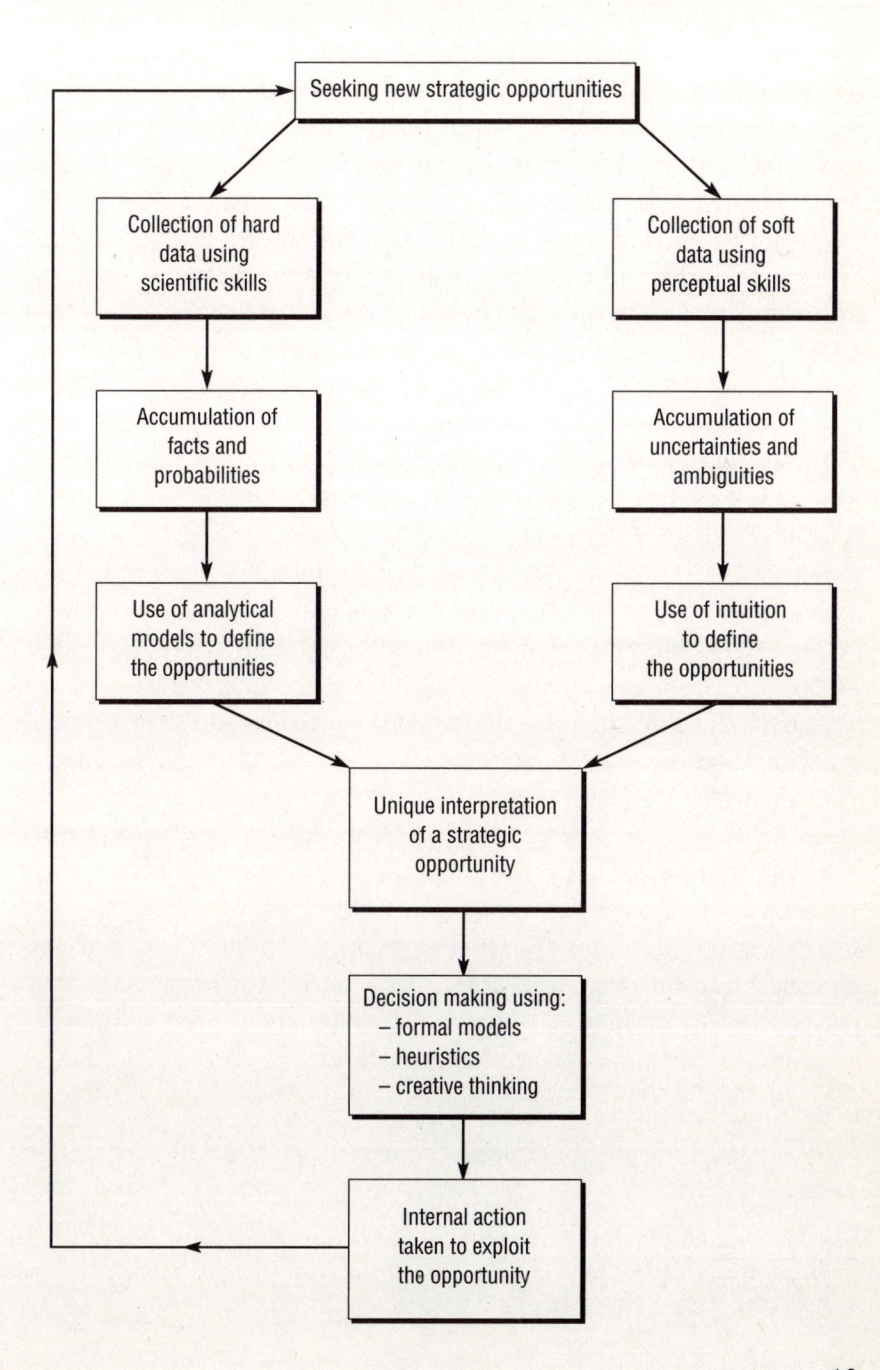

```
                    Seeking new strategic opportunities
                    ↙                              ↘
    Collection of hard                        Collection of soft
    data using                                data using
    scientific skills                         perceptual skills
          ↓                                         ↓
    Accumulation of                           Accumulation of
    facts and                                 uncertainties and
    probabilities                             ambiguities
          ↓                                         ↓
    Use of analytical                         Use of intuition
    models to define                          to define
    the opportunities                         the opportunities
                    ↘                              ↙
                    Unique interpretation
                    of a strategic
                    opportunity
                              ↓
                    Decision making using:
                    – formal models
                    – heuristics
                    – creative thinking
                              ↓
                    Internal action
                    taken to exploit
                    the opportunity
```

13

these 'rich pictures.' They are used to capture a mental picture held by managers about their work or the strategic nature of a set of issues. They can include the use of metaphor and analogy, with linkages between the various sets of issues that are described. At a lower or micro-level we are faced with depictions of processes and relationships between factors which then lead to quasi-mathematical thinking. This would include the use of graphical depictions of relationships and at a more definitive level we have arguable relationships that lend themselves to quantification and mathematical manipulations, for example the use of financial ratios and their interconnections. At this detailed level, the use of statistical methods starts to dominate. It is worth reminding ourselves that at all these levels we are attempting to inform and communicate individual cognitive processes in a manner that is plausible enough to engender commitment and belief.

The most popular meta-model, used to support strategic thinking and identify key strategic issues, is that of 'matching for fit.' Here an attempt is made to suggest a fit or match between the organization and its external environment. In most cases this external environment is applicable to all industries involved in the pursuit of profits over those of their competitors. The wide range of possible external features requires that analysts focus on those features that have the greatest impact on the industry being studied. The external or far environment is further analyzed into four basic areas: political, economic, social and technological. The subdivisions and breakdown within these areas are considered in terms of their potential impact on the firm. In this way, the strategic thinking is informed by a process that identifies the key strategic issues. From this point significant and realistic strategies can be identified that will either take advantage of or protect the firm from the effects and consequences surrounding these issues. At a more local or industry level perspective, the position of the firm *vis à vis* its competitors is analyzed in terms of a series of so-called forces such as:

- the threat from new entrants entering the industry;
- the threat from substitute products or services that will take market share;
- the danger from suppliers who might exert pressures on price, delivery and even takeover;
- the dangers of changes in buyer behaviour;

- the impact of competitive strategies being used by major players in the industry; these would include price competition, advantages gained from product and service differentiation, and their decisions to focus on either the whole customer base or a particular segment.

This process of matching for fit between the firm and its environment is completed by analyzing the firm itself in terms of perceived strengths and weaknesses, which are counterpoised with seizing opportunities and countering threats in each of these far and near environments of the firm. Figure 1.2 illustrates this matching process.

**Figure 1.2**
**THE MATCHING PROCESS**

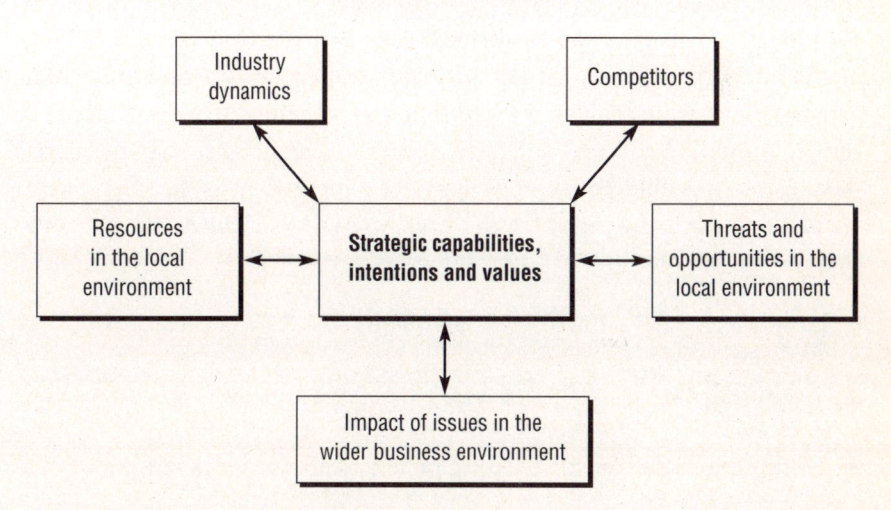

```
                    Industry                        Competitors
                    dynamics
                         ↕                              ↕
  Resources                  Strategic capabilities,         Threats and
  in the local    ↔          intentions and values    ↔      opportunities in the
  environment                                                 local environment
                                    ↕
                         Impact of issues in the
                         wider business environment
```

A more process-based model that is used to seek ways of adding value to the activities of the firm relies on an analysis of what is known as the 'value chain.' Here the firm is seen as engaging in a series of sequential activities that includes sourcing of raw material and goods, transforming these into products and services, distributing these through sales and marketing channels and providing after-sales support. Surrounding these activities are organizational functions such as research and development, human resources management, procurement and the infra-structure of the firm itself. The firm is seen as being part of a wider set of value chains of other firms and in most cases other industries.

The strategic thinking that this type of model encourages centres on finding new and original ways to achieve customer satisfaction by adding value. This is tackled by leveraging and connecting sources of expertise knowledge and resources, while at the same time identifying and seeking to reduce areas of cost that do not add value. Obviously the level at which these processes are analyzed will depend to a large extent on the knowledge and ability of the analyst to represent the reality of the operations of the firm. Too deep an analysis can be just as inappropriate as an analysis which is too superficial. These two models that employ matching and leverage dominate much of the analytical modelling work of the strategic thinkers.

Competition or adding sustainable competitive advantage relies on the notion of increasing market share in order to establish dominance in the industry. This relies on the firm gaining benefits from what is known as the 'industry learning curve' with subsequent use of economies that can be gained from scale and those that can be gained from product and service scope. The model suggested by Igor Ansoff as a way of representing the possible directions of growth for a firm is still used as a fundamental starting point for this area of analysis. This model suggests that a firm can consider growth in four key areas. These areas include:

- continuation with the current products and services in the existing markets;
- continuing in the same market but developing new products and services;
- continuing to deliver the existing products and services but doing this in new markets;
- diversifying into new products and services in new markets.

This last area is seen as the one where the manager is at most risk due to the lack of experience and knowledge of both products and the markets. Vertical integration where the firm moves up the value chain, towards the end user, or down towards the suppliers represent conventional growth strategies. Others include: buying competitors and complementary product firms, strategic alliances and joint ventures. An extreme form of diversification is where the firm decides to move out beyond the boundaries of the industry. This type of growth would be typically associated with the strategies pursued by the conglomerates in the late 1960s.

# COMPETITIVE ADVANTAGE AND GROWTH

Competitor analysis is also an area where managers rely on the use of a range of approaches to understand what it is that other firms are doing that should be copied or thwarted. There are three models that are favoured by managers for analyzing what has become known as the competitive position of the organization. The first of these is the lifecycle model. Here the marketplace is seen as being in various stages of growth from embryonic to mature. Strategies are determined for expenditure on, say, product development and promotion depending on the state of growth that is perceived.

> **Analysis heightens sensitivity, understanding takes longer.**

The second model uses the notion of mapping and relies on identifying the groups of competitors in the industry that are using similar strategies for competing. These group differentiators include: geographic coverage, distribution channels, quality, ownership, research and development capability and so on.

The third model is concerned with the way in which the market is segmented by firms in the industry and the relative market shares of the dominant ones. For example, depending on the way that the market is segmented, differentiation and pricing strategies will have different effects.

Figure 1.3 illustrates how these models are used to inform the various stages of strategy making and implementation. It is worth noting that at each stage and with each model, it is likely that the use of paradox will be a dominant feature of the arguments and persuasive activities that are being used.

We should, at this point, be cautious and not make the assumption that these analytical approaches have any real impact on the perspectives held by the strategic thinkers. They certainly make the managers more sensitive about the significance of the competition and perhaps provide a means of measuring their own performance against the major competitors. But there are other influences that also are impacting on the way that strategic thinking is developed. We will be looking at these other influences in later sections. But for now we need to look closer at how the leaders of the firm and the managers apply their strategic thinking at various levels in the firm. It is a consideration of these levels that will help us to get closer to understanding how the quest for competitive advantage encompasses both the leaders of the firm and the managers

17

PART I · THE WORLD OF THE STRATEGIC THINKER

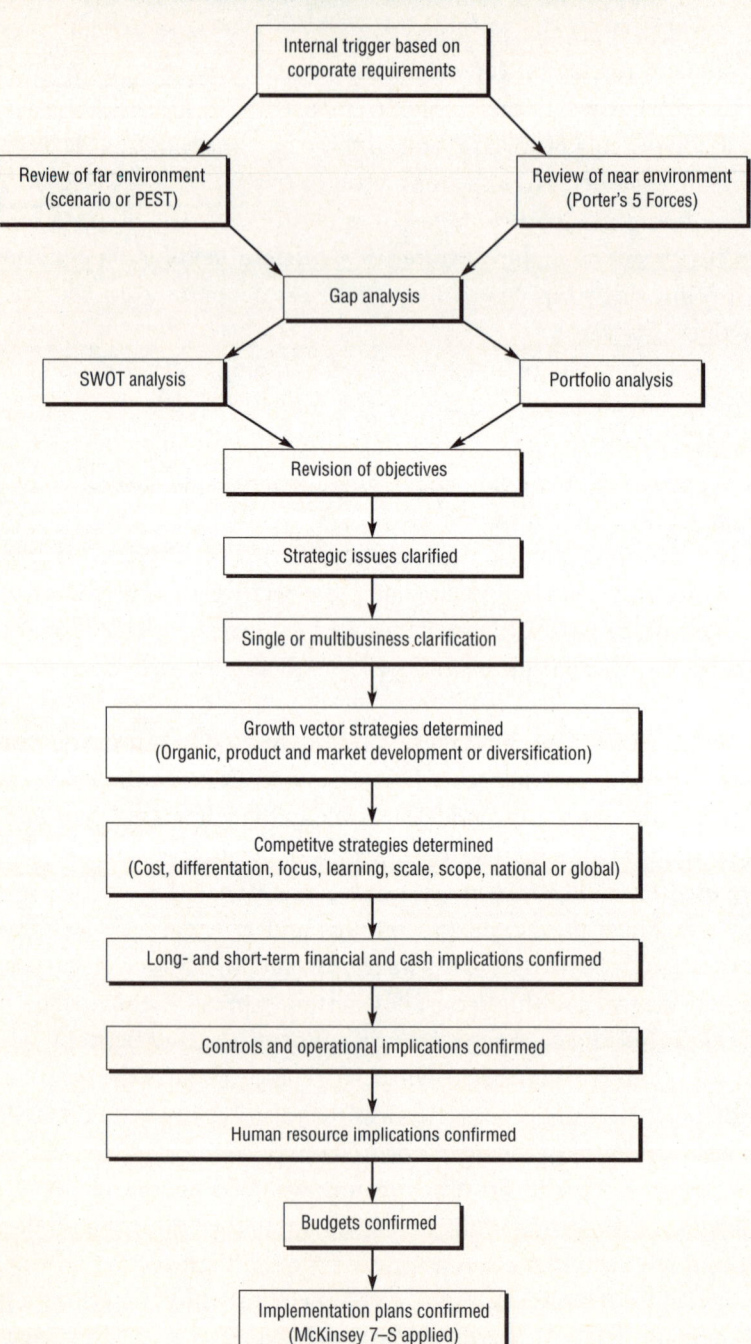

**Figure 1.3**
**THE CASCADING OF MODELS USED IN STRATEGY MAKING**

```
                    Internal trigger based on
                    corporate requirements
                    /                    \
   Review of far environment          Review of near environment
   (scenario or PEST)                 (Porter's 5 Forces)
                    \                    /
                        Gap analysis
                    /                    \
         SWOT analysis              Portfolio analysis
                    \                    /
                     Revision of objectives
                              ↓
                    Strategic issues clarified
                              ↓
                Single or multibusiness clarification
                              ↓
                Growth vector strategies determined
      (Organic, product and market development or diversification)
                              ↓
                 Competitve strategies determined
   (Cost, differentation, focus, learning, scale, scope, national or global)
                              ↓
        Long- and short-term financial and cash implications confirmed
                              ↓
             Controls and operational implications confirmed
                              ↓
                Human resource implications confirmed
                              ↓
                        Budgets confirmed
                              ↓
                   Implementation plans confirmed
                      (McKinsey 7–S applied)
```

themselves. We also need to take a closer look at the notion of an organization being able to generate a collective will or mindset regarding how to compete.

## COMPETITION VIEWED FROM VARIOUS LEVELS

In a firm we will find managers pursuing competitive advantage at two levels. We need to understand the perspectives that they will be using. These levels are those of:

- leaders of large corporations and owners of small and medium-sized firms;
- business unit or divisional leaders.

Looking into the competitive strategies and actions taken at these levels will provide an insight into how paradoxical situations are created and how they are interpreted.

The corporate leaders, of large conglomerates and focused enterprises, are charged with adding value for stakeholders. They achieve this by devising and monitoring strategies that aim to make the best use of the resources under their control. They are also charged with conserving the scale and quality of those resources. Corporate level growth can be tackled in an entrepreneurial way. This means that the firm adopts a set of behaviours that are normally demonstrated by an entrepreneur. This corporate entrepreneurship approach takes three forms.

The first is where the firm sets out to create a new business within the existing organizational set. It is recognized that this approach can take on average some eight years to achieve profitability and some 12 years before return on investment reaches that of the mainstream business. Firms that follow this route create new venture divisions whose continuing existence depends largely on maintaining a close relationship with the main corporate strategies. In the early stages, there is resistance from corporate management to the new business ideas. Senior management fail to be convinced that the new venture will prove viable. The measures being used by the corporate group are typically those of return on investment and pay back period which are difficult to formulate around new ideas.

Here we see a paradox beginning to emerge. The corporate management want the new idea to succeed and recognize the need to give it freedom and space to grow, but at the same time they are driven by a need to justify the investment of resources. A second paradox also emerges at the lower levels in the organization. At these levels, the new idea requires acceptance by the managers who are dealing with the marketplace. They see the new business idea as radical and difficult to define as it does not meet their perspectives of what the organization is capable of delivering. The paradox they perceive is that they know that a breakthrough requires new knowledge, but their very survival is based on old knowledge. In later sections, we will look in more depth into this method of growth and where it constantly is blocked by the existence of a host of insurmountable paradoxes.

The second form of growth is where the organization attempts to transform or renew its very nature. This is approached by the firm altering its resource pattern. This can include restructuring of finances, downsizing, turnaround based on divestments and outsourcing. Many of these activities present the manager with what appear to be mutually exclusive and hence conflicting approaches. The managers find themselves surrounded by unresolvable paradoxes and they are forced to make choices.

The third approach, to corporate renewal, is that where a firm attempts to change the rules of the industry. This framebreaking approach relies on finding new ways of using existing competitive capabilities, which means that the firm is competing on strategies rather than on resources. Firms are increasingly finding themselves either initiating the change or in an industry that is being reshaped by the competitors. This calls for a high level of corporate entrepreneurship and a collective will or mindset. Figure 1.4 illustrates how these three levels operate.

In the smaller enterprise, the owner-manager is often classified as an entrepreneur and pursues adding value in ways that are quite different from that of the leaders of the large corporation. The entrepreneur attempts to maximize value creation by minimizing the resource application while recognizing the point where the risk outweighs the return. This ability to pull out of an investment rather than pursuing events to a loss-making conclusion is often seen as the hallmark of the successful entrepreneur. The approach of the entrepreneur, when faced with a new opportunity, is to

**Success comes from making and learning from mistakes.**

# COMPETITIVE ADVANTAGE AND GROWTH

**Figure 1.4**
**CORPORATE LEVEL GROWTH STRATEGIES**

Required level of corporate entrepreneurship

|  | L | M | H |
|---|---|---|---|
| Timescale for financial return to exceed that of the original business set — M | | Developing the current business set. | Industry framebreaking:<br>• new ways of using capabilities<br>• influencing the industry dynamics |
| H | | Transforming the structure of the business:<br>• downsizing<br>• outsourcing<br>• divestment<br>• alliances | New venture business divisions replace existing business set:<br>• linked to but supersedes original business strategies |

commit few of the available resources immediately, as this would reduce the opportunity to flex when the situation changes, thus minimizing commitment of resource until evidence of success is clear. This approach when coupled with apparent reluctance to own certain resources has encouraged the view of the entrepreneur as being predominantly exploitative. Typical features found in competitive industries which demand entrepreneurial skills would include those where:

- a high degree of resource specialization is required for very short periods and ownership of the resource would not be appropriate
- the flexibility required to be able to withdraw from a new idea or innovation, very quickly, is paramount
- the speed of decision making is vital
- rapid learning from mistakes, as well as successes, is essential.

The effective entrepreneur is also someone who has a very good grasp of both the marketplace and the technology involved in developing and delivering the product or service.

At the second level, that of the business unit or division, the managers approach competition from a predominantly operational perspective. Here the managers have a battery of analytical tools and strategic management approaches available to them. But at a fundamental level, it is operations management performance that they believe creates the truly competitive firm. So we have the business on the one hand seeking to support the overall strategy of the corporation, while on the other pursuing more operationally focused strategies that will enable it to stay ahead of the competition. Managers are attempting to match what they see as an operationally focused strategic posture to the critical success factors in their industry. For many firms, the tension between supporting corporate-driven or longer-term strategies and achieving short-term operational performance presents a paradox. Here two apparently mutually exclusive, but laudable, ideas must be pursued at the same time. Before considering how such a paradox can be tackled, we need to look more closely at the thinking behind improving operational performance as a means of achieving competitive advantage.

The measures used for evaluating operational performance are vast. They include: quality, productivity, delivery times, flexibility, introduction of new products, capability, costs and the ability to continuously improve through innovation. The variations in operational performance between competing firms are largely accounted for by the differences in the design and management of the operations themselves and the associated value chain. In all of these areas the focus is on two features: reducing costs and innovation. In many operational activities, at least in the Western world, labour is a high cost element, and achieving productivity gains and utilizing the creative problem-solving ability of staff is a key area of focus for managers.

Self-managed teams, where front-line workers conduct their own quality improvement programmes and determine the most effective way to deliver products and services, are now an accepted part of the management philosophy. These approaches are expected to produce substantial savings in the number of supervisors and support staff that are required and hence a cost reduction. This drive for efficiency creates paradoxes such as *control* versus *autonomy* and *automation* versus *flexibility* which the operational managers attempt to resolve. Over and above efficiency, we have also to consider the significance of how innovation can contribute to achieving sustainable competitive advantage.

# INNOVATION LEADS TO SUSTAINABLE COMPETITIVE ADVANTAGE

Innovation can be considered at two levels: that of the strategic thinker and that of the operational manager. At an operational level, managers recognize the benefits to be gained from pursuing an innovative approach to improving key processes. But they also recognize the inherent risks, as the impact of the innovation translates directly into measurable performance. This has resulted in firms introducing processes that will select the winning innovations and eliminate the rest. These processes are often detailed and obviously slow down the rate of change, whereas at the strategic level the speed with which innovative ideas can be generated and evaluated is much greater. But as we try to close the gap between strategic thinking at the tacit level, and arguments at the explicit level, then original and breakout ideas are easily lost. Efforts to close this gap often forces the manager to revert to well-tried recipes that deny the new thinking. This is where we find managers presenting their propositions in the form of the paradox. For example:

*We must maintain our flexibility, as an organization, and encourage staff to be innovative and breakout of tramline thinking. At the same time, we must ensure that all ideas satisfy our drive for rapid commercialization and utilization of existing resources and skills.*

*Our future success depends on being able to build on our brand image that represents high quality and value for money in commodity products. While at the same time, we must become known for our ability to bring new and innovative products to the market.*

The risks that follow from making judgement errors at this strategic level are enormous. Unfortunately, they only become obvious as errors after two to three years. The managers have then either moved on, or can easily distance themselves from the outcomes. There are legions of stories that would support this view. Perhaps here we have an example of the danger of believing that managers can learn from their strategic decision making. Our contention is that learning from strategic thinking is possible, but much less so once the strategic decision has been made.

There are some clear conditions that increase the chances of a firm adopting an innovative approach to strategic thinking. These include:

- the extent to which the culture of the firm supports innovative thinking;
- the position of the firm regarding technology, intellectual property management and the customer base;
- the managerial processes used by the firm to capture and spread learning across the various businesses and functions.

Many of these prerequisites become the basis for paradoxical statements that are used to argue for a particular strategic innovation. One of the main arguments that managers would support is that competitive advantage relies heavily on innovation at both strategic and operational levels. But there is a great deal of controversy about how innovation should be approached.

The first approach is one characterized as involving continuous and incremental improvement, whereas the second involves discontinuity. These two perspectives apply equally well for innovations at both the strategic and operational levels. Continuous improvement requires the firm to turn over old products, to refine designs and revisit current competitive strategies. This is the approach most favoured by managers and has resulted in some important developments. Business process re-engineering, lean production, just in time, improvements in technology and processes are all approaches that stem from a perspective of continuous improvement. The major failures of this approach to innovation are associated with poor decision making over capital investment and the resistance to change by people. Much of the management thinking in major firms is more about how to implement change than it is about how to identify where the change is required.

> **The skill is in identifying the industry breakpoints.**

Breakthrough or discontinuous change is a much less well-understood area and is more risk-laden. At the strategic level, it is difficult to ascertain the response in the marketplace or from competitors to radical changes in either positioning of the firm or in a product or service. Also the benefits from a strategic innovation involving, say, an alliance or an acquisition are, at the outset, extremely hard to predict. A popular approach to radical innovation is to identify breakpoints in the competitive cycle that will stimulate a rush of innovation. This is based on the view that there are divergent points where firms compete by innovating to give customers variety and added value. The other breakpoint is labelled 'convergent' and occurs when the divergence is spent. Here processes focused on cost reduction and delivery around the dominant design are pursued.

Anticipating these breakpoints requires a deep understanding of both the firm, the marketplace and the industry. This discontinuous approach to innovation raises an immediate and powerful paradox. Legitimizing diverse perspectives and the development of new capability in the firm clashes with the drive for conformity, focus and control. The tensions that this creates can be used to promote the dynamic capability of the firm or alternatively to expend energy and management time on reconciling two apparently mutually exclusive approaches. Figure 1.5 shows the application of this breakpoint effect.

**Figure 1.5**
**THE BREAKPOINT EFFECT**

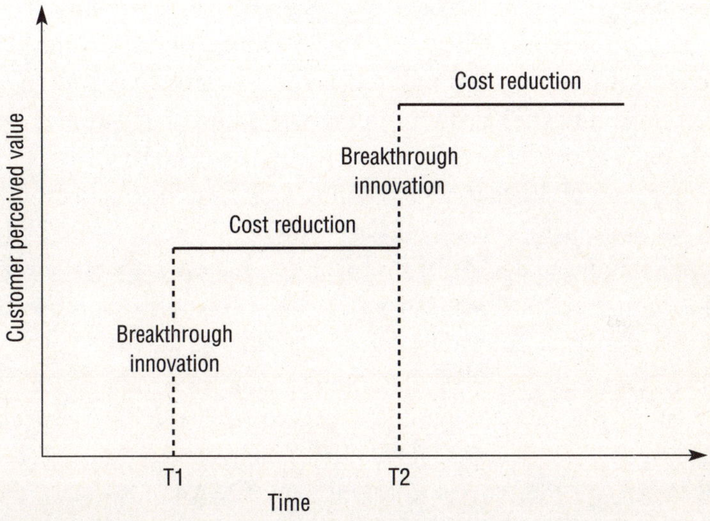

*Note*:
- Cost reduction is achieved through product and process developments
- Breakthrough innovation produces the dominant design
- T1 and T2 are the breakpoints in the competitive cycle

Firms are obviously competing with local- or national-based competitors, and also on a more international or global basis. We need to have an initial look at how firms approach competition at this international level. There are no doubt some very important and powerful paradoxes to be unearthed in that area.

# FIRMS COMPETE IN NATIONAL AND GLOBAL ARENAS

International competition for market share of commodities, products and services is not new. What perhaps is new concerns the rate at which the source and features of the competition can change or be influenced. Although it seems so obvious, it is perhaps worth reminding ourselves that the competition is for sales in both consumer goods and services and those required by industries and national governments. The impact that a nation can have on a firm's ability to compete at an international level is also well-known. The country itself will be attempting to remain competitive at an economic level, influence trade regulations and set up conditions whereby its major companies can help the national economic growth by exporting and doing business in other countries. All of these actions will impact on the ability of a firm to compete.

Firms see the need to take active steps to protect themselves from overseas competitors. They also see tapping overseas markets for resources, skills, technology and outlets for their products and services as being opportunities for growth. Investments and acquisitions overseas, joint ventures and strategic alliances are options open to firms as ways of improving their abilities to compete. Owning or controlling an overseas firm is an approach used to gain access to rapidly-expanding markets. Attractive labour, materials, transportation and energy costs are all factors that would be considered by a firm when considering the advantages of investing in other countries. For some nations, the investment would also be made on the basis of tapping into a skill base that would act as an opportunity for home-based managers to accelerate their learning. An example of this would be where US firms have moved their R&D facilities to Japan in order to recruit local expertise and also learn through collaboration with universities and local competitors. The two areas where the strategic thinking of a firm's managers has a major impact on international competitive advantage are those involving organizational structure and the differentiation of their products and services. It is within these two areas that the use of paradox is seen to have its greatest effect. We will make an initial exploration of these two areas in order to illustrate how these paradoxes arise.

Most managers accept that an organizational structure should be designed to support the strategies that the firm is pursuing. At an early stage of overseas expansion a firm will use the marketing department to set up and manage overseas trade. As the firm grows, then export departments will evolve into either a series of international product divisions or into area divisions. This move towards an international division with the use of overseas subsidiaries, joint ventures, strategic alliances and acquisitions is a natural progression. Our first paradox emerges around the product division organization. Product divisions are usually controlled on profitability and return on investment in order for the corporate group to evaluate the progress of their strategies for international growth. This encourages product divisions to compete with each other for investment through concentration on products and services which

> **The paradox is to want corporate global learning from competing businesses.**

give the best short-term performance, while avoiding those that require special promotion. The managers are also likely to be experts in only one or the other of the potential worldwide markets and hence will avoid those with which they have little knowledge, growth thereby being limited. Thus a corporate policy that advocates product divisionalization in order to achieve profitability through focus on a product is also aimed at achieving effective synergies between the assets and knowledge residing in the firm. This for most managers would in reality present a paradox.

The international or global area division presents us with the second paradox. Here the organization is structured into areas or geographic regions, the managers being responsible for production, finance, staff, marketing and sales, while the products or services are influenced and co-ordinated through a geographic area focus. The manager has scope to become much more responsive to local variations in customer requirements, and hence there is a tendency to reduce the chances of gains from companywide economies of scale and standardization. The paradox is that the corporate policy that is advocating area segmentation in order to provide outlets as a way to profit from investment in new products and services is also relying on integrating the global learning that takes place as a means of standardization and gaining subsequent economies of scale. These intentions are easily seen by area managers as mutually exclusive. We will explore, in later sections, how these and other paradoxes that arise from a view on how to strategize at international levels create tensions from which breakthroughs and new learning can take place.

# Chapter 2

# AGREEING WHAT COUNTS

Identifying the owners  *31*

Corporate level strategies and adding value  *33*

Stakeholder analysis determines the pay-off  *38*

Social consciousness through corporate strategy  *40*

> *The public be damned. I am working for my stockholders.*
>
> William Henry Vanderbilt (1821–85),
> US railway chief

In this chapter, we will be considering how managers view and subscribe to notions of what it is that the firm is trying to achieve, and how these views impact on their approach to achieving sustainable competitive advantage. We will look at historical and contemporary views on ownership and extend this to the way that corporate governance is used to add value to the enterprise. Finally we will look at the current views on stakeholding, and how this area impacts on the ways in which firms and their managers approach strategic thinking.

## IDENTIFYING THE OWNERS

Ownership implies freedom to use the resources and assets in whatever way one considers appropriate. But in the context of the firm the owners are faced with attempts at regulation and the law to curb uses that would harm the populace and the country. Individuals are also operating with a set of values and beliefs that result in varying degrees of responsibility being demonstrated and discharged. It all sounds fairly straightforward, but as many individuals and firms have demonstrated around the world, there are a great many interpretations as to what level of responsibility is acceptable. The managers involved in the strategy-making process are in a powerful position. They are the ones who are able to make choices as to the outputs of the firm and how resources are to be obtained and applied. As we are seeking to increase your power in strategic thinking, we should first look more closely at the process by which this power is applied. We are not attempting to come to any great philosophical conclusions, but we will highlight some of the tensions and contradictions that influence the strategic thinker in organizations.

Owners have historically anticipated a financial return on their investment. A not-for-profit organization is also dependent for its continuation on being able to attract funds and skilled people who see working for the organization both as a means of obtaining a livelihood and contributing to an enterprise whose purpose they value. For both profit and not-for-profit organizations, the pursuit of efficiency in the use of resources is paramount. We can adopt two distinct interpretations of the notion of ownership. First, where the assets being deployed are legally owned by an individual or number of individuals, and second where there is a traceable responsibility for the outcome arising from the use of these assets. The legal form of contract is most likely to apply to the former and the latter moves us towards looking at the part that managers employed by the owners begin to play.

> **Strategy makers are in a powerful position.**

Obviously board members of companies, both executive and non-executive, as well as the managers and staff, are increasing their interest in the outcomes of the firm through share ownership. Their interests are now a lot closer to those historically attributed to the owner or asset provider. What we have here is a consideration of the balance between ownership and control, where the owner and now the equity investor in an enterprise is increasingly only able to exercise power through a chain of agents and intermediaries. The dilution of their power increases as the scale of the enterprise increases. In the UK and the USA, the State is increasingly acting as the third hand in applying controls on corporations through legislation and regulatory bodies. This form of bureaucratic control in some ways protects but greatly reduces the power of the investors.

It also acts to control the actions of the executives and the managers. The macro-level tensions that this produces centre around issues such as the powerlessness of the investors, the irresponsible behaviour of the corporate staff and the local managers, the increasing demand from the public for State intervention and control. Somewhere in all this is the lurking feeling that stark capitalism is really the only way for a nation to prosper:

> *'What's good for General Motors is good for the USA'*

The determination to downsize and the collapse of large employers has and perhaps always will act as a counter to some of the enthusiasm for capitalism and the free-market philosophy. Many governments are now struggling to produce policy that will direct company law regarding the duties of directors and the rights of shareholders and employees, with the aim of creating transparency and co-operation between the investors, firms and the state. An on-going saga which will no doubt have an impact on the strategic thinker and approaches to strategic innovation, competitive strategies, implementation and the outcomes of the activities of the firm. One way to begin to peel this onion of corporate governance and reveal the paradoxes is to look at strategy making in large corporations.

## CORPORATE LEVEL STRATEGIES AND ADDING VALUE

Conglomerates, the darlings of the investors and the financial institutions in the 1980s have increasingly found themselves out of favour. The antipress that they have received stems from a mixture of a drop in the returns that investors received and a growing public concern that their very purpose, of capitalizing on the leverage of under-utilized assets and spreading investors' risks, was no longer in sympathy with the notion of good corporate governance. Conglomerates differ from multinational-focused businesses in that their main purpose is to acquire businesses that can be used to add value to the total value of the parent body. The nature and pursuits of the subsidiary businesses do not necessarily have to have any centrality or unifying characteristics, whereas the executive in the

> **The corporate desire for control denies business independence.**

multinational business has a different mission and perspective, in that there is assumed to be a core business, for example, oil exploration, extraction, processing and distribution, to which strategies for growth and competitive positioning can be applied. Although we have deliberately highlighted the differences between these two types of business organizations we would argue that in both cases the executives who are charged with strategic thinking and the identification and pursuit of corporate strategies are facing the same sets of paradoxes. The executive, in both types of organization, has to decide:

- in which industries and in which businesses the company should invest its resources;
- how best to do this in terms of organic growth, acquisitions, joint ventures, alliances or through divestments;
- what forms of guidance and control the corporate body should apply to the subsidiary businesses;
- how the total should be structured and organized;

- who should be charged with selecting those key figures required to run the businesses and how this should be done.

You will note here that although many if not all of these decisions can be applied at the business level, we are focusing in this section on the corporate level only. All of these areas for decision making are aimed at adding value to the individual businesses through its actions and thus adding value to the corporate body. We can immediately see a paradox in that the corporate desire to guide and control, balance business portfolios and spread risk will all involve decisions on investment and support that appear to exclude the subsidiary business from taking independent action. This paradox creates tensions that in many firms around the world are a daily diet. Enlightened firms have learned from this form of tension and have focused on finding a role for the corporate group that is more about being better than other firms at adding value to their subsidiary businesses.

The phrase 'parenting advantage' has been coined by academics such as Goold, Campbell and Alexander (1994) to capture the notion that competitive advantage can be gained by the parent body engaging in strategic thinking that will lead to advantages for the subsidiaries over their competitors. This advantage being achieved by becoming the best among competing parents. In executing this role, the corporate group can be seen to act in four distinct ways that are aimed at adding value. The four approaches include:

1. Monitoring and controlling the corporate process;
2. Integrating the businesses to create synergies;
3. Providing centralized functions and expertise;
4. Influencing the scope and nature of the activities of the whole group.

## Monitoring and controlling

The first and perhaps the most conventional approach is where the corporate group set out to act as a monitor and control on the strategies and management processes being implemented by the subsidiaries, providing a wider view of the business environment than the individual business would normally have access to and acting as an agent in making expertise available to the subsidiary. The criticism from the business usually centres around excessive control and restrictions on investment and their perception that responsive strategies are the ones that pay off. There is also the danger of the subsidiary telling the parent only the good news and avoiding the bad or not so good. This results in efforts by the corporate to exercise more control and a negative spiral of communication is quickly set up. The local business managers are often perplexed and frustrated by an insistence from the corporate that they engage in strategy reviews, when they are faced with what to them seem and probably are imperatives around cost-cutting and rapid responses to local competition. For many such businesses, a leveraged buy-out, following attempts at declaring their unilateral independence, seems the only route forward. Recognizing and managing these apparently contradictory positions, the dilemma being whether the centre could make a greater contribution to the strategic thinking of the subsidiary than if left to their own devices, form the basis of a paradox that most business managers would recognize. The root of this paradox is probably around the differences in the criteria being used by the corporate and the subsidiary managers to evaluate alternative strategies. The mental models and the recipes being used to formulate their perceptions of how to compete are probably quite different. This brings us back to the central point that we are exploring in this section: that of how to use the tension produced by alternative perspectives such as this to reframe the way that a strategic management issue is perceived.

## Integrating to create synergies

A second approach is where the corporate identifies and creates linkages between the businesses in the group and those outside the group that supersede those that the business could make if left to its own devices. This can include influencing linkages between research and development functions, sources of investment, information management systems, manufacturing, procurement and distribution. It can also include strategic alliances, joint ventures and buy-outs. This approach can result in the creation of a centrally planned system that constrains the strategic development of the subsidiary businesses. These businesses might have operated quite well on the basis of market forces and a strong sense of self-interest among the business managers. The management overheads associated with integration need to be carefully weighed against the benefits before steps are taken to seal the knot. The operations of the major multinationals present many examples of where this integrating activity of the parent company is put to good use. Unilever, Matsushita and many others have demonstrated how integration can add value. They have also shown that it can hamper growth and restrict the creativity and flair of the local managers. The paradox here is that the corporate is seeking to maximize the value of the group resources and knowledge through integration and at the same time the subsidiary business is attempting to maximize their ability to meet business targets by minimizing the management overheads. The businesses may also be seeking to secure their own future by competing with each other, and thus see any attempt at integration as a threat. The notion of sharing knowledge and resources across the businesses would in this case be rejected, at least at the tacit level. Resolving this paradox is a permanent challenge within large corporations and incurs massive management overheads.

**Corporates can add value by centralizing expertise.**

## Centralizing functions and expertise

The third approach is where the corporates add value by providing a focus of expertise and centralize functions that would normally be carried out by the subsidiary businesses, thus offering cost savings and standardization across the businesses. Obvious areas for this would include centralized finance, research and development, technological innovation, public relations, advertising, brand identification, information systems design, servicing and maintenance and the personnel and remuneration functions. By this process of centralization, the corporate is offering benefits, but is also sending very strong signals to the businesses and the outside world as to the activities that it sees as central to the success of the organization. The paradox that arises here is that the corporate control of major aspects of a business are essential to standardization, learning and economies of scale while the subsidiary businesses by their very definition need to internalize the expertise that is contained in these key activities. It appears that these are contradictory states. The advent of the virtual organization that relies on a mixture of outsourcing, co-operative arrangements between suppliers and strategic alliances is at the very heart of this paradox.

## Influencing the total business scope and nature

The fourth and final way in which we suggest that the corporate can add value is by developing the scope of the group's activities. This primarily involves acquisitions and divestments of businesses that are seen as either a realizable asset or a source of potential revenue, sometimes both. In this role the parent is acting very much in the way that an individual would buy and sell shares in order to reduce risk and gain opportunity, the role typically attributed to the conglomerate. The pitfalls of this approach to adding value are legion. Companies are purchased because of what apparently were opportunities to add value by gaining access to markets, increasing share of existing markets and diversifying into new technologies. Often the purchase turns out to be overvalued and the subsequent drain on the group leads to other businesses being sold off and the group being restructured. Figure 2.1 illustrates these different roles for the corporate group.

**Figure 2.1**
**CONTRASTING THE ROLES OF THE CORPORATE GROUP**

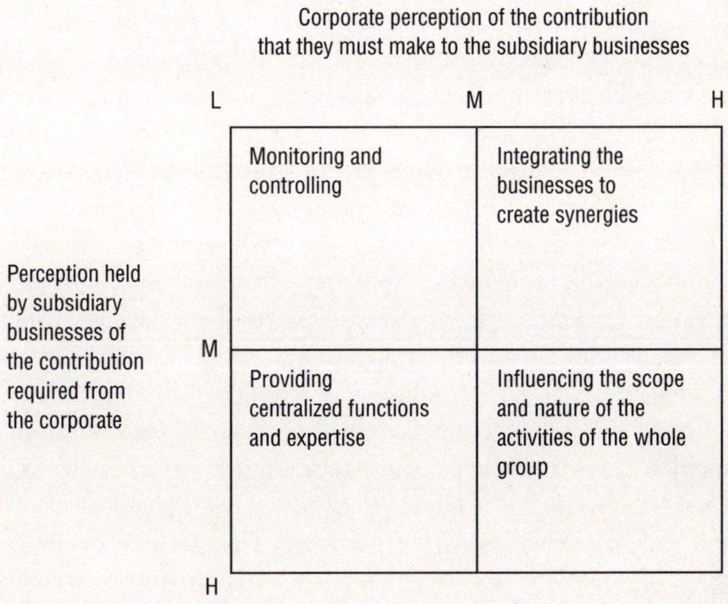

Corporate perception of the contribution that they must make to the subsidiary businesses

Perception held by subsidiary businesses of the contribution required from the corporate

|  | L / M | M / H |
|---|---|---|
| **M (low)** | Monitoring and controlling | Integrating the businesses to create synergies |
| **H (high)** | Providing centralized functions and expertise | Influencing the scope and nature of the activities of the whole group |

Obviously the motivation behind buying and selling companies is to provide the shareholders and owners with short-term benefits and longer-term opportunities. As the question of who benefits from such transactions is at the heart of strategic thinking, we need to look a bit closer at the question of ownership. This wider perspective as to who is most affected by these corporate decisions has an impact on how strategic thinking is formulated and implemented. We need to look at some of the players in this wider stakeholding scenario.

## STAKEHOLDER ANALYSIS DETERMINES THE PAY-OFF

In early industrialized society, and today for some owner-managed firms, the decision makers and beneficiaries from profit-maximizing strategies were easy to identify. In the complex business world that has evolved, the influencers and beneficiaries now range from governments to equity holders, labour unions and special interest groups. This has also been extended to include the employees, suppliers and other firms that form part of the operational value chain, and these are all now seen as being stakeholders in the firm. They are all involved in some way or other with the strategies and fortunes of the firm. Those responsible for the strategic thinking, strategy making and implementation also hold values and beliefs that will influence their perspectives on stakeholder needs. These strategic thinkers will share their views on relative stakeholder power and needs in either an informal way, for example by association or by engaging in a formal planning and analytical process. Any analysis of stakeholder needs, be it informal or formal, will result in a set of declared goals and objectives for the firm that are a compromise. It will represent a view on how important it is to satisfy the various groups and where the power and politics need to be attended to.

What we are starting to expound here is a theory about how firms formulate goals and manage the perceived conflicts of interest among the stakeholders. As we have seen, conflict of interest quickly leads to defensive routines and postures being taken up by managers and paradoxes will be used to frame and win arguments. The conflict arising from a statement of intent by the firm will arise between the owner stakeholders and the manager stakeholders. The managers will be interested in growing a profitable firm that offers them a satisfying job and prospects of continuation, rewards and promotion. They will also be interested in finding ways of increasing their own freedom to make decisions and reducing those of the true owners and other stakeholders. The owners may be more interested in short-term profitability and increasing the share price in order to sell, or increase the attractiveness of the firm itself to a takeover bid. Once again we are presenting what might appear to be a cynical view of business, and there are examples of stakeholder groups that have managed to reach and maintain an equitable and reasonable set of objectives and balanced outcomes. A key feature of stakeholder analysis is that negotiation and compromise over goals and intentions will be part of the process if it is to be effective. To understand how important this negotiation is in practice we need to look more closely at how the process of analysis is carried out.

> **Stakeholder analysis is the start point for the strategist.**

The process will involve:

- identification of the stakeholder groups;
- their financial and tangible input to the firm;
- their intangible input to the firm;
- their ability to co-operate or act independently of the rest of the stakeholders;
- how they judge or measure the performance and outcomes of the firm;
- their relative importance to the firm in terms of an ability to influence outcomes;
- their key values and beliefs.

Figure 2.2 provides a framework for conducting a stakeholder analysis. In order to complete such an analysis, we are assuming that those involved are able to arrive at an objective and valid set of measures and viewpoints concerning the needs, intentions and views of these complex stakeholder groups. We are also assuming that the views of the stakeholder groups do not change extensively over time and can be articulated and declared. This all starts to sound quite daunting and potentially misleading in that many of the interests of these groups would appear to be mutually exclusive. But our premise in this book is that the tension that arises where organizations and their interest groups perceive mutually exclusive goals creates new and enriched understandings. The

## Figure 2.2
### CONDUCTING A STAKEHOLDER ANALYSIS

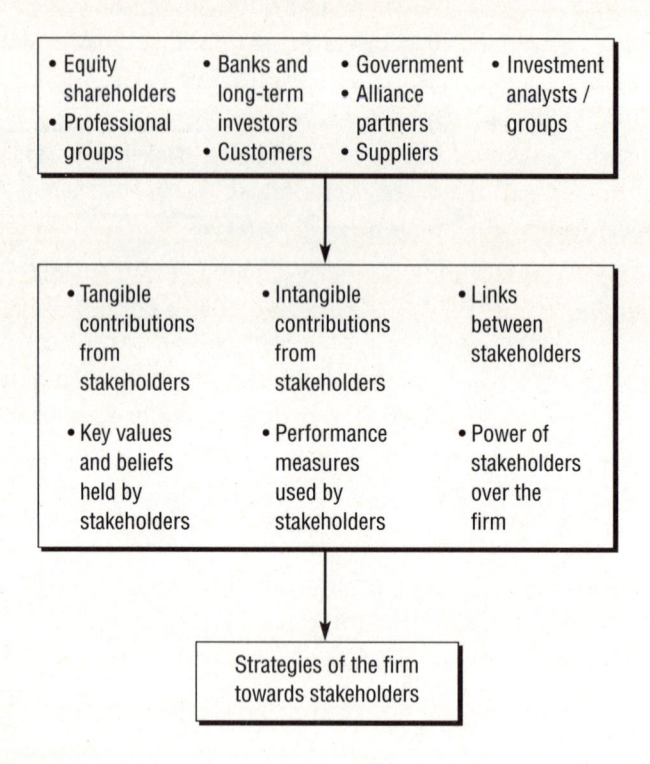

- Equity shareholders
- Professional groups
- Banks and long-term investors
- Customers
- Government
- Alliance partners
- Suppliers
- Investment analysts / groups

↓

- Tangible contributions from stakeholders
- Intangible contributions from stakeholders
- Links between stakeholders
- Key values and beliefs held by stakeholders
- Performance measures used by stakeholders
- Power of stakeholders over the firm

↓

Strategies of the firm towards stakeholders

trap in stakeholder analysis is then to approach this as a set of competing and mutually exclusive interests, rather than as an opportunity to harness the power that is produced. The success of a firm may be most easily measured by conventional metrics such as profitability, asset worth and market share, but we may need to look further in order to reach an understanding of the purpose of the firm and the interests of its stakeholders.

# SOCIAL CONSCIOUSNESS THROUGH CORPORATE STRATEGY

Most managers would agree that the firm has both a social and an economic function which is discharged or energized by the intentions and actions of all the stakeholders. The debate arises when decisions have to be made over priorities and the allocation of resources. The purposes behind the activities of the firm can also be debatable. Most would agree that they include: the production of goods and services that satisfy customers in markets, providing a vehicle for the economic growth and development of the nation and providing opportunities for people to exercise their creative talents. Perhaps all of these can find justification for the support that the world gives to its industries. The interaction and mutual support required between firms and the society in which they are embedded is a feature of modern economic life. The role of the State in providing an infrastructure in which firms can operate with a degree of stability is challenged where firms engage in international trade and there is an increased use of direct foreign investment as a strategy for growth. Although the interest shown in the effects of changes in currency exchange rates and tariffs perhaps brings firms back to recognizing the central role that national politics and policies can play in their success. There is of course an enormous range of perspectives held in different countries and cultures as to what are acceptable roles and activities for the State to adopt and what is acceptable behaviour for the firm. Considerations of the variety of perceptions held in say, China, the USA, Japan and European countries would quickly illustrate the complexity of managing operations in the larger multinationals.

The firm, as we have seen, finds itself balancing the short- and long-term goals of a mixed set of stakeholders which includes those charged with strategic thinking. The State on the other hand focuses mainly on the longer-term, through investments and regulation of sector groups and institutions in ways that provide an infrastructure for the firms to operate in. Firms for their part need to offer attractive investment and employment opportunities for the public. This brings to the fore the notion of the social consciousness of the firm. Here the role and contribution that the firm makes has to reinforce both societal demands and societal values. This can act as both a tempering and constraining force on the strategic thinker. It can also act as a spur and a guide. Here we have a paradox for the strategic thinker in the firm. Attempts to beat the competition and grow require strategies that involve decisions based on maximizing the use of resources, both human and financial, while minimizing the costs. The firm is also dependent for survival and growth on satisfying the needs of the workforce, and working within the wider set of values and constraints established by society. We would need to question the extent to which a set of directors, managers or employees in a firm would be competent to engage in strategic thinking for the firm in a way that was aimed at providing direct benefits to society in general, let alone be interested in doing so. Sufficient to recognize that the strategic thinkers are influenced by a set of values that they hold and by questioning and exposing those values, we may find that the societal focus is being achieved.

The prime focus of the strategist is perhaps to identify the rules of the game in which they are playing and then concentrate on achieving profitable growth, while relying on the checks and balances of legislation and control plus a strong set of ethics and moral values to guide strategic thinking and judgements. On an international playing field, the strategist is of course faced with a wide range of rules for engaging in play. Many of these challenges present dilemmas for the manager, rather than paradoxes where choices are made on moral and ethical grounds. For the multinational firm, this presents questions of control that may be based on values held in the country of the parent group. These may be in direct conflict with those held at the country level. In the next chapter, we will look at the context in which this international and increasingly global perspective impacts on the way in which the strategic thinker approaches competition and the growth of the firm.

> The strategist has to understand the rules of the game.

## Reference

Goold, M., Campbell, A. and Alexander, M. (1994) *Corporate Level Strategy: Creating Value in the Multibusiness Company*, New York, John Wiley & Sons.

# Chapter 3

# FORECASTING THE FUTURE

The global economic dimension  *45*

Competing at international levels  *48*

Forecasting the future or
building scenarios  *53*

Planning as thinking  *56*

> *The new electronic interdependence recreates the world in the image of a global village.*
>
> Marshall McLuhan (1911–81),
> Canadian sociologist

In this chapter, we will be exploring the influence that global economics has on how the strategic thinker approaches business competition and growth at national and international levels. We will look at how strategist use formal planning techniques to forecast the future, and how these techniques can mask the importance of strategic thinking and learning. For the majority of middle and senior managers, the exposure to international trade means confronting deeply held views on what leads to success. These views are often presented in the form of paradoxes. The strategists needs a framework or backdrop against which these can be considered.

## THE GLOBAL ECONOMIC DIMENSION

Firms that focus on globalization strategies see the world as a single market where customers' needs are homogeneous, or at least that is what the firms want people to believe. These firms concentrate on low-cost production, albeit in various locations, and seek standardization in products and services. Promotional techniques such as branding give impetus to these efforts to convince their users that the firm is meeting a universal need (the notion of the global village captures this pervasive idea). Products such as Coca-Cola, Levis, VCRs and industrial goods such as aero-engines are all examples of this globalization strategy at work. Alternatively, the multinational firms focus on competing through differentiation of their products and services. They rely on tailoring their goods and services to local and country needs in ways that enable higher prices to be charged. Considerations as to how effectively a mix of these two approaches can be managed pervades much of the strategic thinking and subsequent planning in international firms. The perspectives of the strategic thinkers in these firms are also heavily influenced by the environments in which they operate. Their thinking is not value free.

Firms that operate on an international basis vary in the degree to which they rely on strategic planning to manage growth. Planning is used to help co-ordinate a complex mix of activities. But as we have seen in earlier chapters, there is a fine line between planning as a means of control from the centre and it being useful to the subsidiary businesses. The challenges facing these businesses are more likely to stretch their ability to respond to rapidly changing local demands and pressures.

**Changes in local demand put pressure on global strategies.**

These pressures primarily stem from the economic conditions prevailing in the country in which the business is situated. Some firms operate in countries that have resource-driven economies, where the market determines the supply and demand, others have a centrally determined economy, and some are a mixture of both.

The tendency in Western countries has been to see a greater degree of integration between governments and firms to influence the way in which foreign business can be encouraged and supported. For developing countries, arguments usually centre around the extent to which governments will support nationalization or privatization. Airlines, oil companies, banks, transport, telecommunications and utilities are all prime areas in the economy where this debate takes place. For the strategist in the firm, these are all areas that need monitoring as they can have a major impact on both competition and profitability. Against this backdrop of national governments' efforts to achieve economic integration, through for example, free trade agreements and the abolition of tariffs, there are opportunities for the international firms. Strategies that include foreign direct investment and forming joint ventures are two of the ways in which firms can take advantage of this national economic integration.

This economic imperative where the firm is focusing on taking advantage of value that has been added at the product development stage is also dependent on the economic developments taking place in the outlet country. This can include efforts by the country to manage its balance of payments, the levels and contributions being made by local competitors to gross domestic product (GDP) and changes in local foreign exchange rates. Some multinationals would see changes in local exchange rates as an opportunity to borrow for investment and others an opportunity to reinvest local profits to aid growth. Managing these risks and opportunities are areas where the strategists will probably take advice but be wary of the difficulties faced when trying to predict the future.

Many of the risks associated with investing and operating in foreign countries can be considered under the rubric of political risk in that the power of the foreign country to support or thwart the international firm stems from an ability to wield political power. One way of identifying these risks involves a consideration of political, general and special investment risk as shown in Figure 3.1.

**Figure 3.1**
**DIMENSIONS OF POLITICAL RISK**

| Level of political risk | Context for the corporate investment strategy |
| --- | --- |
| Low | • Focus on industrial sector<br>• Goods manufactured to supply local demand<br>• Subsidiary only partially owned<br>• Some targeting, by host country, of import and export tariffs and duties |
| Medium | • Focus on service sector industries<br>• Raw materials, used in manufacture purchased locally<br>• Some price controls and taxation applied by the host country |
| High | • Focus on the prime sector industries<br>• The manufactured goods are exported<br>• The subsidiary is wholly owned<br>• Some controls on ownership by the host country |

The political risk is seen as involving restrictions on the transfer of funds into and out of the country by way of tariffs and duties, operational risks that involve price controls and taxation and ownership control restrictions. A second area of risk is that of general investments, which include corporate investment, where the firm is producing goods that are not for consumption in the host country, as they are seen by the host to be of no direct benefit. Other types of investment are goods and raw materials that are used in the final production. The host would see these as being of value as they could also use them for export to other countries. Investments in producing goods that supply a home demand are seen as low threat by the host.

The final area is that of investments that are seen by the host as impacting on the primary sectors in the economy. For example, agriculture and mining incorporate a high element of technology that, if acquired, could be used by the host. Ownership thus becomes a key factor in balancing this area of investment risk. Multinationals assess these risks for each of the host countries and recognize that following an initial investment phase where the host country is in a low-power bargaining position, time will reduce the relative power of the firm. The requirement is to maintain this initial advantage to deter the host from instigating expropriation or interfering in the workings of the firm. With the rapid growth in the economies of the newly industrialized countries, this pattern of investment and associated risk-taking is changing, and with it there is a need for a change in strategic thinking and strategic planning in firms. Global dynamics are creating a moving target for the strategic thinker.

The economies of Japan, Singapore, Hong Kong and Korea have risen more rapidly in comparison to some of the older and more established countries, and the picture is changing in terms of the traditional sources of wealth creation. The United Nations reported that in 1992 there were some 37 000 multinationals with 90% being based in the developed countries. These multinationals accounting for 75% of the world commodity trade and 80% of traded technology. The competition between these multinationals is rising as industries establish operations in the same countries, seeking growth of sales through foreign direct investment.

Changes are also occurring in ownership dominance in major industries, for example, in the steel, electronics and automobile industries where US dominance has been eroded. The expansion of the strategic alliances and joint ventures in high technology industries has underpinned the drive to leverage resources, innovate and improve manufacturing and distribution services in order to get new products to market much more quickly. Newly industrialized countries take advantage of these new technologies and methods. By investing in the manufacture and supply of products and services, their growth relies less on supplying raw materials and more on using the skills and knowledge of the workforce. This changing international scene provides many opportunities for the strategic thinker to add to the competitive advantage of the firm.

**Pursuing economies of scale and scope creates conflict.**

## COMPETING AT INTERNATIONAL LEVELS

There are three key areas that are fundamental to sustaining competitive advantage at international levels. Being efficient in existing operations, managing the business risks and accelerating learning at all levels in the organization. Strategies to support this include making use of resources in other countries and emphasizing benefits from economies of scale and of scope. Pursuit of these strategies will create apparent conflicts and at times appear to require the recognition of the existence of mutually exclusive goals. It is here that we will see the emergence of some of the paradoxes that we are interested in exposing.

So far we have considered competition from other countries as being dominated by labour rates, exchange rates and the abilities of countries to achieve volumes of sales that give them advantages through economies of scale. We have also seen that strategic alliances, joint ventures and direct foreign investment provide competitors with the opportunity to move quickly into new and established markets. These approaches when coupled with the ability of firms to innovate in product, services and delivery mechanisms all create an environment in which competition takes place. Michael Porter (1990) has suggested that there are four factors that determine national competitive advantage and that a firm that wishes to compete needs to understand these in order to form a basis for developing competitive strategies. The approach is shown in Figure 3.2.

Porter's approach is being presented and interpreted here as needing to be viewed from the perspective of a strategic thinker in a firm trying to understand the national features that will give the firm the basis for establishing a competitive strategy. Having unique and available resources such as land, labour and skills would seem obvious requirements, but the way in which local demand creates advantage is more subtle.

Porter argues that the seller receives direct feedback on the product and that this accelerates the demand for innovation to satisfy the customer. This early warning enables the home producer to stay ahead of foreign competitors. For example, the Japanese dominance of the world market for small air conditioners arose from a local demand for quiet energy-saving rotary compressors for use in small houses. The American dominance of the world in both pizza production and in Coca-Cola are other examples of this factor. The requirement for supporting industries also contributes to national competitiveness by providing a lower cost source of service and sub-unit supply than that available from other countries. Competition between these suppliers also creates an opportunity for innovation and cost reduction.

Finally, Porter suggests that the way in which firms are structured should suit the national culture and that geographical clustering gives a

## Figure 3.2
### A PERSPECTIVE ON NATIONAL COMPETITIVE ADVANTAGE

```
                  Development of strategic thinking
                  towards competitiveness in a country
                                 ▲
                                 │
                  Analysis of the strength and
                  interaction between structural features
                    ▲       ▲       ▲       ▲
```

| Unique aspects such as:<br>• Land<br>• Labour<br>• Skills<br>• Materials<br>• Transport<br>• Communications | Extent to which local demand stimulates innovation | Clustering of firms and industries and the location of services and skilled staff | Competition among support services and the impact on growth and costs |

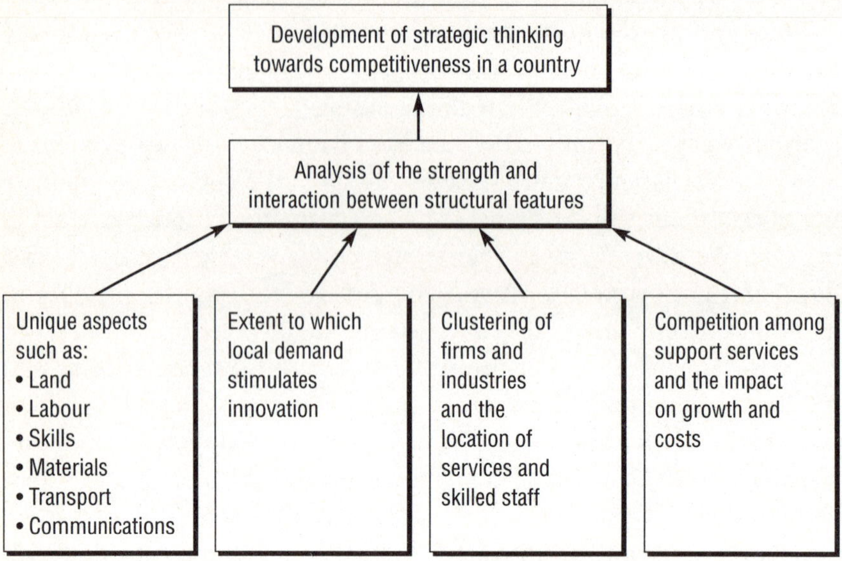

(Based on ideas found in Michael E. Porter, *The Competitive Advantage of Nations*, New York, Free Press, 1990)

focus for skilled workers and support industries. The situation would of course be different for each country, and it is by analyzing the interaction between these four factors that the opportunities for growth in other countries as well as nationally can be identified.

We have touched on the question of globalization and national responsiveness in terms of differentiating the product offering to meet local requirements. Bartlett and Ghoshal (1989) have identified that there are choices to be made concerning the extent to which economies of scale and scope can be achieved by a globalization strategy, and where this conflicts with a growth strategy aimed at responding to country requirements. For a globalization strategy, they suggest that the approach should be to compete on price and seek mergers and acquisitions, whereas with a national responsiveness strategy, the focus should be on creating and acquiring niche firms and gaining support from the host country. In cases where neither economies of scale nor differentiation would result in cost advantages, then a standardization strategy around products and services is likely to emerge.

Bartlett and Ghoshal see the emergence of the transnational strategy being the one that most multinationals would aspire towards. Here integration and local responsiveness are both used by the firm. This is seen as the most challenging and potentially productive stance. We can now see that the strategic objectives of the firm and the means by which these are achieved present many opportunities for conflict. Most of these conflicts will arise from a difference in perspectives on how to decide between these ends and means alternatives. We will look now at the background and key factors that influence these perspectives.

An international perspective on strategy will be influenced by attempts to achieve multiple objectives. These will include:

- seeking efficiency of operations;
- managing the financial and other business risks;
- promoting innovation and learning at all levels in the organization.

This presents the strategists with a wide set of choices and having to balance the conflicts between the various stakeholders. The efficiency strategies rely on taking advantage of national conditions such as labour costs and selecting the correct locations for the various activities in the production or service chain. This will result in being able to achieve economies through the scale of the work being done and to capitalize on opportunities to share or leverage physical resources. The strategic thinker has many sources of information, experiences and analytical approaches to help in making sense of

> **Alliances can be used to bridge industry value chains.**

this complex and changing set of conditions. The field is one for the specialist, and theory has only a small part to play in helping in this sense-making process. But there are some broad pointers that will help expand the thinking of our strategist. The notion of a worldwide value chain can be linked to the notion of economies of scale by focusing on adjusting levels of work at the points in the value chain where advantages can be gained. The balancing of scale and flexibility is of course a key consideration for firms that find themselves in a rapidly changing environment. The more stable environments lending themselves to this optimization of capability through investment in value chain resources and skills.

Another area where a theoretical notion may help is that of sharing resources either within a value chain or between value chains. This would apply to firms that are diversified and can share resources between different products and services. Common use of a distribution channel is one way of sharing such resources and gaining what are described as economies of scope. In following such strategies, the danger is that the efforts to share resources may lead to loosing sight of the flexibility or focus that is essential to success in particular markets (the local responsiveness argument). Also, the management overheads involved in creating and maintaining the integration can in some cases outweigh the benefits. Although driven by the need to gain efficiency, we have at the same time to manage the risks. Aside from the cataclysmic risks associated with events beyond the control of the firm, it is necessary to instigate strategies and policies that will hedge against such things as exchange rate fluctuations and the moves of competitors.

There is also the threat of the core resources of the firm being eroded or made obsolete through the introduction, by competitors, of, say, a new technology or an innovation that changes the way that the industry sector works. The complexity involved in attempting to hedge against these risks is obvious. The need to maximize the opportunities of learning from such a diverse set of activities must therefore become a key concern for the strategists. We have suggested that this whole area is fraught with conflicting theories from economists, country experts, brand and imaging devotees and the believers in analyzing processes involved in value chains and the management of the political and financial world. Among all of this, our strategist will find a number of common paradoxes being used.

The most common exhortation is to think global and act local. Easier said than done. We have just seen that globalization separates different elements in the value chain, locating them at geographic points where costs are lowest and then maximizing throughput to benefit from economies of scale and the learning curve effect. This will eventually lead to specialization of activity by location. It would appear that attempts to form strategies that focus on leveraging local learning and responding to local country and market requirements are at odds with this globalization strategy. Another paradox arises around learning. Here the global strategy leads to centralization of expertise and those functions that the firm believes are part of their core competence and the feature that gives them their competitive edge. But at the same time the firm seeks to maximize learning from the various subsidiaries and country variations in requirement, seeing this as a key part of their information-gathering network for new innovations.

This drive to centralize expertise and learning while wanting to maximize learning from the subsidiaries appears to present mutually exclusive goals. A final paradox arises where investing in local subsidiaries, in order to obtain growth and local efficiency, will detract from the attempts to build in flexibility. Changes in demand, factor costs and economic changes that effect exchange rates and investment opportunities require a global value chain that is flexible. Investments, particularly those involving plant, infra-structures and training of the local workforce will all militate against retaining the flexibility that the multinational seeks. These paradoxes are obviously all context-dependent and have to be considered against the objectives of the firm and the dynamics of the industry. This brings us to the next consideration for the strategist: that of attempting to forecast a changing future.

## FORECASTING THE FUTURE OR BUILDING SCENARIOS

The problem with most good ideas is that they become over-used and misused. Attempts at forecasting the future of an economy, an industry, a technology or a firm is a notion that has engaged many great minds over the last century. If the forecasts turn out to be correct, then the managers quickly move on to the next set of forecasts. When a forecast fails to materialize, then the procrastination centres around either having set the wrong objectives in the first place or around the inadequacy of the forecasting method or on the abilities of the forecasters. Usually the rain-makers are then called for, and if they are successful, then forecasting and all that goes with it is treated with scepticism. It seems that forecasters are always going to get a rough ride.

Strategic thinking about how to tackle the competition and grow the firm requires some reflection. For example:

- How has the firm performed in the past?
- What strategies and key actions have been taken?
- How is the firm performing today?

Exhortations from the management gurus will also encourage thinking about the future and how to renew or change the firm's competencies such that the future can be shaped or captured. This involves establishing some form of shared vision of the future that is sufficiently exciting, but at the same time realistic enough to be credible among the stakeholders in the firm. Strategic thinkers are managers, they know about targets and they know a lot about commitment and control. They also know a lot about problem identification, how to select options and tackle implementation. Forecasting the future is easy to do, but getting people to believe in the forecasts strongly enough to deal with and accept the unfolding evidence that comes with time is another matter. No doubt Christopher Columbus had to sell himself as a credible forecaster, as he set out to find the New World. While we can all readily identify and agree with these homilies, there is still this problem of how to approach strategic thinking, when forecasting the future is such an imprecise activity. There are two approaches open to us – well, three – but we will eliminate the option of ignoring the future.

> **Management consultants live by their models.**

The first approach involves persuading ourselves and our colleagues that by using quantifiable data in mathematically based models and relationships we will be able to extrapolate, with a known degree of confidence, a future. This future assumes the continuance of many of the facets of our current industry environment. Identifying the models to be used and the sources, validity and reliability of the data will all have to be agreed. But this is a conventional and familiar approach that managers consider to be reasonably reliable. Intuition can be added to the analysis, at the various stages, such that the pathways to the future become more concrete. This use of tangible evidence, to make sense of uncertainty about the future, involves rational processes of thinking and is the first step in creating a sense of control and order where none previously existed. These approaches rely on having a systematic forecasting and planning process that is credible and well-understood. The management consultancies make a lot of money by supplying their clients with such models. These models become the cornerstone of strategic planning activity in many companies. Their contribution to the activities of strategic thinking is much more debatable. So what approach can be offered to help the strategic thinker approach the future?

Shining a light into a darkened cupboard is an analogy that captures the notion of scenario planning. Depending on where you shine the torch, you get a slightly different picture, but putting all these small pictures together may enable you to anticipate what you will experience and the posture you will need to adopt when you switch off the torch and step into the cupboard. Scenario planning is a technique that involves creating various accounts of how the business environment might develop over time. This involves extensive use of creative techniques and 'what if' questioning. The approach helps the strategist to grapple with a complex set of factors that are related to envisaging and dealing with an uncertain future.

This scenario-building process is used to help surface the mental models that those engaged in the strategy process use to link information about the environment. It also draws out the premises that they use to make sense of that environment and consider action. One of the main benefits of scenario planning is argued to be the way in which 'groupthink' is overcome and learning that has been built into the minds of the participants is made explicit and challenged. By this process, managers are encouraged to confront differences that arise over misunderstandings in the way business language and management concepts are being used. Experience gained from using this technique has highlighted the importance of linking the scenarios that are generated with the vision held by the corporate group. These scenarios also need to be tested against the views of the business and operational managers, particularly in areas such as competitive positioning and operational capabilities.

What we are exposing here is a learning process in action. Strategists are pooling and confirming the range of experiences and expertise that they have on possible future scenarios. This is then tested out using various 'what if?' questions to test the boundaries of these scenarios. The scenarios that emerge are then matched against the views and mental models of business and operational managers who are much closer to the realities of competitive positioning and operational experiences. For firms that use this approach, the conventional strategic planning process then follows. The emphasis of this scenario approach is to avoid the temptation to predict the future. The process encourages managers to explore possibilities and to exercise their imagination, moving closer to the stance of the strategic thinker rather than that of the conventional planner. An outline workshop showing how to undertake scenario planning is provided in the later sections of this book. So how far is planning from thinking?

PART I · THE WORLD OF THE STRATEGIC THINKER

## PLANNING AS THINKING

Planners prefer to opt for a systematic and logical approach to formulating strategy as this provides a sense of order and control. Their aim is to be able to understand how the firm operates and how these operations impact on performance. The operations can then be redirected or re-arranged, in order to achieve a clear set of business objectives. As any one attempting to raise a loan for a small business or project will know, a business plan is the first requirement. The more clear and believable the plan, the more likely it is that the funds will be made available. Plans provide the investors with a sense of control over the thinking and action of the enterprise. It will always be this way. What we are arguing here is that the value of the thinking behind the espoused plan is the important element and that this thinking will determine how the plan is played out.

Plans seek to capture thinking as facts or 'hard data', which is then used to predict the outcomes of a set of actions taken by another group of thinkers. The fault in this logic starts to become apparent in that those taking action may well make a markedly different set of interpretations of events as they unravel. Here we see how control comes into play as the means of implementing the plans. This presents a clear paradox in that effective strategic thinking depends on being able to mentally suspend the constraints surrounding the firm, and its operation and yet effective strategic planning rests on being able to represent these thoughts as 'hard facts' in ways that can be measured and controlled in order to begin implementation. Finding the root of this paradox is one of the central questions addressed in later sections of this text (see *Chapter 11*). Here we just need to explore this interface between thinking and planning a bit further in order to open up our thinking.

It would be silly to argue that having a plan against which managers can monitor progress and learn is unhelpful to a firm. A plan enables the managers to see clearly the sequencing and priorities of activities and the points in time where evaluation of progress against objectives are to be made. Plans also provide stakeholders with the sense of confidence that is so vital to maintaining their support. If the future was predictable to the point of near-certainty, then we would assume that all of the firm's competitors also had access to that information. In such a case we would expect that firms would seek either to dominate the sector in which they were competing, by being smarter or quicker than the rest, or else they would try to change the nature of that certainty. Much of the effort around branding, advertising and promotion is aimed at breaking the certainties that other firms have attempted to create. What we see here ties in with our intuition that planning is based on assumptions not only about our forecasts of the future, but also on what we think the competitors are likely to do to secure their forecasts for the future.

Our strategic thinking can now move beyond trying to forecast the future. It can include trying to describe what we expect the future to be like, while recognizing that there are likely to be as many views on this as there are managers. Competition between firms is therefore being posed as competition between strategists and decision makers. It is the thinking and sophistication of mindsets that is the key to resolving the thinking, planning paradox. The planning processes and methodologies that are used to capture and represent this thinking as a set of definitive plans become the output rather than the input of our strategic thinking.

> **Plans provide stakeholders with a sense of confidence.**

To ask how strategic thinkers make sense of the signals in their local and far environments and how they re-adjust and adapt their mental models or industry recipes is probably a more fruitful way of understanding the power behind this particular paradox. We must avoid the temptation to join the battle between the supporters of logic and predictability and those who rely on intuition and the ability to be responsive. How to live and prosper in a turbulent and dynamic world rather than trying to create stability and order will be the central argument tackled in the next chapter.

## References

Bartlett, C.A. and Ghoshal, S. (1989) *Managing Across Borders: The Transnational Solution*, Boston, Harvard Business School Press.

Porter, M.E. (1990) *The Competitive Advantage of Nations*, New York, Free Press.

# Chapter 4

# CHAOS OR CONTROL

Riding the waves or navigating the ship  *61*

Logic is still a powerful tool  *64*

Empowerment and control  *66*

Innovation as a challenge to implementation  *69*

> *He that will not apply new remedies must expect new evils: for time is the greatest innovator.*
>
> Francis Bacon (1561–1626),
> English philosopher

Managers are rarely rewarded for doing silly things, in spite of all the exhortations from the guru Tom Peters. Making clear appraisals of messy situations and acting in a purposeful and straightforward manner is still seen as the hallmark of a good manager – so we are encouraged to believe. But is this the way that we expect our strategic thinker to behave? In this chapter, we will look at some of the perspectives and organizational pressures that influence strategic thinking. We will show how individuals exert power and influence in groups by the use of logic and argument. Logic and control have also been linked, in contemporary management, to the notion of empowerment, and we need to see how this impacts on strategy making. Innovation is argued as being the pathway to success for those strategists who set out to achieve competitive advantage. The guru's advice is that the winning firms are the ones capable of stimulating a burst of innovation, followed by a total organizational focus on efficiency and commercial delivery. This type of thinking can be seen in the automobile industry and is now being adopted in the pharmaceutical and high technology industries. We will explore the realism behind these notions and their impact on the deliberations of the strategic thinker.

## RIDING THE WAVES OR NAVIGATING THE SHIP

Analogies as we know are attractive and easy to use. Their use in organizations is one step beyond that of the joke or good story. The danger is that they encourage us to narrow our perspectives and start to believe that the analogy is a perfect illustration of the point of view that we hold. They encourage us to take action as though we were inside the analogy: it becomes almost real.

The analogy of surfing is a powerful one, even if you have never been near a surfboard and have no intention of doing so. The strategist as a surfer, paddling along, going with the current and then riding the big one. The feeling of exhilaration is contagious, and for some strategists provides that spur or nudge that causes them to abandon their familiar logical thinking processes. The pressing desire to gather hard data in order to formulate their viewpoints is suspended. The more extreme and wealthy, management gurus adopt this stance, exhorting and encouraging strategic thinkers to let go of tried and tested recipes and processes, and arguing that benchmarking gets you alongside the competition, but to get ahead you need to break out and do new things. The attractiveness of this advice is not based on the use of logic, but more on a feeling that chaos might be a way of having some fun and capturing the spirit that true entrepreneurs and geniuses enjoy every day. But one of the disappointments that follows from adopting this view is that how to apply the approach is then prescribed, and unfortunately, the prescription is presented as the old familiar logic. It seems that the freedom of thinking that appeared so attractive is quickly lost.

**Innovation is the pathway to success.**

But to get back to our surfing analogy. Strategy making, it is argued, is like a game where the players make a discovery, take action and then react to the consequences of the impact of that action on others. Is our surfer engaging in a game against other surfers or possibly the wave? Perhaps the surfer sees it as a sport in which the aim is to reach a determinable standard of performance. Achieving the standard will then result in public acclaim and fame. Alternatively our surfer may have been trapped into proving a point to a group of peers and is trying to minimize the risk of failure while not appearing to be a coward. We could continue, but the point that emerges is that we have used the surfing analogy to describe a state where the strategist is deliberately setting out to create a mindset and seeking a context in which the element of surprise is likely to be high, one in which there is no logical or reliable way of predicting the outcomes and actions that will ensure success. If we became concerned about the way that our analogy was starting to appeal to the strategists, then we might want to try a more conventional analogy: the sea captain who we rely upon to navigate a safe passage for our ship.

The ship analogy is better. It gives us a feeling of stability and control. We assume that our captain has read the weather charts and is familiar with the working and capabilities of the ship and the crew. Although he is prepared to compete with other ships for a good sea-going position, and to manoeuvre so that we are the first in the queue going into harbour, we would not expect any surprises or unpredictable behaviours.

The captain is formulating strategies, making decisions and learning from every facet of a controlled environment. If perchance our captain ran into some freak weather conditions, we would put this down to bad luck and the power of the elements. It would be very rare to expect disaster.

What differentiates our two heroes? Is it that good surfers self-select and the bad ones disappear? In that case, as long as we isolate the strategist who is following the surfer analogy and only expects a few wins, then we will be all right. Our expectations of breakthrough would be quite low, and we would on occasions be pleasantly surprised with success.

On the other hand, our strategist following the sea captain analogy is a much better bet. Presumably, we have carefully selected our strategist and arranged an environment in which performance based on predictability is almost guaranteed. Yes, the problem is that there are plenty of examples of where the planned strategies have not worked out. Steel might seem like a fairly predictable business to be in, and strategies easily produced and implemented. But many firms in the steel and other apparently stable industries seem to have got things wrong. Perhaps we need to select an approach that suits the conditions.

**Mental models are our way of making sense of a mess.**

So if we can predict the conditions, we can select the strategy, and then select the type of implementers that will enable us to achieve our goals. Sounds easy, but once again a lot of great minds have failed to achieve a viable and sustainable approach. Perhaps we have a paradox. We know that breakthrough requires an ability to encourage and engender chaos, but on the other hand we know that stability and control are powerful ways to achieve successful outcomes.

Learning to accept and manage both, rather than argue for one or the other would seem a good approach, but what is at the root of this paradox? We would suggest that it is around the way that our strategist thinks and makes sense of the environment, the mental models that are understood and have been at the root of previous successful actions. There are many other factors that will impact on the way that our strategist makes sense of the environment and is able to persuade others that the sense-making is acceptable. One of the key factors is the way that logic is used.

PART I · THE WORLD OF THE STRATEGIC THINKER

# LOGIC IS STILL A POWERFUL TOOL

The use of logic has enabled puzzlers and seekers after the truth to make sense of a confusing world. Our strategist would not and should not ignore or abandon the power that resides in the use of logic. But we need to consider the place for logic in strategic thinking and how it is used to influence perspectives. Strategy making is bedevilled with constant references to probabilities. Managers quickly learn that although they would like to be able to use logical deduction from a set of hard data to reach a certain and indisputable conclusion, this rarely proves to be the case. Where science and engineering are concerned, we are familiar with a process of argument that states the validity of a set of conditions and then uses a deductive process to reason a logical connection to a conclusion. This scientific process of reasoning is aimed at producing an outcome that is proven or certain. The reasoning is based on the use of intrinsic deductions from a set of agreed principles. Use is made of a set of principles or laws of nature that are universally recognized and agreed.

For the strategist, the objective is not to attempt to arrive at certainty, but to reach a state of conviction where the use of probability is a reality rather than an option. The strategist seeks and elaborates on the contingencies surrounding a situation or problem. The data is always contingent upon a host of assumptions and probabilities. Dealing with ambiguity, uncertainty and the equivocality of information is the daily diet of the strategist. Although we are arguing that seeking certainty through a process of logical deduction from a set of data is not a credible approach for the strategist, this does not mean that it is not used. The arguments are usually presented in rhetorical or persuasive form. An example of how this might be used in the strategic deliberations of a large transport and logistics firm is given below.

- *Our competitors want to change the way that the retail industry looks at distribution and are likely to offer open book contracting for their logistics management.*
- *We know that our competitors want to change the retailers' outlook.*
- *Therefore we must move to open book contracting.*

This illustrates a conclusive form of reasoning. Here the first statement presents a major premise which is not easily refutable, and evidence, if called for, could be found to back this up. The second statement is a minor premise from which the final conclusion is quickly reached. Another example is where a wholesale firm is deliberating over the further investment in information technology systems.

- *A large wholesaler who wants to be a major player in the next ten years is likely to take advantage of the Internet.*
- *We know that our main competitor wants to continue to be a major player in the next ten years.*
- *Therefore they are likely to invest heavily in order to acquire that capability.*

This example uses rhetoric rather than logic, but the difference is easily overlooked when the presenter of the argument is both credible and powerful. But though the use of probability is central to the argument, the way that the argument is presented often masks any discussion around the strength of that probability. There are four main approaches used by those offering rhetoric as a way of structuring and presenting an argument:

1. By presenting antecedents and the subsequent events that have arisen:
   *By focusing entirely on our global branding strategies over the past five years, we have allowed our local competitors to capture our traditional home markets.*

2. From a consideration of motives and drawbacks:
   *We have been seeking world dominance and rapid growth. Neither of these have been achieved.*

3. By presenting opportunity:
   *The marketing department and their pursuit of brand strategies created the opportunity for us to be attacked by local competitors who concentrated on product differentiation.*

4. By concentrating on cause and effect:
   *It is the marketing focus on brand strategies that has caused the decline in our home market share and the downturn in sales and profitability.*

5. By resurfacing opportunity:
   *We can recover if we invest in strategies that promote product differentiation.*

6. By resurfacing consequences:
   *The outcome will be a strong home sales performance and a means to feed our overseas markets with a range of products that will capitalize on local variations and taste.*

One of the purposes of this rhetorical approach is to present an argument that appears to be logical, but is in fact a series of unproven premises. The intended outcome is that it becomes impossible, for the other party, to present a counter-argument. This may sound slightly academic and far from the notion of an objective, value-free set of corporate colleagues sitting down to discuss ways of revitalizing the firm. But some readers may be able to reflect on some very similar scenes occurring in their own organizations. The use of logic and rhetoric in arguing a strategic case suggests that there are games to be played, and winners and losers will be determined as a consequence. If at the same time we are trying to harness the creativity and innovative capabilities in the firm, we need to look at some other approaches to managing.

## EMPOWERMENT AND CONTROL

Strategists have been sent many ambiguous and some downright contradictory signals about how to capitalize on the creative talents of staff in the firm. These signals have been generated, in all good faith, by academics, gurus, consultants and those reporting the progress of firms in the media. One of the key areas of advice has centred on the importance of organizational structure and on re-engineering processes within the firm. The focus here is on improving efficiency and making firms more flexible so that they can deal with changes in their markets and environments. Another contemporary and far-reaching piece of advice has been to embrace downsizing. This is aimed at improving productivity by reducing the number of workers and linking this to improved processes. Improving processes is an admirable objective as long as it is complemented by an increase in market share. Productivity without growth in sales is a recipe for disaster.

As many firms quickly discover, all of these approaches to success depend on the support and imagination of the managers and the workers. We know that a successful strategy is one that:

- promotes ways of doing business with fewer people;
- improves management and operational processes;
- encourages continuous improvement in processes and procedures from everyone;
- promotes creativity that will regenerate the firm;
- over time will restructure the way that the industry operates.

All of the above rely on two key factors. First, that the managers and workers are empowered to take action and apply their creative talent, and second that there is a control mechanism in place that can set targets, measure performance and implement corrective action. We can see an immediate paradox in the above statement. On the one hand we are advocating freedom of action for all, and on the other a determination to control or at least restrict choice and freedom. This is more than just a question of degree. We need to explore this paradox from some alternative perspectives.

**How can we get creativity with control?**

Some of the most popular and influential management books and ideas have come from the minds of Gary Hamel and C.K. Prahalad. We can seek their advice on empowerment.

> Although the voices calling for a new organizational paradigm (leaner, flatter, virtual, modular, etc.) have been numerous and vocal, there has been no concomitant clamour for a new strategy paradigm. We believe, though, that the way many companies 'strategize' is just about as out of date, and just as toxic, as the way they organize. However lean and fit an organization, it still needs a brain. But the brain we have in mind is not the brain of the CEO or strategic planner. Instead it is an amalgamation of the collective intelligence and imagination of managers and employees throughout the company who must possess an enlarged view of what it means to be 'strategic'.
>
> *Competing for the Future*, Gary Hamel and C.K. Prahalad (page 26)

Knowing about and being able to make everyday decisions with an eye to the overall strategies being pursued is now recognized as being a key feature of successful firms. What we have here is a determination to empower people as an extension of the strategy making and management process. What we need to avoid is suddenly withdrawing that power when decisions that could lead to key learning are presented. This is where the paradox starts to become a battleground rather than a representation of a dynamic set of tensions and opportunity.

Empowerment involves freeing up people to make decisions based on their own perceptions, values and judgements. Strategies that encourage continuous improvement around total quality management imply that staff are being encouraged to apply all of their potential to the job in hand. This presents conventional management systems, based on rewards for performance against a set standard, with a dilemma. On the one hand, rewarding performance against set standards is measurable and justifiable, but you also need to reward people for managing a changing set of conditions and standards. The problem is no longer static but becomes one of rewarding against a changing set of circumstances. The conventional approach would be to decide which decisions can be decentralized, how this will be done and over what timescales the decision-making effects will have to be monitored and controlled. A less conventional approach would be to ignore the notion of central control.

The following two examples help to understand this empowerment control paradox. They also suggest that the context and culture of the firm may be a bigger determinant than logic or rhetoric as to the final approach taken to determining a winning strategy.

> To survive in modern times, a company must have an organizational structure that accepts change as its basic premise, lets tribal customs thrive, and fosters a power that is derived from respect, not rules. In other words, the successful companies will be the ones that put quality of life first. Do this and the rest – quality of product, productivity of workers, profits for all – will follow.
>
> At Semco we did away with strictures that dictate the 'hows' and created fertile soil for differences. We gave people an opportunity to test, question and disagree. We let them determine their own training and their own futures. We let them come and go as they wanted, work at home if they wished, set their own salaries, choose their own bosses. We let them change their minds and ours, prove us wrong and when we are wrong, make us humbler. Such a system relishes change, which is the only antidote to the corporate brainwashing that has consigned giant businesses with brilliant pasts into uncertain futures.
>
> *Maverick – The Success Story Behind the World's Most Unusual Workplace*, Ricardo Semler

The second example that we are using to understand the empowerment control paradox comes from reported efforts at Banc One. The headquarters are in Columbus, Ohio and the company grew rapidly in the early 1990s to become one of America's leading banks. Here the bank adopted a strategy on empowerment that integrated tight policy and decision-making guidance with decentralized decision making. Managers were free to choose their own portfolio of customer products dependent on local market needs and set their own pricing policies. This decentralization of decision making was supported by an information reporting system, so the success of different local strategies could be shared among the branch managers.

These last two examples illustrate attempts by companies to close the gap between the local knowledge that managers have of the markets and customers and their potential for producing innovative solutions to growing the business. This all sounds like sound advice, but we still need to know how this will contribute to our quest for building strategies that are sufficiently innovative that they will secure the future. Empowerment of managers and staff will take us partway, assuming that we can harness the power of the empowerment and control paradox. But we need to move towards a way of managing innovative strategies that will secure the future while delivering promises made yesterday.

**Innovation can be radical or incremental.**

## INNOVATION AS A CHALLENGE TO IMPLEMENTATION

We have been encouraged to take the view that the way to achieve sustainable competitive advantage is to engage in some form of strategic innovation. We are further encouraged to believe that strategic innovation can take two forms. It can be approached in an incremental and continuous manner or it can be tackled in a discontinuous way where the existing set of organizational paradigms about how the industry and the firm interact and behave are challenged. This later approach is believed to result in more radical outcomes than those achievable through the incremental approach. For the strategist, who is focusing at the business or operational level, the incremental approach seems intuitively to be the one that is most likely to lead to implementation of predictable outcomes. It is easier to attract support when seeking to implement an improvement programme, and make approaches such as empowerment much more easy to introduce and manage. There is evidence that companies use a mixture of these approaches. For example,

GE incorporates what they call 'multigenerational programmes': starting a new programme with proven technologies and trying radical innovative approaches only when the product development seems to be failing.

This may be fine at an operational or product level but many strategists work at the corporate level, encompassing many separate businesses. At this corporate level, where the firm is operating as a multi-business, then the need for innovations that are based on a radical change are essential. Corporate renewal and regeneration will depend on these radical changes, as will the introduction of major new products and services. Some of these products and services, that are central to the core mission of the firm, may involve timescales of some 5 to 20 years before a pay-off is determined. If it is accepted that innovation, at a strategic level, is essential to the survival and growth of the firm, then we need to have a view as to the impact that this has on the pace at which implementation can proceed. A rapid innovation process, moving from idea selection, through to development and application, sounds like the best way to proceed.

Our first concern would perhaps be on how to generate a batch of radical ideas. Setting up think tanks and new ideas groups to spark off radical ideas is a well-proven approach. How then to transfer these ideas to a business and achieve commercial reality has challenged the minds of many great business leaders. Conventional wisdom tells us that successful transfer will depend on having the right organizational culture in place. If not, then we have to change the culture. Creating a climate and culture that encourages new thinking and does not punish mistakes. Easier said than done, as most firms have found to their cost. Companies such as Motorola have focused on creating such a climate, and they have reaped the benefits of an investment that has taken 10 to 15 years to pay off. If a firm establishes a process and climate in which new ideas can be generated, then these ideas have to be filtered. To do this, we need a process that can be seen to be fair and open, in order that ideas are not sacrificed for expediency or political reasons. Once again – not an easy management task.

It is not unreasonable that such an organization would become over time more proceduralized and systematic. Implementation is key to commercial success and although innovation is required at every stage we can see that routinization must be an objective. This would seem to mitigate against bringing in radical ideas and approaches. The very process that we saw as being vital to renewing the firm. The focus shifts away from radical breakthroughs to a more incremental approach. For those firms where radical breakthroughs involve changes to the processes and operating technologies and procedures, then the innovations have an obvious end point.

We then have two cases to consider. First, where the strategic innovations are about renewing the firm in terms of the way that it operates and the cultures that exist to support the mission of the firm, changing the core competencies and capabilities. Second, we have the strategic innovations that are aimed at repositioning the firm in terms of the products and services being produced and attempting to match the firm to the business environment and manage a network of external relationships. This presents a paradox. On the one hand, the firm is searching for new ideas around radical products and services for the firm and changing the firm's industry positioning, the radical innovation strategy. While on the other hand, it is trying to improve the processes of the firm around the existing products and methods of working.

The tensions that this produces have resulted in some extreme approaches being employed. Some advocate the use of change leaders or champions to push the changes through. Others promote organizational development programmes that attempt to produce a culture that supports the change strategies. In some companies, groups of people are encouraged to work away at new ideas in spite of the focus of the firm. These have been appropriately labelled, by gurus such as Tom Peters, as 'skunk works.' All of these approaches are central to the paradox of innovation and implementation. Many have their champions and advocates. But they have all failed to identify clearly and then tackle the root of the paradoxes that abound. Balancing thinking and action brings us closer to these roots and in the next chapter we will begin to unravel some of the core beliefs that surround these issues.

## References

Hamel, G. and Prahalad, C.K. (1994) *Competing for the Future*, Boston, Harvard Business School Press.

Semler, R. (1993) *Maverick: The Success Story Behind the World's Most Unusual Workplace*, London, Random House.

# Chapter 5

# MYTHS AND REALITIES OF STRATEGIC PLANNING

Planning as strategy  *75*

The manager as a strategic thinker  *78*

Making sense of a complex and dynamic organization  *81*

Dialogue helps to create new knowledge  *83*

> *There is always some accident in the best of things. The thought came to us because we were in a fit mood; also we were unconscious and did not know that we had said or done a good thing.*
>
> ..........................
>
> Henry David Thoreau (1817–62),
> US writer

## PLANNING AS STRATEGY

The intention or end sought by the planner is to be able to control. The intention or end sought by the strategist is to be able to sense or see how to achieve satisfaction for stakeholders. Planning is about management, and strategy is about loyalty and duty, a role that is conventionally assumed to be that of the directors. What we are suggesting here is that the strategists are ultimately responsible for the health of the corporate body. This assumes that their strategies are accepted by the business, and can be clearly linked to the actions that will ultimately lead to commercial success – quite an assumption given the complexity of business decision-making and action. We are taking a strong line here in arguing this deterministic role for the strategies that are developed. Much of the conventional wisdom takes a much softer line, promoting notions such as 'strategic intent' and 'having a strategic architecture in place'. If this deterministic role is to become more than rhetoric, then the strategist needs to have the power to influence implementation. The strategist position therefore differs from that of the planner in that the inferred duty to care means that business judgements are central to all strategic thinking and actions, the role of the planner being much more instrumental.

The conventional view of a good strategy is that it must be seen as viable by those involved in the decision-making and action loop. The strategy must meet two criteria, if it is to be accepted by the business managers. It must be desirable, in that it supports the current objectives of the business, and secondly, it must be feasible in terms of the current capabilities and the resource base. It is this pragmatic thinking that drives the strategist into the arms of the planner. As the strategist moves from thinking towards identifying options and making choices, the need for help from the planners becomes more pressing. The strategic thinking moves into the realm of decision making. Strategic decision making takes place against a background of uncertainty about the future, the ambiguities associated with the business objectives and the means required to achieve them.

The interactions between the various strategies and their relative impact on business outcomes are also, at best, not understood. A traditional way to structure the decision-making process has been to make explicit statements about the criteria being used to evaluate alternatives. In determining these criteria the strategist takes into account the impact of the thinking and hence strategic alternatives on the stakeholders, the competitors, the marketplace, the industry, the nation, the environment and themselves. In an ideal world, each group would warrant the identification of a set of criteria. The reality is that most strategists have strong beliefs about the primacy of one group of stakeholders and the relative importance of the criteria being used in the decision-making process. They will be trying to balance these conflicting demands and rely on being able to exercise their best judgement when faced with hard choices –

**Business judgements are central to strategic thinking.**

for example, balancing the short-term interests of the shareholders with those of the longer-term interests of the firm. An academic view on this would be that the strategist, when faced with these complex choices, creates order by adopting a perspective based on bounded rationality. This is where the strategist rationalizes as to what is feasible in the circumstances and makes decisions on that basis, putting boundaries or limitations on the information that is accepted as relevant to the decision. The strategist moves into the domain of the planner at this point, seeking to systematize the way in which the decisions on strategic choices are to be made.

Strategists often find their thinking and decision making pressurized by two types of stakeholders: those that want to use the firm as a tradeable asset and the managers and workers that are inside and rely on the firm as a source of livelihood and satisfaction. The constant challenge is in finding where to strike the balance between these two perspectives, on what represents continuing success. The conventional approach is to adopt the classical strategic perspective. This relies on the identification of a vision and supporting mission for the firm that is aimed at achieving satisfaction for all of the stakeholders. The drive is to secure the sustainable competitive advantage that follows from market positioning and the pursuit of excellence. This pursuit of excellence is measured in terms of:

- the enhancement in image and reputation through product and service provision and responsiveness;

- how value is added through leveraging knowledge and expertise in the various parts of the value chain;
- the way capital is used to gain competitive advantage through investments and acquisitions;
- the approaches used to encourage staff to commit themselves to the goals of the firm.

The strategists know that effectiveness has to be balanced with efficiency, and value the importance of having some measures of control over the outcomes. These would include conventional measures such as:

- market share and growth rates;
- accounting ratios such as debtors, creditors, contribution, overheads and cash flow forecasts;
- capital ratios such as earnings per share, share prices, etc.;
- asset ratios such as return on capital employed, profit margins and liquidity.

From the above it becomes clear how quickly planning becomes strategy made explicit. The reality is that corporate success will be assessed by financial measures. These will become the ends to which strategy is being directed, rather than just indicators of the efforts of the managers to deal with and learn from a series of actions taken against a background of strategic intent. The strategist is attempting to make the best use of a set of resources and circumstances over which there is almost no control in the sense of cause and effect. The attempts by planners to produce a set of devolved actions and linkages that stem from these espoused strategies are part of a mindset that demands control and accountability. Having identified an enormous gap or disconnection between the role of the strategists, in visioning and thinking about how to best apply the resources of the firm, and that of the objective planners and seekers of control, the academics have offered some explanations and advice.

> **Strategic intent and performance must be linked.**

Two pieces of advice stand out. First, that strategies need to be reflected and supported by a culture or set of espoused values and beliefs among the employees, so that a connection between strategic intent and performance can be made. Second that strategist and managers should work together to identify core competencies in the firm and that these should then be built into capabilities that are sustainable. The sustainability will depend on these capabilities:

- not being easily copied by competitors;
- adding value to the service or product being offered to the customer;
- being competitively unique.

The strategist, and the managers in the firm, are thus brought together through this process of identifying competencies. Formal planning techniques and processes are then used to express the thinking in a way that links into the investment and decision-making processes.

What has this told us about strategic planning? We have argued that the roles of the strategist and the planner are not naturally connected. The strategist is more involved in formulating vision, mission and strategic intent, acting in a stewardship role and balancing the demands and interests of the stakeholders, while the planner's contribution is to take the broad goals, that arise from this strategic thinking, and convert them into an ends/means programme. The business manager then attempts to work to these plans and deliver against the performance measures. The performance, against plan, is used as an input to an on-going strategic evaluation process. The strategic intent drives all of this activity and is surrounded by a supportive culture and an appropriate leadership style. How realistic this is, in terms of the extent to which the manager can be influenced by strategic intent or can contribute to the strategic thinking activity, will be explored in the next section.

## THE MANAGER AS A STRATEGIC THINKER

We have been making the point that strategic thinking, as a means of developing strategies for an organization, can be viewed as either a top-down activity or as deriving from the bottom-up. Conventional wisdom would suggest that the source of strategic thinking stems from the power holder or influencing group. Because of this view many managers spend time and energy attempting to be part of that group or at least secure sufficient influence over the process so that their interests can be promoted and protected. Business process re-engineering and many programmes aimed at influencing the thinking of managers and the ways that they interact have failed to overcome the interface between the way that managers think about strategy and the way that they act. The action part of a manager's job or daily life is where most learning takes place. Making sense of messy situations, handling crises, making decisions that are at best made under a set of uncertain conditions, all create a heady and exciting environment for the active manager.

Reflection – more likely about daily activity than about a distant future – tends to be a less familiar and rewarding activity. The popularity of the 'away day' or the setting up of study groups to generate ideas and suggest where change is required supports this view that longer-term thinking has to be done 'off line'. The reality is that strategy is created through daily operational decision making and that the separation occurs only at the reflective thinking level. The business and operational managers become the strategy makers, creating strategies from actions that are driven from a set of mental models, in the minds of the managers, about how the firm should be proceeding, and only capturing and making them explicit through reflection and description.

An analogy for an 'off-line' process for creating strategy is that of trying to drive in the fog while looking at the rear-view mirror – perhaps a bit extreme for an analogy, but this is an important point that needs arguing out. We are presenting here quite a radical view compared to one where managers follow a set of guidelines that stem from an analysis of the best way to achieve a set of predefined objectives. If there is any credence, in this fairly radical view, about managers driving strategy, then we need to look more closely at how these models can be surfaced, understood and perhaps influenced.

We are arguing the view that managers use a range of mental images about how the organization works to guide their action, and further that where longer-term thinking is concerned, these images about what the firm should be doing exist but are perhaps less likely to surface. Therefore the imperative is to encourage managers to make their thinking about the longer-term explicit. This becomes central to the task of closing the gap between the daily action of managers and the development of a robust process for improving the strategic thinking capability of a firm. Personality traits, leadership styles, organizational processes and culture will all have an impact on how managers develop and share their thinking about the future. A strong mental model can encourage a manager to argue and win the case against all comers. Alternatively, some believe that appeasement and harmony, with a great deal of compromise, is the best way to gain acceptance of their view of the world, or at least the firm. These apparently opposing approaches present a dilemma. The root of this lies in the need to obtain commitment from others to your ideas. Most people rarely experience commitment, and in many cases feel that compliance is quite sufficient.

To encourage the surfacing of mental models, we need a degree of formalization, we need to become systematic. The danger is that we can very quickly move from systems that encourage and facilitate thinking to those that attempt to generate the thinking itself. The aim should be to create a process that acts as a catalyst, rather than as a control. Some firms encourage informal exchanges of ideas and views on business problems faced by managers as a way of sharing mental models. Others use the long-range forecasting and budgeting processes as a means of smoking out views and making changes. There are some that create formal processes where managers are expected to advance and defend their views against other managers. These approaches have their devotees, but it is important that they are set in the context and culture of the firm. For example, in Japanese or Far Eastern firms, the focus on a shared vision or mission may be much more central to the way that mental models are formed about the firm than in Western firms, where the focus is much more on plans, objectives-setting and control.

Whichever view is taken, the role and contribution of the manager, as a key element in the development of the firm's capability in strategic thinking, is guaranteed. But underlying this we can see a paradox. We want managers to share their mental models, as we see these as being the key to understanding the sources of new strategic thinking. At the same time, we want strategy to incorporate past experiences on how to achieve goals, and we want managers to support controlled implementation. These are apparently mutually exclusive requirements and represent the new thinking versus *status quo* paradox. Learning is central to this paradox, and in the next section we will look at how managers make sense of the complexity that organizational action taking can present.

> **Dealing with ambiguity is the key skill.**

## MAKING SENSE OF A COMPLEX AND DYNAMIC ORGANIZATION

All organizational life is messy. When involved in strategy making, the two features that quickly add to the mess are that the future is uncertain and that the strategies that are being followed are at best unclear and at worst contradictory. Any manager that has used multivariate analysis to help determine the underlying relationships between a number of causal factors will have first-hand experience of the dangers of believing that strategies are acting independently of one another. In competitive situations, where other firms are pursuing strategies that may well conflict with those of your own firm, we are likely to face dealing with an even bigger mess. The wider environment, albeit on a global scale, and the local environment, which includes the marketplace, are all changing in ways that are difficult, if not impossible to anticipate and control. But in spite of all this uncertainty, the strategic thinker still tries to work with colleagues to make some sense of what is going on. We will first look at how ambiguity is dealt with.

The strategic thinker is likely to see a lot of the strategic information as being ambiguous. One view is that corporate management is best equipped to establish an unequivocal meaning for such information, and should do so using deductive processes. This will result in managers lower down the organization being able to use the interpreted information to influence their actions directly. An alternative view would be that the important information required for strategy making resides lower down in the organization, and that what is needed is a way of communicating this information among members of the organization and encouraging them to form their own interpretations. The cynics who see vision and mission statements as an example of corporate excess will be groaning at this point. But many believe that the confusion that strategic thinkers experience when trying to make sense of ambiguity results in new ways of thinking about the firm and leads to the creation of new knowledge. Nissan's CEO, Yutaka Kume, has been reported as having used the phrase, 'Let's change the flow,' to capture the notion that creative approaches to strategic thinking can be stimulated by promoting constructive chaos in the organization.

By creating an open attitude to the ways that information is interpreted and routine mental models challenged, new perspectives are established. This process, of questioning interpretations, leads to the establishment of an agreed order that may be fundamentally different from that which was previously held to be true. We can see here a far different approach to that where the purpose of interpretation is to find a solution to a given problem, using a tried and tested set of rules and methodologies. The emphasis, where ambiguity abounds, is one of agreeing a definition of the problem and using the tension that ambiguity creates, rather than seeing it as something that has to be clarified and resolved in order to apply a known algorithm, and reach a solution.

Obviously and perhaps thankfully the strategic thinker is not continuously in this state of creative tension and chaos. But the reflection that it encourages will cause the thinker to question some of the values or preferences that are being used in the strategy-making process and to be careful as to the significance of some of the so-called hard data that is being used to establish facts about the firm and the external environment.

Uncertainty is the other dimension that surrounds the complexity that the strategic thinker faces. Organizations can be thought of as systems that respond to attempts to implement strategies. The outcomes of implementation decisions are at best uncertain and at worst impossible to predict. Attempts to manage this uncertainty rely on the use of mathematical theory and modelling to predict how the introduction of small changes to the strategies will influence performance over time. This uncertainty theory implies that negative and positive feedback features in the organizational system produce either a re-inforcing or dampening effect as strategies are implemented.

Alternatively, the organization may react in an entirely unpredictable fashion by flipping between the two states. Breaks in technology and major environmental disasters are believed to be two of the triggers that result in the firm being flipped between these two states – not exactly a vote of confidence for the promoters of this modelling of uncertainty approach. The paradox that this presents is that implementable strategies have to be found that will result in achieving predicted outcomes in an uncertain and ambiguous future, while at the same time the strategies must be capable of seizing opportunities as they arise.

If we believe that the future is unpredictable, to the degree of accuracy required, and that the outcomes of our strategic action taking are uncertain. We need to adopt an approach that emphasizes the short-term, adaptability and rapid learning. This has resulted in the growing belief, among strategic thinkers, that a drive towards continuous innovation and the creation of new knowledge, through a combination of loose networks of managers and an emphasis on the use of dialogue, points the way forward.

We have explored the way that our strategic thinker approaches making sense of a messy set of data which is at times ambiguous and at others uncertain. The three approaches to making sense of such information include those that rely on:

- a rational and logical set of models;
- algorithms, a heuristic or rule of thumb which is based on experience and intuition learned from previous action taking;
- a creative approach that breaks out of the existing paradigm and set of beliefs about how 'sense making' is usually approached.

Once this stage is completed, the strategist would then attempt to persuade colleagues that the sense making was both valid and consistent with the way that the interpretation had been made. The arguments that follow are then made in the form of a series of linked premises, some of which may be true and others may be false. We will revisit the way in which premises are used to link strategic thinking and action in later chapters. But before that we need to take a look at how such arguments and dialogue can impact on this sense-making process.

## DIALOGUE HELPS TO CREATE NEW KNOWLEDGE

Conventional wisdom would encourage the strategic thinker to set out to build a firm sufficiently dynamic to survive in a changing world, but at the same time one that could also forge a new future. It sounds like an exhortation, but, as we have seen so far, the tools and methods available to support this advice, are a bit lacking, although an approach that has gained acclaim involves accelerating learning from experience and creating new knowledge.

Organizational life, for most people, centres around management processes and procedures. The use of information technology and the drive to cut cost through systematizing procedures has perhaps been at the expense of true dialogue. We are differentiating here between discussions aimed at defining or resolving a problem and reaching a decision on action, and those aimed at dialogue. With a dialogue, there is no predetermined set of definitions or intentions to produce an outcome. You may ask why the author is bothering to make what appears to be a small and potentially academic point. The reasoning is that in discussions the intention is to put across your viewpoint and then to argue with others, or at least make your point tell. Some areas in organizational life are never discussed, or at least not openly, and others are assumed to be private. We would agree that discussion, as a means of communication and problem solving, is appropriate for the mainstream organizational activities. But where the need is to produce new knowledge, then dialogue is more appropriate.

Dialogue involves encouraging people to share the mental models that underpin their thinking. A great deal of the content of these models will be based on deeply held values expressed in the form of opinions. The knowledge that the strategist has acquired consists of that which is held at the explicit level, and easily shared and recognized by colleagues, and that which is hidden or tacit. This will also apply among those implementing strategy in that their tacit knowledge is shared through subtlety of language and behaviour. One of the dangers here is that of making an incorrect assumption concerning the knowledge being used to support the thinking.

> **True dialogue relies on not anticipating any outcomes.**

Sharing tacit knowledge is therefore a key step in creating new knowledge among a group. The purpose in using dialogue, as opposed to discussion, is to create the conditions under which this new knowledge can grow. Having surfaced and recognized the mental models being used, the challenge is then to build a shared model of how the strategists see the firm developing. This can be done by using metaphors and analogies. Creative techniques can also be used to help diverge and converge the thinking in order to look at the model that emerges in many different ways. Thus the individual strategic thinkers have the opportunity to test out the incoherence in their thoughts and models. To do this effectively requires individuals to suspend their assumptions, seeing each other as colleagues rather than adversaries who hold contrary opinions.

The following extract from Peter Senge's book, *The Fifth Discipline*, helps make this point more clear.

> For example, in a recent dialogue session involving a top management team of a highly successful technology company, people perceived a deep 'split' in the organization between R&D and everyone else, a split due to R&D's exalted role at the company. This split had its roots in the firm's history of a string of dramatic product innovations over the past 30 years, literally pioneering several dramatic new products that in turn became industry standards. Product innovation was the cornerstone of the firm's reputation in the marketplace. Thus, no one felt able to talk about the 'split,' even though it was creating many problems. To do so might have challenged the long cherished value of technology leadership and of giving highly creative engineers the autonomy to pursue product visions. Moreover, the Number 2 person in R&D was in the meeting.
>
> When the condition of 'suspending all assumptions' was discussed, the head of marketing asked, 'All assumptions?' When he received an affirmative answer, he looked perplexed. Later, as the session continued, he acknowledged that he held the assumption that R&D saw itself as the 'keeper of the flame' for the organization, and that he further assumed that this made them unapproachable regarding market information that might influence product development. This led to the R&D manager responding that he too assumed that others saw him in this light, and that, to everyone's surprise, he felt that this assumption limited his and the R&D organization's effectiveness. Both shared these assumptions as assumptions and not as proven facts. As a result, the ensuing dialogue opened up into a dramatic exploration of views that was unprecedented in its candour and its strategy implications.
>
> *The Fifth Discipline*, Peter Senge (1990)

In this chapter, we have highlighted the difficulties that the strategist faces in promoting new thinking, while at the same time needing to build on the existing knowledge within the firm. This quest is at the heart of the strategic innovation process, where the firm is seeking new ways to use existing resources and identify those core competencies and capabilities that are likely to be essential to sustainable competitive advantage. The key to harnessing the knowledge and experiences of the managers, in tackling this challenge, is to surface mental models. The majority of these models will be held at a tacit rather than explicit level. The convention of using logic and formal approaches, to make sense of ambiguity and uncertainty, becomes a serious block to creating new strategic thinking. The power of using dialogue, as opposed to conventional discussion and debate, opens up the possibility of achieving a breakthrough in strategic thinking. We now have an alternative approach to making sense of organizational complexity, a chance to extend and harness the use of organizational conversation as part of our strategy-making process.

We have also completed the first part of the book – capturing what it is that the strategists are trying to do and how they set out to do it. Some of the ideas and approaches may clash with the views that you hold. This is a good thing, as our approach, in Part I, has been to set the stage for providing an understanding of how paradox is formed and used in organizational argument and strategy making. The strategist is obviously central to this and we now need to look more closely, in Part II, at how strategic thinking has become embedded in the language of business, what is central to the beliefs that are held, and how these beliefs are taken as truths in action.

## *Reference*

Senge, P.M. (1990) *The Fifth Discipline: The Art and Practice of the Learning Organization*, London, Random House.

# Part II
# STRATEGIC THINKING REVISITED

Chapter 6

# UNDERSTANDING THE ORGANIZATIONAL MIND

The truly dynamic organization  *91*

The transition from evolution to revolution  *96*

> *My people and I have come to an agreement which satisfies us both. They are to say what they please, and I am to do what I please.*
>
> Frederick the Great,
> King of Prussia 1712–86

In Part II, we explore some of the notions that influence the thinking of the strategy maker. We begin by looking at the notion of the thinking organization. Most of us are quite happy to talk about an organization taking action and behaving in a manner that suggests that there is an organizational mind at work. Organizations are described as being 'customer-focused', 'caring' and 'responsive'. Senior managers and the management gurus tell us that the ideal organization is one that demonstrates dynamic behaviour and can achieve self-renewal. If this notion is credible, and the holy grail that all gurus and organizational designers are trying to find, then we need to find some good guides for the journey. This takes us deep into uncharted territory and we will need to consider the language that managers use in order to make sense of the terrain. Perhaps the language has become the terrain.

Our guides, to continue with that analogy, are the management gurus who have become the experts in helping managers understand the terrain. In this chapter we present the ideas of some of the more well-known gurus in order to check out the foundations of our own strategic thinking. Much of their work has become embedded in the belief systems of firms, as to how strategic thinking and implementation should be approached. We start by exploring some of the thinking behind the notion of the truly dynamic organization.

## THE TRULY DYNAMIC ORGANIZATION

Management is concerned with taking action that uses resources to obtain a desired goal or changed state. Individual managers learn different things as a result of taking action but where a group works together, and produces consistent outcomes, we attribute this to group learning. This learning is then applied to achieve the required levels of organizational performance. As long as the required levels of performance and organizational behaviour continue to be met, then the group learning is not questioned. The organization is seen to have learned how to perform. This all sounds very reasonable and it seems logical to accept that the performance of larger groups, who constitute the staff of major

## Figure 6.1
## SINGLE- AND DOUBLE-LOOP LEARNING

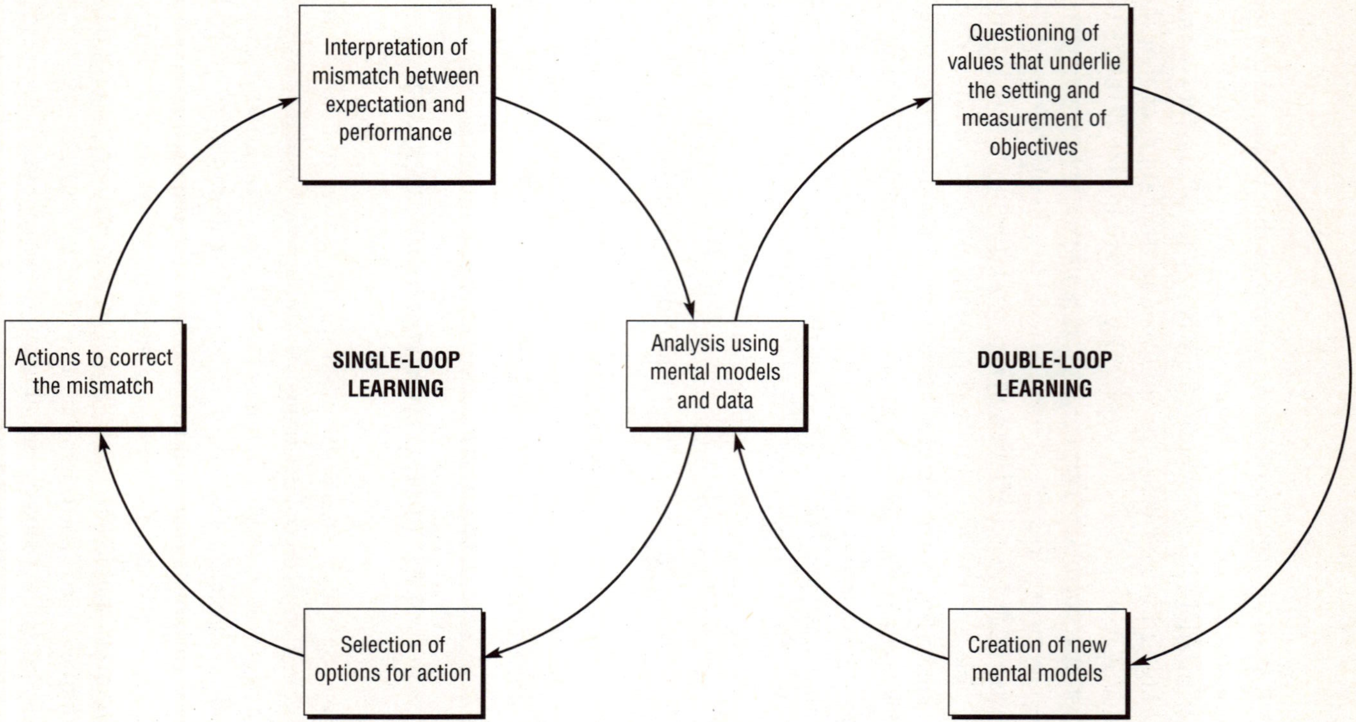

**DOUBLE-LOOP LEARNING**

- Questioning of values that underlie the setting and measurement of objectives
- Creation of new mental models
- Analysis using mental models and data

**SINGLE-LOOP LEARNING**

- Interpretation of mismatch between expectation and performance
- Selection of options for action
- Actions to correct the mismatch

corporations, are capable of learning how to behave. Much of the past 50 or more years of management theory and practice has been aimed at finding ways to ensure that organizations can be made to behave in the ways that managers dictate, with resulting efficiency and effectiveness, leading to the achievement of sustainable competitive advantage.

Many of these theories cannot be tested in the range of contexts that organizations operate. It is therefore difficult to convince managers that applying the theories will lead to achieving the required organizational behaviours. The theories become exhortations and best practice approaches, that managers are expected to adapt to the particular circumstances of their organizations. The impact of a particular theory is also hard to determine as there is rarely evidence available to demonstrate if it was used and if it was applied as specified. An example of this is where the strategic thinker is exhorted, and encouraged, to move from single-loop to double-loop learning. Single-loop learning is where the mismatch between intention and outcome is noted, and action taken to close the gap. Double-loop learning, attributed to Argyris and Schön (1978), is where the strategist, having detected a gap, is encouraged to question the beliefs and values that underlie the setting and measurement of the objectives. By changing these values and taking new action, the thinker moves into a higher level of learning. Figure 6.1 illustrates this notion of double-loop learning.

It is easy to grasp this as a notion or concept but applying the approach in practice, and knowing if it has been applied rigorously, is quite a different matter. Not surprisingly, the theories that become popular are those that can be most easily observed. 'Management by objectives' might be one that springs to mind. Finding out how best to create dynamic managers in dynamic organizations is a continuing challenge to the management gurus. By looking more closely at contemporary views on strategy making, we will get an insight as to how this quest is being pursued.

Recognizing that group learning is at the foundation of organizational level learning has moved us towards the view that organizations are dynamic. The strategy makers, within the organization, are in a unique and powerful position to influence the opportunities that the managers have for learning. The strategy makers, by striving to achieve sustainable competitive advantage for the organization, create the conditions for learning and hence the dynamics. There are two contemporary views of how to approach strategy making that will illustrate how the dynamics of a business are promoted. The first is where the firm is seen as being part of an industry and economic set of pressures, and it is these that influence the competitive position. This is known as the 'product market view' of the firm. The second is where the firm is seen as a set of resources that, if configured in a particular way, will enable the firm to achieve a position of sustainable competitive advantage, the 'resource-based view' of the firm. These contrasting perspectives are shown in Figure 6.2.

### Figure 6.2
### MARKET POSITIONING AND RESOURCE-BASED PERSPECTIVES

| Market positioning | Resource-based |
| --- | --- |
| Balancing a portfolio of products and services | Establishing core competencies |
| | A focus on arranging resources to create capabilities |
| A focus on cost leadership, differentiation and market segments | Cost reduction |
| Product and market development | Process re-engineering |
| Diversification | Quality improvements |
| Alliances and joint ventures | Operational improvements |
| Acquisitions and mergers | Outsourcing |
| | Financial restructuring |
| | Building and protecting the intellectual asset base |

Both of these views rely on the strategy maker gaining a deep understanding of the external and internal aspects of the firm. The acronym SWOT has been emblazoned on the hearts of all strategy makers and business managers. In the product-market-based view, the emphasis is on understanding the industry structure, and how the strategies of competitors, suppliers and customer behaviour, determine the posture and positioning of the firm. The strategist is expected to learn, through analysis of all the environmental factors, the best way to position the firm, anticipating the moves of competitors in order to maintain any competitive advantages. This view is questioned by those who believe that future changes in the external environment are impossible to predict with sufficient accuracy, and that the complexity of the interactions of strategies can never be fully understood, although the firm itself would appear to be dynamic, in relation to others in the industry, even if it held all of its strategies constant. The fact that things are changing around it would give it every appearance of changing itself.

The second view of strategy making is where the strategist sees the firm as having a set of core competencies and that by configuring these in particular ways a competitive capability can be achieved. The dynamic becomes obvious in that the strategist is making decisions about which competencies to acquire and develop, and which of these can be supplied by outside sources. This view is further supported by the notion that within a firm, it is the management processes and norms that provide what are called pathways through which competencies are developed. Where a firm has developed a set of strategies, based on core competencies, it is likely that they will not be easily imitable by other firms, unless these firms also build in the appropriate management processes. This interweaving of management processes and core competencies is seen by many strategists as being the key to creating sustainable competitive advantage. The dynamic of the organization therefore derives from an integration of management processes, core competencies and the knowledge of the people within the firm. The strategies that the firm follows then create the opportunities for managers to accelerate their learning.

**Core competencies establish sustainable competitive advantage.**

The rate at which the learning acceleration needs to take place, if a firm is to remain truly dynamic, will depend on the industry and the intentions of the strategists and managers. The emphasis here is on the ability of the management to address the question of how flexible it needs to be in the light of changing circumstances. If the firm concentrates too much on refining and making incremental adjustments, to its capabilities, then its resources may become too specific and its processes too rigid. The strategic capabilities which have been so painstakingly obtained, may be the very thing that limits the ability of the firm to take advantage of opportunities and deal with major threats. The strategic challenge is to balance the dynamics with the need for stability.

PART II · STRATEGIC THINKING REVISITED

# THE TRANSITION FROM EVOLUTION TO REVOLUTION

The ideal firm is one that can evolve to the point where it satisfies the needs of all of the stakeholders in an ethical and moral manner. Our ideal firm is also able to detect the point where it has to make a rapid and radical change in order to deal with either changes in its environment or in the needs of its stakeholders. All of this, in a perfect world, would take place in a natural way without the need of interference from either the strategic thinker or the business managers. The problem with this vision is twofold. One difficulty is that the economy relies on competitive market behaviours, from both suppliers and customers, and the second is that firms are owned and run by people who are notorious for their ability to see things in different ways. The people in these firms are also learning and likely to resist any attempts at control beyond, what in reality is, a superficial level, and the firm, through its people, demonstrates that it has a mind of its own that dictates the pace of change and the direction in which it is prepared to move. So the strategist is faced with trying to make sense of how to help the firm to evolve and determining when revolution may be the only way forward.

We have seen that firms pursue competitive strategies that involve making decisions in the short- and medium-term. The strategic focus is most likely to be on which products to develop and which markets to pursue. Most firms adopt this evolutionary and market-driven approach to growth. The assets required to support this growth are acquired and become fixed as do the business processes. The business reliance on achieving cost-efficiency results in adoption of conventional notions such as:

- how to take advantage of the learning curve effect
- pursuing economies of scale by creating manufacturing and distribution centres
- seeking economies of scope by making common use of manufacturing and distribution facilities for the various products
- developing the product and the distribution and customer support services in ways that will differentiate the firm from its competitors.

Alternatively where the firm takes a longer-term perspective, then the notions will include:

- investment in skill development and competencies
- re-engineering management processes
- investment in advanced manufacturing facilities
- finding ways of making the behaviour of the firm more entrepreneurial
- finding ways of undertaking corporate renewal.

Here the strategic view is longer-term, but still based on an evolutionary perspective. The strategic thinker can be contributing to this evolutionary strategy-making activity, while at the same time being concerned with detecting when a more radical approach may be required. One person's evolution represent another's revolution and the strategist needs to be aware of the attraction of seeing the promotion of radical change as their primary role. So on the one hand there is the drive to make profits, from the investment made in developing skills and acquiring resources. This requires an evolutionary approach to growth. Seeking economies of scale, market dominance and providing high customer value, with low cost delivery, all require a strategy based on building knowhow and capturing competencies. On the other hand, the nature of customer behaviour, changes in the marketplace due to competitor action, technological developments and economic fluctuations require a strategy that senses and is able to respond to or initiate rapid change.

An example where the failure to address this base paradox led to almost total failure for a firm is that of the Ford Motor Company in the early 1920s. Ford had evolved a process for manufacturing automobiles that resulted in market dominance and lowest-cost production. Massive investment in their River Rouge plant, based on an almost perfect example of vertical integration and continuous process improvement, had made them the envy of the industrial world. General Motors, their major rival led by Alfred Sloan, had decided to compete on product differentiation. Ford was now faced with having to change direction and learn how to compete on product development. The investment at Ford and the management processes and philosophy had to be changed. It is alleged that the River Rouge plant had to be closed for 12 months for retooling, and that market leadership, on the scale previously enjoyed, was never recaptured.

There have been many examples of failure to address this fundamental paradox since that time, and the IBM experience with the battle between the mainframe and the personal computer is another one. Plenty of advice is available from the gurus on how to survive and grow in both stable and chaotic conditions. In stable conditions, the advice is to adopt the conventional management approach that centres around institutionalizing procedures and establishing clear plans and controls. In chaotic conditions, the advice is that the firm should adopt a style more usually attributed to the entrepreneur rather than the corporate planner or strategist, a style that has been termed 'corporate entrepreneurship'.

Small firms are often owned and driven by entrepreneurs who demonstrate an ability to be flexible and take rapid but calculated risks. Bureaucracy and routinization of procedures and processes are seen as counterproductive by the managers in these firms. Perhaps not surprisingly, many medium-sized and large firms are now trying to behave in an entrepreneurial way and reduce the use of bureaucracy. This is demonstrated by their efforts to be more creative in formulating strategies and in relaxing control over decision making by managers in the subsidiary businesses. The danger here is that the very process of bureaucracy may be the feature that supports their ability to make sustainable profits.

> **Large corporations are learning how to be entrepreneurial.**

The determination to become more entrepreneurial starts with the leader or power group deciding that the firm's performance requires a change to existing strategies and business processes that goes beyond improving on what has been done before. In these circumstances, the leader is driven by a mixture of intuition and an acute awareness of the difficulty of trying to make objective sense of the complexity surrounding the business. Ricardo Semler, in deciding to turn around Semco, a medium-sized firm in São Paulo, Brazil, provides a classic example of the way in which personal ambition and drive can trigger this determination to create an entrepreneurial organization.

> When I took over Semco from my father 12 years ago, it was a traditional company in every respect, with a pyramidal structure and a rule for every contingency. But today, our factory workers set their own production quotas and even come in on their own time to meet them, without prodding from management or overtime pay. They help redesign the products they make and formulate the marketing plans. Their bosses, for their part, can run our business units with extraordinary freedom, determining business strategy

without interference from top brass. They even set their own salaries, with no strings. . . . For truly big decisions, such as buying another company, everyone at Semco gets a vote.

*Maverick – The Success Story Behind the World's Most Unusual Workplace*, Ricardo Semler

Obviously the strategic intent and ambitions of the leader have to be communicated and taken up by the top team, if the outcomes are to be realized. This is where the leader, who is often the strategic thinker, sets out to make the strategic issues facing the firm clear, as opposed to broad and open to misinterpretation. Some leaders will emphasize an external threat in order to get the top team to focus on one or two key strategic issues. To move the top team to action and commitment, it is also necessary to help them to see the way in which a solution or set of actions will lead to success. Many firms fail to address this aspect adequately and the managers either resort to calling in consultants, as a means of prevaricating, or they rationalize that they are doing their best in difficult circumstances. If an early demonstration of success can be achieved, through introducing new strategies that lead to overcoming a major performance gap, then the momentum for change grows.

The ultimate pay-off from adopting an entrepreneurial approach is where the firm is able to implement strategies that change the way in which the industry and the associated markets operate, in effect, changing the rules of engagement in a way that competitors cannot or will not respond to. Obviously not all firms aspire to become industry frame breakers. Those that do gain a rapid advantage over the competition, while others simply enjoy the flexibility that comes from encouraging the entrepreneurial approach. Corporate renewal takes time, and some firms may be looking for quicker ways of achieving a breakthrough in performance. We need to look at how the strategic thinking is likely to operate and develop in these firms.

Rapid and radical change in the strategies that the firm is pursuing sounds attractive, but proves to be more difficult to implement than the evolutionary approach. When considering radical change, we are faced with all the problems of the:

- sheer size of the existing investment in current strategies;
- traditions and working practices that have been institutionalized;
- vested interest in maintaining the *status quo*;

PART II · STRATEGIC THINKING REVISITED

- inherent skills, knowledge and capabilities in the firm;
- investment in becoming competent in a set of technologies;
- existing customer expectations;
- relationships and expectations of suppliers and network partners.

Change is not something that is welcomed in organizations that have been pursuing strategies aimed at efficiency and the institutionalization of procedures and practices. Conventional wisdom suggests that large firms operate from similar recipes on how to compete and operate in a particular industry context. They pursue strategies that result in convergence in technology and competitors' offerings, with radical change only occurring at fundamental breakpoints. These breakpoints occur around events such as technological breakthroughs or a reconfiguring of base factors involved in production and environmental disasters. Firms with large research and development investments would be prime examples of how these breakpoints are sought. If a smaller firm attempts to introduce breakpoints, and sell the knowledge and rights, as a way of making their profits, then the larger firms will attempt to capture the intellectual property rights or buy up the firm. In this way, large firms are able to stabilize their markets and the industry pattern. The pharmaceutical industry presents a prime example of this type of strategy in action.

Faced with these barriers to introducing radical change, the strategy maker relies on two fundamental approaches. The first involves introducing changes to the management processes used by the firm. For example, through promoting a focus on business process re-engineering, total quality management and instituting changes to organizational structures that allow radical innovations to be identified and introduced. The second approach is more fundamental, and here the focus is on changing the beliefs and values held by the power figures and managers. This latter approach is described as attempting to move away from the current organizational paradigm and to change the *status quo*. In both of these cases the strategy maker has to create the organizational climate and conditions in which radical changes to the current strategies can be both considered and implemented. This involves taking a view on whether the longer-term interests of the firm depend on being able to introduce radical changes to its strategies.

> **To create a breakpoint you need an entrepreneur.**

By exploring the notion of the dynamic and thinking organization, we have highlighted the role that the strategy maker plays in influencing the mind and behaviour of the organization. The decision to rely on an evolutionary approach to strategy development or whether to seek a more radical approach are choices that the strategic thinker faces. Being able to recognize the arrival of breakpoints in the industry, either in the technologies used or the products, is a key skill that the strategist has to acquire. Deciding to be the instigator of a breakpoint relies on the ability of the firm to behave in a dynamic or entrepreneurial manner. For the strategist, longer-term views on the application of more radical strategic innovations have to be balanced with a concern for using the resources and skills of the firm in the best interests of the current stakeholders. But within the organizational mind, there is one aspect that will probably have a wider bearing on making sense of the complexity being faced than anything else. That is the way that language is used to frame and argue the competing perspectives and theories about how to operate and grow the business. We need to explore and understand the business lexicon, as it will underpin our efforts to grasp and use the power within the organizational paradoxes.

## *References*
Argyris, C. and Schon, D.A. (1978) *Organizational Learning*, Reading, Mass., Addison-Wesley.

Semler, R. (1993) Maverick: *The Success Story Behind the World's Most Unusual Workplace*, London, Random House.

# Chapter 7

# LEARNING THE BUSINESS LEXICON

Language as organization   *105*

The impact of language on strategic thinking   *114*

> *Good work in language presupposes and depends upon a real knowledge of things.*
>
> Annie Sullivan (1866–1936),
> US Teacher

Every industry and profession develops its own language. Management has over the last 60 years become a recognized activity sufficiently complex to have developed its own language: a language that purports to clarify the thinking behind the management activities involved in running and developing businesses. The reality is that the confusion is increasing, as the language now includes fashionable ideas in many cases simply used as exhortations rather than as attempts to communicate solid managerial experience. Some academics from the older disciplines would argue that as management does not have a strong theoretical base, then it cannot develop a language of its own and has therefore borrowed concepts and descriptors from sociology, economics, philosophy, science and cybernetics. The term 'management' has also been widened to embrace the activities that are carried out by the functional specialists within the firm, as well as those of the top team or corporate group.

In this chapter, we will highlight the way that managers use language to describe their mental models and perspectives on complex business issues, and demonstrate how sharing concepts and notions on best practice in business management has created a common management language. The language is being constantly updated by the consultants and management gurus, and this chapter will bring the reader up to date, while at the same time uncovering the generic ideas that are driving the changes. Management language has a huge impact on the work of the strategic thinker and on the process of implementation, in particular where it is used to frame ideas in the form of organizational paradoxes.

## **LANGUAGE AS ORGANIZATION**

One of the great hopes expressed during the so called 'Age of Enlightenment' was that a systematic and orderly world existed that was the same for everyone and that if we pursued investigation and argument we would eventually agree on a universal meaning about its nature and form. How enlightened have we become and is there a shared language that explains clearly what it is that management is all about? Furthermore, are there any rules that will enable us to grow successful businesses? We find it fairly easy to agree what is meant by the notion of a corporate group, the activities of various organizational functions and what profit, growth and other such everyday expressions convey. It is unlikely that there would be any fundamental disagreement. But as soon as we started to take action based on our understanding, then differences would quickly appear, and where we went beyond discussion over our interpretation of these words, and started to construct and progress our arguments, then we would find that confusion and disagreement would be unavoidable.

> **Power is demonstrated by control of the language.**

We are arguing here that the way language is used, to determine action and share understanding and concerns about complexity constitutes the organization. The language itself represents and influences how the firm behaves. A complex and intricate language becomes the basis for dynamic behaviour. Language is an aspect of organizational control that has not been overlooked by those seeking power and influence. This is perhaps an obvious assertion and we know that many firms go to great lengths to introduce procedures and rules that control the way language is used. Definitions of what is meant by terms such as 'return on investment', and instructions as to how performance parameters are to be defined, measured and evaluated are all ways in which the organizational language is controlled. This form of control is accepted and seen as helpful to managers in their everyday activities. The language becomes a type of shorthand and enables actions to be taken and procedures to be followed. But where the managers are engaging in argument to persuade, engaging in negotiation or in attempting to understand another manager's perspective, then we realize that controlling through language is both complex and powerful.

The organization can be seen as streams of decision making, each manager forming their own judgements as to the impact that their decision will have on other parts of the operation and how their decision will be interpreted by others. Both the judgements made by individual managers and views that others hold about them will be communicated and elaborated through the language and the institutionalized systems and ways of working in the firm. This can be seen when a manager joins a new firm and has to decide the extent to which independence and personally held values and beliefs are to be sacrificed, or at least submerged, and what is to be fought over. Integration into the new firm will depend on how these decisions are played out. The firm will be attempting to integrate the new manager into the ways in which decisions are made and the way language is used to enforce these ways or rules. Individuals quickly learn how to cope with any mismatches between their perceptions of what is important and those held by the power group. Defensive routines are learned and conflict suppressed. The group manages to preserve social relations by, in effect, hiding the thinking that is behind the views of its individual members. When a group experiences a major shock or failure to perform, then it is likely that, beyond rationalizing over the outcome, there may be some attempts to seek deeper understanding behind the perspectives and mindsets of its individual members.

This may sound all very defeatist, but for many managers a few moments' reflection will remind them that this is a very common pattern in firms. Hence an opportunity for the legions of academics, gurus and consultants to ply their trade in trying to explain why this happens, and offer remedies as to what can be done about it. In this chapter, we are adding to their ranks by suggesting that the way language is structured and used has a major impact on both helping and hindering the strategy making and implementation activities in a firm.

We all know that joint action, albeit in teams, is the hallmark of an effective firm. But only if the outcomes of that joint effort are considered by the stakeholders, or power group, as constituting a success. So the first issue that the manager has to negotiate, through language, is that of agreeing the required outcomes and how any trade-offs between competing demands for resources will be made. In a conventional and orderly world, we would envisage a staged process being set up with consultation, negotiation and agreement against a set of objective criteria. But we all know that managers operate from a mixture of historical understanding and frame their perspectives in relation to learning that they experienced in similar situations. They have a desire to be seen to perform well as a manager and will want to represent their view of a situation in a way that will gain the support of those involved in the discussion, hardly a simple set of constraints and decision points, but we all experience and get through these stages many times each day – well, perhaps once a day for big issues and ten times a day for the minutiae of the work.

There are two distinct views on how we do this. First, there are those that see us as formulating a view followed by a thought out set of arguments and then we engage to win. Others see it as individuals putting out their perspectives and viewpoints to others, so that these viewpoints can be changed and the recipient re-informed, the outcome being that the firm gains from this shared understanding, because the firm now has a new way of interpreting a situation that has been made explicit, and can now become institutionalized into the procedures of the firm. The reality is much less straightforward. Managers have an agenda and their level of capability in the use of language varies. Language is not a value-free commodity in most firms. We will explore this proposition in later chapters when we consider how paradoxes are used in organizational language and argument. But in this chapter, we want to focus on how language can impact on the strategic thinker and we need to identify some of the contemporary as well as traditional ideas that underpin conversations around strategic thinking.

> **Contemporary and traditional ideas underpin strategic thinking.**

There are hundreds of notions that have become part of the corporate language. Here we have highlighted some that you will be familiar with, and others that are perhaps rarer or just very difficult to understand. We are not setting out to provide a definitive list or a prescription that should be followed. What we want to do is to engage in a form of conversation or dialogue with you, so that we can tackle the complexity of paradoxical thinking in later sections with a shared understanding. In some areas, you may disagree with the way that some of the notions are framed: this is to be expected, and is part of the process that would occur with a one-to-one conversation in a business setting.

## Vision and mission

*The mission statement is a dream only in the sense that it required imagination, ambition, and sensitivity from the leader about what is achievable. It should not be dreamlike in terms of achievability. If it does not look feasible, it will not be credible and, eventually, it will just be ignored.*
             *The Strategy Workout*, Cyril Levicki (1996)

What the above quotation suggests is that the vision captures a wish or long-term ambition for the firm and that the mission describes what the firm has to acquire in terms of assets and abilities in order to support the vision. An example is when British Airways, in 1987, declared that it was to become 'The World's Favourite Airline.' At that time this appeared to be very fanciful thinking, but some five years later their rating and public image was certainly very close to the dream come true.

For many organizations, a prescriptive approach to developing the mission statement will be followed by a clear identification of objectives. Strategies will then be determined that support the mission and will deliver the objectives. In following this approach, the views of stakeholders, the ambitions and drive of the leader or CEO and the organizational culture are just a few of the features that will influence the statements that are produced. It should incorporate values and beliefs that are comprehensible to all of the stakeholders and be recognized as being feasible. There are many firms that find this approach a waste of time, and would see the 25-year mission statements from Matsushita as a lot more than wishful thinking. Such firms see the future as much more uncertain, and might be feel more comfortable with a mission statement that differentiated the firm from competitors and encapsulated what has become known as 'industry foresight', coupled with strategic intent.

## Industry foresight and strategic intent

> *Industry foresight must be informed by deep insight into trends in lifestyles, technology, demographics, and geopolitics, but foresight rests as much on imagination as on prediction.*
> Competing for the Future, Gary Hamel and C.K. Prahalad (page 89)

Achieving this foresight requires that the existing mindsets of the strategic thinkers and corporate leaders may need to be changed or at least temporarily suspended. Not an easy task, when intuition and experience will be the very things that have created the existing mindsets. Much of the advice on how to do this depends on seeing the firm as a collection of resources that need to be reconfigured and focused in order to become more competitive.

> *Strategic intent also implies a particular point of view about the long-term market or competitive position that the firm hopes to build over the coming decade or so. Hence it conveys a sense of direction. A strategic intent is differentiated; it implies a competitively unique point of view about the future.... Strategic intent has an emotional edge to it: it is a goal that employees perceive as inherently worthwhile. Hence it implies a sense of destiny.*
> Competing for the Future, Gary Hamel and C.K. Prahalad (page 142)

These ideas are what is known as 'end-' or 'goal-directed' as opposed to being prescriptive. They set goals that are described in sufficiently meaningful terms to be the basis of action-taking, but do not suggest how the goal should be achieved. The achievement is in many ways linked to the notion of core competencies.

## Core competencies

There is a growing interest in analyzing the firm as a set of resources that can be reconfigured and focused in order to gain and sustain competitive advantage. This resource-based view of the firm goes beyond the operational analysis that most managers are familiar with, that leads to reducing costs and increasing efficiency. The base unit is described as a core skill which the firm see as the key to being able to compete in the future. This could range from a technological skill to an operational skill, such as warehousing and distribution. Integration of these core skills then creates what are known as 'core competencies.' The criteria that are used to distinguish key core competencies from the myriad that might at first appear are that they:

- make a major impact on adding to customer value;
- must be sufficiently differentiated from those of the competitors to give a unique advantage to the firm;
- must be capable of creating the basis for new products and services beyond those currently being provided.

There are many criticisms of this notion of core competencies, and much of these have come from small and medium-sized firms that do not have the management skills to carry out the required development programmes. There are also those that believe that an approach such as this needs to be more prescriptive and less of a retrospective viewing of success stories. Not surprisingly, the core competence approach has been extended to include capabilities-based resources.

## Capabilities-based resources

The view here is that the core competencies need to be extended to embrace financial and market-based resources. These capabilities are seen to include an integration of core competencies to form key business processes that are used to seize market opportunities. This involves:

- the creation of infrastructures that will link together parts of the firm;
- having a leader who can promote and sustain this resource-based view of the firm.

Focusing on capabilities, for example, by creating an effective and flexible distribution chain, would seem an obvious extension to the core competencies approach, and links closely to the notion of leveraging points in the value chain.

## Value chain and value system analysis

The notion behind the value chain is that organizations consist of activities that when linked together enable value to be added to the total business. Further that all organizations have such internal chains and that these combine, in an industry, to create a value system. The firm's value chain is split at the level of primary and support activities. 'Primary' including the main production and delivery activities, and 'support' being functions such as human resource management. The primary activities range from logistics to after-sales service, and the added value at each stage is expected to be greater than the cost of performing the activity. This approach involves a detailed knowledge of the various operations in the firm and an ability to allocate costs and calculate added value. In many ways, the value of the approach lies perhaps less in conducting a precise analysis and more in determining how activities can be reconfigured or linked to give greater or unique forms of added value. One of the major problems is that these changes to configuration require support from the functional managers. This often presents a mismatch between intention and execution. To help focus the decision-making and elicit support for any planned changes to the value chain configuration, the notion of identifying critical success factors has been developed.

## Critical success factors

The factors critical for success in an industry are the resources, skills, relationships and features of the firm that are essential to delivering value to the client. This notion is used when considering the way that the firm fits into the industry and the extent to which external features of the environment and the marketplace are being utilized to provide competitive advantage. The range of success factors will vary between industries and countries. But once identified, their presence or absence in the firm can indicate where investment and focus is required. This need to focus is seen as particularly important when resources are scarce, and they need to be applied to ensure that the critical success factors are maintained. In this way, an identification of success factors such as service levels or the ability to innovate around new product features becomes the focus for strategic analysis.

## Strategic analysis

A key notion behind the idea of strategic analysis is that of fitting the resources and capabilities of the firm to an external environment. The idea is of course extendable from a national to an international base and can be approached from a resource-based and a marketing-based view of the firm. The analysis of the external environment can utilize what is known as a PEST analysis where the features of the 'far' environment that are likely to impinge or be useful to the firm, are analyzed. This presents a problem in that most of the areas involved, such as government and political changes, economic trends, social developments, changes in demography and technological developments are difficult to measure, let alone predict.

Strategists therefore identify the factors that are most likely to be of interest to the firm and agree ways of measuring and monitoring these, setting breakpoints or threshold levels that, if broached, will give the firm an early warning system against which actions can be determined. The more local environment is also analyzed, using the notion that competitors follow generic strategies such as price, differentiation and market focus.

This analysis, of the local environment, is used to establish strategies in four key areas. These strategies are used to:

- guard against new entrants coming into the marketplace
- anticipate and protect the firm against threats from substitute products, services and delivery systems
- reduce the impact of suppliers that become powerful and start to dictate price and delivery

- combat the threat created when customers change their requirements or form alliances that give them more power over the products and services being offered.

This focus on the near or competitor environment encourages the firm to view its products and services as competing for market share and profitable segments. This links into the notion of the firm having a portfolio of products and services that need to be managed in relation to strategies being pursued by the competitors.

## Portfolio management and market positioning

The notion of a marketplace growing in size and firms competing in that marketplace for economies of scale, through obtaining a dominant share, has cycled from prominence in the 1980s to disparagement in the 1990s. The underlying idea here is that it is possible to identify where the firm's products and services are located on a matrix that contrasts market growth rate and market share. Conventional wisdom holds that, in a fast-growing market, the way to gain market share is to invest in advertising, product development, reconfiguring distribution chains and leveraging image through brand loyalty. Where the market is static, and even declining, then market share can be improved by accepting lower margins and reducing development expenditure.

The Boston Consulting Group notion of the proverbial cash cow became infamous in the world of the corporate planner. The criticism levelled at this method of analysis was that market share and growth rate were only two variables in the competitive equation, and also that new innovative products do not figure well on the matrix and the tendency is to eliminate these as not being profitable. The reality is that products, markets and industries have life cycles. Hence firms need to balance their commitment to the longer-term development of sustainable competitive advantage, with the need to produce cash flows and maintain margins.

**The strategic thinker comes armed with biases and complex mental models.**

These few notions represent just the tip of the iceberg for the student of business language. The proliferation of textbooks and journals, propounding the language of business, are testimony to this claim. But the definitions and the meanings, behind business language, are context-dependent and certainly not value-free. The complexity of the language thus both helps and hinders the strategic-thinking process, as we shall see in the next section.

## THE IMPACT OF LANGUAGE ON STRATEGIC THINKING

Conversations between senior managers about the firm and its activities will be based on a wide range of mental models. These will have been built up from experience and the language they use to share or understand each other's models. This is the arena in which the strategic thinker, already starting to describe possible futures on a sheet that is far from blank, has to operate. A rich collection of mental models are already in place and these will determine action and behaviour. Some are shared or socially constructed and others are more personal and rarely articulated or tested. We have all experienced situations where managers, from a particular function, have used language that is either unintelligible or so convoluted that we either switch off or are too intimidated to express our lack of understanding. In this section, we will identify some of the more personal or individually constructed models that are used and those grounded in the business language.

We all have a clear view about our role in the firm and where our expertise and experience is best demonstrated and applied. This view is bound up with the way that we see our relationships with colleagues and the ways that our close colleagues prefer to work and relate. Much of this is at the tacit level and rarely surfaced or shared. Our models about how the firm works, the priorities and pressure points, are discussed much more explicitly and are likely to be the subject around which most problem-solving takes place. For the strategic thinker, there will be models that are used to:

- evaluate how the firm is performing against internal targets
- compare performance and the strategies being used by competitors
- gauge the urgency and timescales over which the strategies are expected to pay off
- determine what goals are desirable, from the stakeholders perspectives, and how feasible these are in relation to the resources and capabilities of the firm.

Obviously these mental models or frameworks are linked and overlap, and it is unlikely that any individual would be able to describe them readily. They become explicit through the use of language and argument, and drive thinking and action in areas where strategies are being made. The 'glue' that holds these models together and determines the extent to which individuals are prepared to make them explicit and argue their relevance is made up of two elements. First, the personality and style of the individual. This can be seen by the way problem definition and solution seeking are approached. One extreme is where the individual wants to identify the background data and constraints surrounding the problem prior to exploring the way forward, and the other is where the start point is seen as arbitrary if not irrelevant. Some would describe this as a contrast between creative and adaptive styles of problem solving. But whatever your style, it is likely to be at odds with the preferred approaches of some colleagues.

The second element is the extent to which the group have been exposed to and can share a common business language. We have seen, in the previous section, how the concepts used in business language are complex, context-dependent and are linked to the experience of the individuals involved in the strategy making. In order to create new ways of thinking about strategies we have to rely on our ability to use the business language to expose and argue our mental models. One way to expose these mental models about strategy making is to point out what might be called extremes. In some cases these will represent a paradox. We need to see where some of the boundaries or extremes of these models have been set. This can be approached by posing a series of broad questions in order to expose the key elements of these models.

*What are some of the sources of the strategies of a firm?*

The arguments here would revolve around corporatists' views and operationalists' views, illustrating the extent to which the board or corporate level power figures determine the vision and the investment. If they are seen as the guardians and founders of the firm, and those with the greatest insight into what is required and possible, then a top-down model will be presented. Alternatively a view may be promoted that those involved in the operations of the business are much more likely to be able to interpret where short- and long-term changes are required. This represents a middle-up or bottom-up view. The argument is likely to be influenced by the extent to which the firm is seen to be driven by the leader or CEO and how far this influence extends into the culture of the firm. Where a crisis has occurred, or following a take-over, conventional wisdom suggests that the leader should be advised as to what is possible within the existing culture. Arguments as to how far the prevailing culture is the problem, behind the crisis, and the extent to which this culture can be changed, will quickly follow.

Many managers have experienced attempts to change cultures and will no doubt be wary of claims made about how quickly this can be achieved and whether it will have any lasting impact on the performance of the firm. Alternatively, many strategists will view the stakeholders as being the start point for any strategic thinking. For others, the historic view of the shareholder as the true source of stimulus for strategy is still dominant. Achieving profit after tax, that can be turned into dividends and re-investment, along with a share price that will hold off predators, is still central to the thinking of many strategic thinkers. This raises the question of the extent to which strategic thinking is believed to be about doing new and original things, with the resources of the firm, and the extent to which it is about making better use of what is already available.

*As the future is both uncertain and ambiguous should we approach our strategic thinking from a belief that we need to predict and plan or should we rely on allowing our efforts to improve on what we are doing to take us forward. Seizing opportunities as they occur?*

This is quite a fundamental question for strategy makers, as it hits at the heart of the planned versus emergent strategy arguments and thinking. Many strategists will have experienced both approaches and have found some successes and a lot of failures when trying to post-rationalize about strategies that have been launched. Those who see the firm being in a short-term crisis situation or attempting to deal with a downward trend in performance will be looking more to the short- and medium-term for their strategic signals or guides. Some will see the short-term problems as having arisen due to previous short termism, and attempt to argue for the longer-term thinking, leaving the short-term to fate and those who revel in the recovery situation.

> **Incrementalists like organic growth but hate radical change.**

There are two extreme ways of looking at ways to develop and grow a firm. The first subscribes to the view that incremental adjustments to where and how the firm operates and a programme of continuous change are the only realistic way to grow. Others will offer a more radical, or step change approach, and see their strategic role as being that of the breakpoint identifier and actioner.

The incrementalist is also likely to support what is known as the organic growth model. Here the firm grows within existing markets and products, perfecting features and reducing costs in line with quality as a way of gaining market share and competitive advantage. The radical change strategist on the other hand is looking for ways to break out of the existing paradigm of the firm and to find ways of creating unique competitive advantage that is not easily copied by the competitors. Diversification may be seen as a strategy that falls within this radical category. Both views are aimed at adding customer value and cutting cost, but the radical strategist has perhaps more of an eye on the competition and the long-term than the incrementalist. This brings us to our third and last broad question which is about the views held concerning the best ways to compete.

*Competitive advantage seems to be a key focus for successful firms. What is the best way to reach a position of sustainable competitive advantage?*

A number of mental models dominate in this area. The four broad categories, under which we can group these mental models, are those based on:

- market positioning;
- development of core competencies and capabilities;
- the ability to leverage the technology;
- a view of how to compete on an international level.

The market-driven view will include ideas about positioning in the marketplace based on parameters such as price, differentiation and focus. The importance of developing an image through success with one or two products that can be used to gain leverage from branding, will probably dominate in the larger firms. Capturing market share through excellence and being able to reach the customer through controllable distribution channels is seen as a key determinant to success by the users of these models. The notion of the firm having to manage a portfolio of products and services will also be a main part of this view of strategy making. Anticipating and responding to the strategic moves of the competitors in both the short- and longer-term will be seen as a recipe for success.

Those using a resource-based view will emphasize the significance of core competencies in the firm, and the way that these are configured to provide a set of dominant capabilities. They will also have strong views about how a deep knowledge of the critical success factors in the industry will enable scarce resources to be focused on areas that will create unique competitive advantage. They will favour using the notion of the value chain and the industry value systems to leverage advantage by original deployment and linking of resource competencies and core skills. The use of benchmarking, process re-engineering and quality improvement systems are all seen by the resource-based strategist as essential aspects for delivering success. Innovation around products and processes as well as the ways in which the firm configures itself on a national and global basis are also key elements of these models that focus on gaining sustainable competitive advantage. Where the strategist sees the firm driving the competition from a position of strong technological investment and strength, the thinking will be about how to build and harness that strength and where to find new areas that can be developed and exploited.

Alternatively, some strategists will favour a follower approach where the pathfinding is undertaken by the competition, and the firm observes and imitates. Following is a high-risk strategy in some industries as the time taken to catch up can be longer than the product life cycle. Gauging the prospective life cycles and the investment and knowledge required in order to be a successful follower is an art form that not many firms have yet perfected. Particularly in the high-technology, high-margin industries. The final category is where mental models have been developed around the best way to structure an organization that is involved in overseas trading and foreign direct investment.

Some strategists will favour an approach that relies on the economies of scale and scope that follow from having a global product that relies on branding and universal applications. Others will be supporting a more decentralized approach where the local resources are used to cut transport and factor costs and the products are tailored to local needs. How best to switch resources between countries, make investments and take profits will all be involved in the thinking that surrounds these models.

We have made the point that the strategic thinker will have to hand a range of mental models that will be expressed through a combination of personal models about self, the role that they are playing, and how to approach strategy making. As the strategist uses these models, there will be a need to test their relevance using both hard or quantifiable data and some of the more soft or motivational data. Testing out these models, in the particular context of a firm, will involve the strategist in seeing the strengths of some of the models and the weaknesses of others. Not an easy task as the strategic thinker will have acquired some favourite recipes.

This chapter has emphasized the important part that mental models and language play in the way strategy making is approached. We have also shown that many of the models are presented as choices, or alternatives, and as the argument strengthens, it is likely that the alternatives will become mutually exclusive. We are beginning to see how paradoxes are indicators of the ultimate goals that individuals would aspire to, and that detecting when a paradox is being presented and how it is being described creates a very powerful tool for the strategic thinker to use. These paradoxes also represent the strength and dynamism created by the experiences of a particular set of individuals in an organization. In the next chapter, we will look at what the gurus can tell us about how to approach strategic thinking and how far they have managed to harness the power of paradox.

## *References*

Hamel, G., and Prahalad, C.K. (1994) *Competing for the Future*, Boston, Harvard Business School Press.

Levicki, C. (1996) *The Strategy Workout*, London, Pitman Publishing.

# Chapter 8

# LEARNING FROM THE STRATEGY GURUS

Simon on decision making and choice  *123*

Ansoff on planning  *125*

Porter on competitive positioning  *126*

Mintzberg on emergent strategies  *127*

Quinn on logical incrementalism  *127*

Peters on chaos  *128*

Hamel and Prahalad on competence  *129*

Ohmae on critical issues  *131*

Goold, Campbell and Alexander on corporate parenting  *132*

Senge on learning organizations  *135*

Heijden, Wack and De Geus on scenario planning  *137*

Nonaka and Takeuchi on knowledge creation  *139*

*We are inclined to believe those whom we do not know because they have never deceived us.*

Samuel Johnson (1709–84),
British lexicographer

The impulse to pick up a copy of the latest book on strategy or *How to Grow a Winning Business* to read on that plane trip or while on holiday is something that we have all experienced. Giving managers advice is a business that some say provides $15 billion each year to the consultancies and the gurus. Getting advice from McKinsey, Arthur Andersen or attending a seminar given by the likes of Tom Peters, Gary Hamel, Bill Gates, and a host of other big names, is part of the lifestyle of corporate leaders and aspiring strategy makers. It seems that someone out there must have worked out how to make sense of this complex business world. They have and for a fee are prepared to share the secret.

In our quieter moments, we would reflect that advice such as this can be taken on two levels. First, it makes us feel good and encourages us to try harder – this is no bad thing. Second, it gives us a framework within which we can try to fit the particular experiences and understandings that we have about our own situation. The matching of the advice and our own realities is not always easy, and we are perhaps troubled by the fact that all of our competitors are getting the same advice. The differentiator must then be in the way that we interpret, communicate and apply that advice. We would argue that in the area of strategy making, the differentiator lies in the way that we think about strategy.

In this chapter, we will therefore be looking to our gurus for advice, not on how to manage our firms or frame our strategies, but on how to approach the thinking process that lies behind strategy making and action. We have selected the gurus who have the most to contribute to our quest to understand the strategic thinking process. In particular where they have indicated that the source of power in strategic thinking lies within the notion of paradox.

## SIMON ON DECISION MAKING AND CHOICE

Herbert A. Simon would not match the stereotype of the modern day guru and would probably be horrified to be labelled as such. His writings date back to the mid-1940s and focus on trying to understand administrative behaviour. The contribution he makes to our quest, to understand how to approach strategic thinking, is in the area of decision-making and choice. Here Simon emphasized the way a premise is used to construct and support the thinking that results in decision making. For example, he saw the polarization of arguments into either/or situations as fruitless in that the decision itself is made up of a myriad of sub-decisions. To express the final choice in a polarized form was therefore not very sensible. Simon saw polarization of the ideas in an argument, followed by the use of a statement made in the form of a premise, the premise then being used to force a convergence in the thinking of the decision maker.

By using this process, the decision maker behaves in a way that suggests there are limits to the extent to which rationality will work, seeing the outcome more an attempt at satisfying, rather than making a totally rational choice. For example, in business expressions such as, 'making sufficient profit', 'obtaining a reasonable market share', 'keeping up with technological developments' all point to this ability to generally satisfy rather than to aim to maximize or select the best option. Simon argues that it is this muzziness that is the very characteristic that enables the manager to make decisions, about what actions to take. Being able to do this without all of the information that ideally could be collected. As these decisions are aimed at achieving some end-goal and involve choosing between alternative approaches, they themselves will have both an ethical and factual content.

The point being made here is that decisions involved in strategy making are based on both ethical and personal preferences as to intermediary and final outcomes. The selection of the data to use in conducting a strategic analysis is arbitrary and reflects the outcomes that the decision-maker finds acceptable. The process is far from one that relies on using strict logic. We know intuitively that this is the case when we reflect on our own attempts to make decisions where the pathways between means and ends are not certain. But Simon gives us two key pointers to help our strategic thinking. First, that managers are likely to seek 'satisficing' rather than maximizing outcomes when engaged in decision making. Second, that the decisions made are likely to be based on a mixture of facts, ethical, and personal views about intermediate as well as final outcomes.

In arguing for a particular decision, it is thus likely that the strategist needs to be aware of the extent to which satisficing is taking place and the extent to which ethics are being mixed with the facts. The persuasive style used in making these arguments will rely on the use of premises or assertions and paradox will emerge as the end-goals become more driven by values and beliefs than by facts.

## ANSOFF ON PLANNING

H. Igor Ansoff is a great advocate for those that believe that a firm can have objectives that are distinct from those of its members. Most of his key ideas were developed during the early 1960s. They have been the underpinning of the rational approaches to strategy making still used by large companies. The notion is straightforward. Objectives are set, strategies selected, controls determined and implementation commissioned. The outcome, if all the steps are followed, is achievement of the original objectives. The recommended approach to strategic thinking is essentially one of 'top-down'. The senior team deciding on the performance 'gap' that the firm faces, and then determining strategies that will best lead to achievement of the goals. The strategists are seen as thinking in three distinct modes:

- a planning mode where they are trying to position the firm in terms of product – market scope and diversification to new activities
- a responsive mode where strategic issues that arise need to be addressed
- a strategic implementation mode where the task is to overcome the resistance that Ansoff called 'organizational inertia,' which some might nowadays describe as the culture.

A distinctive feature of the type of strategic thinking that this suggests is that of consciously separating the strategist's work into these three areas. At an extreme, it suggests that the strategy-making activity can be completely separated from the front-line workers and managers who are implementing the strategy.

# PORTER ON COMPETITIVE POSITIONING

The key feature of the strategic thinking promoted by Michael E. Porter is that competition, in an industry, is founded on the economic structure of both the industry and the country. That to understand an industry strategy, the thinker has to embrace the views and language of the economist. Seeing the firm as representing sources of economic rent and that marketplace competition will work to drive down the rate of return on invested capital. Competitors are thus seen as creating forces that influence the returns available from the market and for the firm. The strategist is encouraged to find a position for the firm where it can both defend itself from the market-driven forces and take advantage of those where it has an edge. The competitors in an industry are seen as being mutually dependent and therefore not willing to engage in competitive action that might bring reprisals. The overriding pressures on the firms stem from structural features in the particular industry: for example, a slowdown in growth, low switching costs, changes to supporting industry technologies. The strategist is encouraged to establish the firm's position or stance with regard to the underlying causes behind changes in these structural forces.

Porter also suggests that the thinker should be aware of how generic strategies such as cost leadership, differentiation and market focus can all be used to cope with the effects of these industry-based structural forces. The two strands of strategic thought thus revolve around gauging competitor behaviour and being aware of the evolution in the industry.

Porter would also encourage the strategic thinker to see continuously adding value to the end customer as being the only way to maintain a position of sustainable competitive advantage. To do this, the focus should be on how the activities of the firm work to provide this value and how the value chain of the firm fits into the value system of the industry. When one attempts to conduct an analysis of where value is being added to the activities of the firm, the amount of detail required is daunting. The knowledge about cost allocations defies the intricacies of most accounting systems. But the framework that Porter provides is still valuable in helping the strategic thinker to focus on the key issues for deploying and allocating scarce resources in the firm.

## MINTZBERG ON EMERGENT STRATEGIES

One of the key features that Henry Mintzberg brings to our exploration of strategic thinking is that there is a difference, at least in timing, between a strategy that is planned and the strategy that emerges. Having a planned strategy suggests an ability to make a clear link between ends and means which can be followed as though it were a signposted pathway, whereas the emergent strategy is seen to be one that occurs in the absence of intentions or at least in spite of intentions. Mintzberg saw these as extremes, and as such only useful depending on how the current position of the firm was seen in the mind of the strategist. Here one person's view of a strategic action to be taken by the firm might be seen by another as tactical and therefore capable of some fairly detailed planning based on a reasonable level of certainty about both ends and means. We are also encouraged to think carefully about how much understanding we require of the firm, its capabilities, and the industry context in order to be effective as a strategic thinker.

> Sometimes, of course, the senior managers do have the capacity to think strategically, but are too detached from the details of the organization's operations. Then they had better find ways to get themselves back in touch, or else ensure that the power over strategy making is decentralized to those who are.... Either the leaders must be able to probe deeply into the organization or else people deep inside the organization must be able to influence the strategies that are formed.
> *The Rise and Fall of Strategic Planning*, H. Mintzberg, 1994

## QUINN ON LOGICAL INCREMENTALISM

In the late 1970s James Quinn promulgated the notion that firms change their planned strategies in ways that he described as intuitive and driven from management processes. Some of these are written down, but many result from informal ways of working that develop within the firm. These ways of working are represented by, what he described as, systems that produce or rely on hard data, for example, how funds are allocated and the definitions about market segmentation and products. He saw other systems in the firm creating soft data, for example: management style, relationships with customers, innovative capabilities, etc.

PART II · STRATEGIC THINKING REVISITED

What Quinn is offering the strategic thinker is an insight into the nature of the strategy-making process that is much less predictable and quantifiable than some of the more rationally based frameworks. The positioning and posturing of the firm resulting from interpretations made by the incumbent management of events that are in effect not predictable. Quinn thus suggests that strategy making is more of an iterative process and that the firm will edge its way forward driven by managers who are cautious about their interpretations of events and seek confirming data for each move, the incremental moves stemming from a mixture of political consensus and interpretation of organizationally confirmed information.

This notion of strategic management being about managing and reconciling the evolving dynamics, created by sub-systems within a firm, is a key idea behind what has become known as logical incrementalism in strategic management. Quinn saw the strategic management process as being one that is defined and agreed among the managers, with clear goals and policies for the firm being spelled out, and then the process being used to co-ordinate and control the on-going experiences and learning that surround decision making.

## PETERS ON CHAOS

Although Thomas J. Peters is an academic, consultant and recognized management guru, his contribution to understanding strategic thinking is often seen as frame-busting and a clear challenge to the *status quo*. In many ways, Peters advocates a view of strategic thinking that embraces chaos. The conventional rationalist approaches are presented as inappropriate in that they encourage:

- an over-emphasis on financial analysis and cost reduction;
- a restriction of entrepreneurial activity;
- managers to fail to take advantage of the motivational power that resides in individuals.

This would not appear contentious to the average manager, but does provide a spur to the strategic thinker. The spur is that in order to bring some originality to a group involved in strategy making it may be necessary to behave in ways that shock or challenge the existing organizational culture and norms of behaviour.

We are also encouraged, by Peters, to think of strategies being played out by small units in the organization or by subsidiary firms that are freed from the pressures and constraints of the main operational business. The notion of pursuing size, market share and the resulting economies of scale benefits are seen as ways of approaching strategic thinking that should be resisted. The notions of lean manufacturing and 'just in time' are offered as examples of how strategic thinking needs to be linked to the operational practicalities and the ability of both the marketplace and the technology to change rapidly. Although Wal-Mart and Coca-Cola in the USA might suggest quite the opposite.

The need to create a holistic approach to thinking about new strategies was an outcome of the work of Tom Peters and Robert Waterman while working at McKinsey, the consultancy firm. This approach encourages the strategic thinker to consider not only the strategies that need to be pursued and the supporting organizational structure, but also the softer aspects of the organization. These would include: the systems and processes that are required, the way in which management present and represent themselves, the staff levels and skills required, plus the shared values needed to support the strategies as they develop. By considering the relative emphasis and hence impact of the softer values on the strategies, the thinker is seen as being able to gauge the likelihood of key outcomes being achieved.

## HAMEL AND PRAHALAD ON COMPETENCE

The advice for strategic thinkers is to forget about strategic fit and matching the strengths and weaknesses of the firm to the environment or market. The danger of this approach, we are told, is that it encourages imitation from our competitors and repetition of behaviour from our managers. The strategic thinking should emphasize promoting ambition and entrepreneurial activity that will lead to leveraging resources in order to create a sustainable competitive advantage. This represents a resource-based view of the firm as opposed to a market-based view.

The approach relies on the notion of the firm being able to create a vision of the desired future state of the firm and the industry structure in which it will be working. This is described by our gurus as clarity about strategic intent. This intent is driven by a desire to dominate emerging opportunities using existing and new competencies within the firm. These competencies are the skills and capabilities that give the firm its unique meaning and differentiate it from competitors. It is this differentiation, based on unique competencies, that is seen as creating the sustainable competitive advantage. The notion of creating a sense of what the firm intends to do to add value for the customers and how this is to be delivered produces what Gary Hamel and C.K. Prahalad (1990) call the 'strategic architecture' of the firm.

In many ways these are conventional approaches to thinking about strategy. The strategic intent is seen as coming from the top management and being stable over a period of time sufficient to be in a position to manage the development and implementation of declared strategies. The outcomes or goals for the firm are seen clearly as gaining sustainable competitive advantage over competitors. The means of achieving this are seen as emerging and flexing as circumstances change and learning grows. The challenge is obviously one of being able to identify, develop and co-ordinate resources, skills and knowledge such that these competencies can be realized. This takes time and would presumably be tackled while the firm was still generating revenues based on perhaps more market-based views. Hamel and Prahalad recognize this problem of facing the realities of needing to run and sustain an existing business, while at the same time pursuing new aspirations.

> We believe that it is essential for top management to set out an aspiration that creates, by design, a chasm between ambition and resources. An explicit emphasis on the notion of 'fit,' and the way in which the idea of fit is embedded in strategy tools often deflects managers from the enormously important task of creating a misfit between resources and ambitions. Of course, at any point in time there must be a loose fit between short-term objectives and near-at-hand resources. But even then the fit should not be too tight.
> *Competing for the Future*, G. Hamel and C.K. Prahalad (page 160)

This resource-based view of the firm presents many challenges for the strategic thinker. These range from:

- how will the existing and new competencies be identified?
- who will want to claim ownership and control of these competencies?
- how will the value of investment in developing the required new competencies be calculated in order to make choices as to which ones to support?

Hamel and Prahalad approach some of these difficult questions by suggesting that the resource-based and market-based views of the firm should perhaps coexist. That the main purpose of the competence approach is to influence the perspectives that managers have on the identification and protection of key resources that are represented by the skills and knowledge of the managers and the workforce in the firm. The notion of using the competence perspective, as a first step in managing a pathway to the future for the firm, is a powerful message that we will revisit in later sections.

## OHMAE ON CRITICAL ISSUES

Kenichi Ohmae champions the art of consensus and incrementalism in strategic thinking. He emphasizes that successful strategies stem from the state of mind and enthusiasm of an individual or group and not from analysis, arguing that analysis is used only to stimulate the creative process. This process relies on the notion of focusing strategy building on what he calls the strategic triangle: company, customer and competition. He draws a clear distinction between strategies that are aimed at gaining competitive advantage and those that are aimed at operational improvements, seeing the strategist's real task as that of coming up with strategies that are aimed at surprising and clearly putting the firm ahead of the competition. For a strategy to be effective, he suggests that it need not be aimed at achieving perfection, but simply capable of improving the performance of the firm in relation to the main competitors.

The paradox that Ohmae presents is that of avoiding perfectionism, while at the same time being extremely thorough in completing the analytical work involved in testing strategic options. Our management guru offers a number of guides to strategic thinking. When approaching strategic thinking, it is suggested that identifying the critical issues in the situation is the first step. These critical issues would then be analyzed into concrete measures and grouped into a series of problem areas. Abstractions, or the causal factors behind these grouped problems, are then raised prior to formulating solutions that are based on a hypothesis that can be tested. It is this movement between analysis and abstraction followed by a testing phase that underpins the approach. Not relying on rigorous analysis nor relying on unrestrained free thinking and intuition.

Ohmae in this way avoids the trap of setting strategic analysis and intuition as a paradox. It is this combination between analytical method and mental elasticity that he calls 'strategic thinking.'

## GOOLD, CAMPBELL AND ALEXANDER ON CORPORATE PARENTING

Michael Goold, Andrew Campbell and Marcus Alexander provide the strategic thinker with a framework to use when operating at a corporate level. They focus on firms that have subsidiaries and offer the notion of the corporate group acting in the role of an effective parent, its task being to provide more added value to the subsidiaries than another parent could. This is an alternative view of the role of the corporate that is normally presented. The conventional view being that the corporate makes decisions that are directly linked to the subsidiary improving profitability and return on investment. Whereas our academics are suggesting that the key decisions should be aimed at improving parenting advantage.

In conventional conglomerates and multibusiness firms, the role and functions of the corporate group are defined and driven by power figures and in many cases a financial and hence controlling perspective dominates. The tensions between corporate staff and the businesses are usually presented around this central versus decentral paradox. The corporate group wanting to control from the top while recognizing the value of giving freedom of action to the subsidiary businesses. Three areas have been identified where these tensions exist. These are presented by our academics as a mixture of paradoxical questions and premises. For example:

- How can part-time board members, who are remote from the business, improve on what local management can do?
- Business managers are free to form their own links between the various corporate businesses – so why do we need the interference from the top?
- How can a corporate board, or an in-house unit, make better strategic sense than a third-party consultancy that is developing strategies for firms every day?

Faced with having to operate in this environment, the strategy maker is encouraged to focus on understanding the characteristics of the corporate group in terms of:

- the mental maps that are used;
- the structures and processes that have been set up;
- the functions that are carried out for controlling services and resources;
- the extent to which the subsidiary businesses are allowed to make investment and strategic decisions without corporate approval.

The main areas of thinking for the strategist should then be around:

- amalgamation or separation of the businesses in order to improve competitiveness;
- the creation of new businesses;
- buying businesses cheaply;
- re-alignment of the portfolio of businesses in order to better fit the parenting characteristics.

The basis for the thinking would be that there was a clear agreement among the strategic development group around what our academics call the nature of the heartland business. Reaching agreement on this requires that two areas are clearly defined:

- First, identification of the criteria that define the type of business that is the focus of the strategy. This would include the industry, technology and market descriptions.
- Second, the types of parenting opportunities that are being sought and the critical success factors that will be used to focus and evaluate the parenting strategies.

Obviously the approaches and emphasis used by large corporations vary according to the nature of the industry, their history and the intentions of the key power figures. However our academics identified broad patterns in parenting styles, among the companies that they studied, and it will help our task of recognizing how tensions can arise by taking note of these style differences.

The three obvious style differences that indicate sources of tension between the power figures in the firm, are those that emphasize:

- strategic goals and competitive positioning more than centralized financial control;
- a focus on balancing financial targets and strategic targets;
- tight financial control and short-term performance.

The three styles emphasize the degree to which short-term financial performance dominates the strategic thinking. The firms where the focus was on strategic planning are those characterized by their seeking consensus between the corporate group and the subsidiary businesses through a formalized planning process. In these firms, the business managers were rewarded more as a result of the health of the overall corporate group than on the performance of their own business. Our academics identified companies such as British Petroleum, Cadbury Schweppes, Shell, Banc One and Canon as demonstrating this style. But they caution us that there are few companies that follow a fully fledged strategic planning style.

Companies such as 3M, Asea Brown Boveri, RTZ, Unilever, ICI and Courtaulds are seen to fall into the middle ground, balancing short-term goals with more strategic approaches. In these companies, the subsidiary businesses are encouraged to work within broad guidelines set by corporate level directives, the role of the parent being one of questioning rather than dictating the decisions. Here the emphasis is on decentralization of decision making around strategies, with financial targets being balanced with achievement of strategic milestones.

The third style is dominated by the pursuit of financial control. Here the subsidiaries are expected to structure their own business and to survive or fail through the pursuit of their own market- or resource-based strategies. There is little evidence of any formalized central strategy-making process. Capital investment decisions have to be approved by the corporate group and control is through a tight monitoring of performance against annual budgets. Companies associated with this type of style include: BTR, GEC, Tarmac and Hanson. It is important that we are able to recognize these styles at work in the firm as this will have a major bearing on how we approach the analysis of how paradoxes can be identified and used to understand and influence strategy making in firms. But once again we need to be cautious about how flexible firms and their corporate strategic thinkers can be about a change in style.

The parenting style of a company follows from the basic beliefs of the parenting team about how relationships between the parent and the businesses should be handled, and about how the parent can add most value. It reflects the experience, philosophy, and values of the chief executive and his or her team. As such, it is deeply ingrained and difficult to alter. We have found that companies seldom voluntarily change their basic styles without a change in chief executive. A crisis may force a sudden change in style, and, over time, a gradual evolution of a company's style can occur. But a planned move from one style to another, without a major shift in the composition of the top team, is rare.

*Corporate Level Strategy; Creating Value in the Multibusiness Company,*
Michael Goold, Andrew Campbell and Marcus Alexander

This quotation suggests that styles, and hence the behaviours of top teams in multibusinesses are not amenable to change other than when faced with a crisis. The more optimistic view offered in this book is that by understanding how managers construct paradoxes and argue through the use of premise, it is possible to harness latent tensions and bring about a change in behaviours. Many activities, in a firm, encourage consistent behaviour from the managers. But we would argue that the process of strategy making and the dynamics associated with strategic thinking are an area where behaviours can be changed to suit the drives of the business rather than be a captive of the learned styles of the managers and the corporation. This points to the challenge and the opportunity of using the power of paradox in strategic thinking.

## SENGE ON LEARNING ORGANIZATIONS

Here we are encouraged to see learning as the key focus for our strategic thinker. Peter M. Senge saw the need for organizations to engage in a process of continuous updating of their knowledge base in order to maintain and gain competitive advantage in a turbulent environment. The idea is simple if not easy to implement, the notion being that individuals and organizations are continually engaging in activities, at both operational and corporate levels, that provide opportunities to learn. He also encourages organizations to consider unlearning as a key activity. As ways of working based on previous learning do not always fit the present let alone the future environment in which the firm will be operating. Senge provides some guidance for the strategic thinker.

His focus is that organizations act as a set of interconnected subsystems and that learning has to be seen as 'systems thinking', i.e., the decisions that are made in one area of the business have implications for other parts of the business. This is perhaps not an earth-shattering notion but for Senge it is significant in that it encourages the individual to embrace the complexity of organizations as opposed to adopting what he calls the 'pervasive reductionalism' of Western culture, that is, the pursuit of simple answers to complex issues. While focusing clearly on how to create a particular type of learning organization, Senge does offer a challenge to the strategic thinker or perhaps an opportunity to influence the way other managers approach their learning and hence thinking. He promotes the notion of dialogue as distinct from discourse as a way of promoting team learning, arguing that in a dialogue you are not trying to win, but to gain insights into the way that others are thinking and have constructed the mental models that they are using.

Complex issues are explored and assumptions suspended in terms of using them to win arguments. Instead they are freely communicated to colleagues in a risk-free way. In order to then reach some consensus and action taking, there is a need to revert to the conventional discourse approach where cases and positions are argued and defended in order to reach a decision. This is obviously not an easy area for a busy manager to tackle and many would-be followers of Senge might have been daunted at the prospect of challenging tried and tested ways of managing discussions and debates in the firm.

As we move into the second half of the book we will revisit this complex but valuable topic and offer some practical guidance on how its power can be brought to bear when tackling strategy building in teams. Senge also offers some advice, to the strategic thinker, in terms of the need to expose and understand the mental models used by others. Once again not an easy area, but in later sections of the book, we will explore how scenario building can be used to expose these mental models. Senge also emphasizes the importance of having a shared vision.

> For years, systems thinkers have endeavoured to persuade managers that, unless they maintained a long-term focus, they will be in big trouble. With great vigour, we have proselytized the 'better before worse' consequences of many interventions, and the 'shifting the burden' dynamics that results from

symptomatic fixes. Yet, I have witnessed few lasting shifts to longer-term commitment and action. Personally I have come to feel that our failure lies not in unpersuasiveness or lack of sufficiently compelling evidence. It may simply not be possible to convince human beings rationally to take a long term view. People do not focus on the long term because they have to but because they want to.

*The Fifth Discipline*, Peter Senge

The role that the strategic thinker is encouraged to adopt is closely aligned to that of the change agent. The assumption is made that someone has to identify opportunities for capturing the on-going learning that is taking place in the organization in a way that will provide tangible benefits to both the firm and the individuals. The start point for the strategist is perhaps the determination that there is a pay-off for adopting this learning-focused approach and then finding ways of getting others to join. Much of the work of gurus who promote this approach centres on making explicit the meanings and interpretations that are associated with taking action. The notion being that much of the key knowledge in organizations is held at the tacit level and that making this explicit and in effect institutionalizing or proceduralizing this knowledge is a key task for the strategy maker.

## HEIJDEN, WACK AND DE GEUS ON SCENARIO PLANNING

Here we are immediately given some clear guidance on the crucial elements in strategic thinking. Work with Shell enabled Kees Van Der Heijden, Pierre Wack and Arie De Geus to identify what it is the strategic thinker has to be able to achieve. These include:

- changing the mental models of decision makers;
- understanding what is predictable and what is uncertain;
- introducing new perspectives to the decision makers based on a mixture of critical analysis and deep intuitive thinking.

They promote, once again, the importance of strategic conversation in the organization, and the use that can be made of the notion of scenario building. The basis of this thinking is that strategies suggest ways of developing profit potential by harnessing unique competencies that need to be regularly updated in order to maintain competitive advantage. The strategic thinker is thus encouraged to identify where customer value can be created, create ways of linking this to the distinctive competencies in the firm in order to deliver this value, and hence establish competitive advantage. This Heijden refers to as 'creating the generic business idea.' This represents an integration of the Michael Porter positioning approach with the resource-based view of the firm promoted by Hamel and Prahalad. To take advantage of this approach, we need to take a closer look at the way that the notions of strategic conversations and scenarios can be used by strategy makers.

Scenario planning involves managers in looking at multiple futures which contain uncertainties and have inherent ambiguities. By engaging in this process, the managers are encouraged to be creative in proposing strategies that will enable the firm to achieve sustainable competitive advantage in environments where the uncertainties have been recognized and agreed. A knowledge of these structural uncertainties then enables the managers to consider alternative interpretations that they would place on these future contexts. The process is one of thinking through the key features of the contextual environment for the firm, say five years hence, and attempting to agree where the associated uncertainties in these environments cannot be reduced. The whole purpose of establishing these scenarios is to engage in conversations that will surface deeply held values and mental models. The generic business idea is then tested for robustness against these scenarios in terms of the way that both distinctive competencies and the choice of businesses to pursue have been made.

The value of this approach is that managers are required to agree on the driving forces in this external contextual environment in a way that separates them from the internal company issues surrounding the selection of strategic options. We know that reaching consensus is not an easy task among experienced managers. Promoting organizational action involves both consensus and personal commitment from the majority of those involved. The conventional approach to achieving this is through the use of rational argument and persuasive evidence. But in this situation we also want to promote diversity in the thinking in order to be able to provide unique responses to changes in the competitive environment. As we increase the ability of the group to reach consensus, we potentially decrease their ability to promote and recognize differences. The conventional approach to this organizational paradox would be to seek a compromise or balance between obtaining consensus and maintaining differences. What we are promoting in this book is an approach that harnesses the tension that this paradox creates in order to improve the robustness of our strategic thinking.

## NONAKA AND TAKEUCHI ON KNOWLEDGE CREATION

Building, capturing and leveraging knowledge in organizations in order to gain sustainable competitive advantage is now accepted as an effective strategic approach. The advice on how to set about doing this varies from creating institutional knowledge data bases to establishing cultures that encourage the risk-taking that is associated with creativity and learning. Ikujiro Nonaka and Hirotaka Takeuchi have provided some clear guidance for the strategic thinker based on work carried out in companies such as Honda, Canon and Seven Eleven in Japan.

The focus of their advice is on how to capture the new organizational knowledge that drives innovation. This new knowledge is captured in the form of systems, procedures, products and services that form the basis on which innovations can be sustained and competitive advantage achieved. Once again the strategic thinker is encouraged to adopt the role of the change agent. Drawing out the tacit, taken-for-granted, knowledge that managers have built up through experience.

Four steps, or modes of thinking, are required in order for the strategic development team to be able to expose and harness the tacit knowledge of its members. The first step is where the team engage in activities that permit shared experiences on the belief that the mere transfer of information will often make little sense. Creative dialogues are set up that go beyond the conventional brainstorming meetings which we have all experienced at one time or another. Use is also made of observation of experts at work, in order to gain deeper insight into how the tacit knowledge is being used. Creating a forum in which the customer can be engaged in a continuing dialogue is seen as a key activity in this exploratory phase. The second step seeks to turn tacit knowledge into explicit concepts. The tacit knowledge being transformed through an identification of shared metaphors, analogies, concepts and models. The use of metaphor and analogy is seen by our gurus as the key to the success of this conversion process.

> 'Using an attractive metaphor and/or analogy is highly effective in fostering direct commitment to the creative process. Recall the Honda City example. In developing the car, Hiroo Watanabe and his team used a metaphor of "Automobile Evolution." His team viewed the automobile as an organism and sought its ultimate form. In essence, Watanabe was asking, "What will the automobile eventually evolve into?"
>
> 'I insisted on allocating the minimum space for the mechanics and the maximum space for the passengers. This seemed to be the ideal car into which the automobile should evolve. The first step towards this goal was to challenge the reasoning of Detroit, which had sacrificed comfort for appearance. Our choice was a short but tall car. Spherical, therefore lighter, less expensive, more comfortable, and solid.
>
> 'This concept of a tall and short car, "Tall Boy," emerged through an analogy between the concept of "man maximum, machine minimum" and an image of a sphere that contains the maximum volume within the minimum area of surface, which ultimately resulted in the Honda City.'
>
> *The Knowledge Creating Company*, I. Nonaka and H. Takeuchi, 1995, Oxford University Press, Inc. (page 65)

The metaphor is used to express an association between two things in a way that does not explicitly identify the differences between them. For example, where the culture in a company is described as being 'driven by the *prima donna* behaviour of the business divisions.' This presents a contrast between a behaviour that is united and consistent and one that is the subject of emotionally driven and unpredictable outbursts. The single expression '*prima donna*' being used to connect these two thoughts. Analogy is then used to find the commonality and differences between the two thoughts in ways that will make the formulation of a rational argument possible.

For example, if an analogy for an organization was presented that suggested that it was like an orchestra whose members considered that they could interpret the score without the help of the conductor. The analogy would then be used to help the team create an explicit concept or model for the organizational behaviour that could become the subject of analysis and subsequent action taking. When we are looking more closely at how paradox is used in organizations, then this use of analogy as a bridging device will become increasingly important.

The third step in the process of creating new knowledge is that of combination. Here the team are engaged in turning concepts into a knowledge system and taking advantage of knowledge that may reside outside of the firm. Computer data bases are then used to facilitate the conversion which emphasizes the sharing and interpretation of explicit knowledge. This leads to co-operation between functions and the development of new products and services.

The final step is that of making this explicit knowledge tacit. Here the new knowledge is captured, in the form of procedures and instructions, and involves people in taking action to help internalize this knowledge. Our gurus also suggest that having a supportive context, in which this way of thinking, and the resultant creation of new knowledge can be utilized, is crucial. The strategic thinker is again being asked to help build an organizational climate or culture in which strategic intent is made clear to all of the managers. Within this individual managers and groups can be given the freedom to help make the strategic decisions. Here an element of chaos and equivocality is recommended in order to build tension and encourage creativity.

The reality, for most of us, is that organizations are at different stages of development, staffed by a wide range of personalities and operating in markedly different contexts. What we will therefore provide in the second part of this book are approaches to strategic thinking that are generalizable to a wide range of organizational contexts. These approaches will form the generics and foundations for strategy making.

In this chapter we have identified key areas of advice from the leading management gurus on how to approach strategic thinking. Much of this advice will have been encountered in one form or other by the managers that you will be working with when doing your strategic thinking and building strategic direction for the firm. Many will have been exposed to the school of thought that sees organizations as being both victims and beneficiaries of their historic learning experiences. They may not be as enthusiastic as Senge and Nonaka and Takeuchi about introducing some structured approaches to learning, but they would probably quickly recognize the approaches as valuable, if at times hard to reconcile with day-to-day pressures. Faced with a determination to rethink and renew the firm, it is likely that the learning frame of reference will gain a lot of support from managers.

Other managers will have followed the rational approach to strategic planning and recognize from their own experiences the inherent uncertainties and ambiguities associated with predicting the future. Ansoff will be popular because of the familiarity and comfort that such an approach brings but the more seasoned managers will probably be happier with a mixture of Quinn's incrementalism and the notion of emergent strategies as outlined by Mintzberg.

Those managers that are prepared to take a more change-orientated or dynamic view of strategy making would no doubt be happy to follow the scenario building route promoted by Heijeden and Wack, although this route, as we have seen, does require a great deal of skill in the management of the thinking processes. Where the managers are involved either at a corporate level or in a subsidiary business, then the approaches to parenting and the associated styles that are involved may strike that note of realism that the busy manager seeks when approaching strategic thinking.

The two outstanding contributors to contemporary strategic thinking must be Michael Porter and the Gary Hamel and Keith Prahalad partnership, Michael Porter through the promotion of tools for competitive positioning and generic strategies, and Hamel and Prahalad for the promotion of strategic intent, strategic architecture, stretch and fit and of course core competencies. In among all of this advice we have noted that the use of paradox, or, as some gurus call it, 'the dichotomies,' reigns supreme. We saw some examples of business situations that set out to polarize viewpoints in order to be persuasive and win arguments. There was also evidence that when the emergence of dichotomies are likely to lead to total confrontation, the advice is to use the tension created but to also seek a compromise in order to come to a consensus. This consensus allows the thinking and subsequent action to proceed.

Nearly all of our gurus promoted the value of generating strategic conversations as a means of sharing and developing meaning among the managers, the inference being that the strategic thinker has to be either totally omnipotent or endowed with the skills of a superb change agent in order to instigate and manage this complex process. In the second half of this book we will look at how the use of paradox in organizations can close the skills gap that the reader may have, and give some clear guidelines as to how to use the power of paradox in strategic thinking and to improve the sustainable competitiveness of the firm.

## References

Ansoff, H.I. (1965) *Corporate Strategy*, New York, McGraw-Hill.

Goold, M., Campbell, A. and Alexander, M. (1994) *Corporate Level Strategy: Creating Value in the Multibusiness Company*, New York, John Wiley & Sons. Reprinted by permission of John Wiley and Sons Inc.

Hamel, G. and Prahalad, C.K. (1994) *Competing for the Future*, Boston, Harvard Business School Press.

Kees Van Der Heijden *et al* (1996) *Scenarios: The Art of Strategic Conversation*, Chichester, John Wiley and Sons.

Mintzberg, H. (1994) *The Rise and Fall of Strategic Planning*, Europe, Prentice Hall.

Nonaka, I. and Takeuchi, H. (1995) *The Knowledge Creating Company: How Japanese Companies Create the Dynamics of Innovation*, Oxford University Press, Inc.

Ohmae, K. (1982) *The Mind of the Strategist*, New York, McGraw-Hill

Peters, T.J. and Waterman, R.H. Jnr. (1982) *In Search of Excellence: Lessons from America's Best-Run Companies*, New York, Harper and Row.

Porter, M.E. (1980) *Competitive Advantage: Creating and Sustaining Superior Performance*, New York, The Free Press.

Prahalad, C.K. and Hamel, G. (1990) 'The Core Competence of the Corporation,' *Harvard Business Review*, May–June, pages 79–91.

Quinn, J.B. (1980) *Strategies for Change: Logical Incrementalism*, Homewood, Illinois, Irwin.

Senge, P.M. (1990) *The Fifth Discipline: The Art and Practice of the Learning Organization*, London, Random House.

Simon, H.A. (1945) *Administrative Behaviour*, New York, Macmillan.

# Part III

# UNDERSTANDING THE POWER OF PARADOXICAL THINKING

Chapter 9

# AN INTRODUCTION TO THE USE OF PARADOX

The paradoxical statement  *150*
The use of tension  *153*
The use of premise  *158*

# INTRODUCTION TO THE USE OF PARADOX

Any attempt to describe how organizations actually work quickly confirms our intuitive feelings. Organizations are very complex. Our efforts to make sense of the dynamic interactions that are constantly taking place result in the production of some very simple models and sometimes misleading explanations. Misleading in the sense that they set out to represent the complexity as manageable and controllable, with conflict and confusion being states that one has to try to stabilize. We see organizational effort being expended on obtaining and maintaining what might be described as a state of internal consistency.

For example, a systems-based perspective argues that negative feedback is used to dampen down any excessive swings in performance, whereas a human behaviour perspective would look for ways of establishing common purpose and balancing out of differences between people. Most conventional, and therefore acceptable, approaches to managing organizations rely on eliminating differences and conflict. This is achieved through a mixture of control and alignment of people to a single cause or purpose. Conventional management wisdom tells us that the successful organization is staffed with people who are able to articulate a consistent, overarching vision and identify with the key strategies that are being pursued. We are encouraged to believe that this shared understanding ensures that long-term and short-term decision-making are executed with a clear constancy of purpose. But experience tells us that this is rarely the case, and that individual interpretations of purposes and events create a constant tension within organizations.

These tensions, and how we manage them, provide the stimulus for individual learning at one level, and inter-firm competition at another. Yet we strive to eliminate the presence of contradiction and mismatch, between perspectives and opinions, particularly around key areas of thought and action in the organization.

This presents an apparent contradiction or inconsistency in our theory about how we manage. On the one hand, we want to create shared meaning and agreement on which actions to take in pursuing our drive for success. On the other, recognizing that encouraging individuals to pursue their own meaning and develop a sense of purpose will help harness the unique talents and creativity of both managers and staff. Some top managers use this apparent contradiction or paradoxical statement as a basis from which to argue for a major drive to improve communications and make changes to the culture. Others argue that the best way to proceed is to adopt an approach that emphasizes the differences between people. Each of these approaches are then underpinned with a management activity that includes: controls, reward systems, and management processes as a means of ordering the organizational behaviour.

> **We want people to conform but at the same time be creative.**

This apparent and simple contradiction, in the way we interpret the world of work, has presented us with a paradox. The paradox becomes very powerful as it presents choices around clear alternatives. A rallying point around which to focus and simplify the diversity of views held by managers. In order to take advantage of this powerful organizational dynamic, we need to understand how these paradoxes – and there are many – arise and are used in organizations.

## THE PARADOXICAL STATEMENT

Most explanations of complex notions begin with a definition.

*A paradox is a statement that contains contradictory and apparently mutually exclusive propositions that are argued as being present as real phenomena, and being able to operate at the same time.*

When faced with a paradoxical statement, one is not expected to make a choice over one or other of the propositions as would be the case when presented with a dilemma. Neither is it to be read as a statement which is to be interpreted as presenting an opportunity for us to demonstrate ambivalence over which is the more attractive of the two apparently conflicting but individually desirable propositions. We are not in effect being asked to choose one in such a way that the other would have to be abandoned. With paradox, we are being invited to accept both of the apparently mutually exclusive propositions. This is the strength and power of the use of paradox in our organizational language and thinking. Paradox can in this way be seen as representing a rich metaphor for understanding organizational conversation and thinking. This is particularly relevant in the area of strategic thinking where managers are predominantly using intuition and tacit knowledge that they hold about the firm to argue and make decisions concerning strategy development. Understanding paradox, in this sense, can lead to a transformation in the way that we think about strategy making.

Paradoxical statements surface more readily when managers are faced with describing changes or discontinuities in their environment and when they are presented with new and potentially threatening experiences. For example, as the ability of firms to trade on a worldwide basis accelerated and switching between sources of labour and markets became easier, then the notion of dealing with a global economy became a reality. John Naisbitt (1990) addressed this growing concern in his book *The Global Paradox*. The challenge was presented as a simple paradox: *The bigger the world economy, the more powerful its smallest players.* Although the paradox was presented as an apparent contradiction, Naisbitt saw its understanding as a means of unearthing not only the fallacies surrounding some of the thinking about globalization, but also as a means of establishing a more robust view of how to manage some of the inherent complexities. He applied the global paradox to companies such as IBM, Philips and General Motors, arguing that they had all responded by restructuring to become a series of small entrepreneurial companies no longer driven from a central point, but still sharing their expertise through networking. This, he argued, led to large firms pursuing economies of scope as a way of achieving flexibility rather than pursuing a traditional economies of scale strategy.

As a writer and champion of the use of paradoxical statements, to expose management thinking, Naisbitt is unique. He uses the global paradox statement to explore not only entrepreneurial networks and downsizing, but also re-engineering, the virtual organization, decentralization of power and control, ownership, strategic alliances, quality and deregulation of financial markets. This gives us a clear signal as to the power of the paradoxical statement in helping to explore issues that are vital to the growth of a business. It also demonstrates how new knowledge and understanding can be developed, among groups of strategic thinkers. We can use the ideas within the global paradox to demonstrate how its power relies on our ability to hold two apparently mutually exclusive thoughts in our minds at the same time.

Let us look at some conventional wisdom, around in the late 1980s, on how multinationals should frame their thinking about worldwide strategies. This was encapsulated in the statement, *Firms need to think global and act local.* At first glance, this seems like some good homespun advice, but on closer inspection it presents a paradox which provides a rich metaphor for describing the complexity involved in creating strategies for multinational companies. 'Thinking global' suggests that a worldwide brand image can be used to promote products and services, and that economies of scale and scope will result from the increased sales volume and standardization of design and delivery processes. To act local, on the other hand, suggests that manufacturing strategies should be developed in sympathy with local conditions and government policies, that products and services should be tailored to suit the local needs, and that investment in the local infrastructure would follow from any profitable trading. These interpretations are, of course, arguable, but the point being made is that the statements are mutually exclusive, although one can see them existing at the same time. Framing them in this paradoxical way means that they can be considered for their individual strengths. Identifying areas where they overlap and synergy can create a breakthrough for the business.

**The secret is to frame the paradox as an opportunity for new learning.**

There are many examples where paradox occurs naturally in organizational activities:

- the drive for centralization of decision making and control, while knowing that decision-making at the local level needs to be responsive and unique to the interpretations of the local manager;
- the desire to organize the work into division and separate groups, knowing that combinations and cross-fertilization of ideas and experiences enable firms to create superior performance;
- the urgency to organize production to achieve lowest cost, while recognizing that the customers' perception of value added will probably demand higher quality and support, and hence higher manufacturing costs;
- the determination of the strategist to obtain fit between the organization's capability and the environment while knowing that it is detecting and seizing the incongruities between the organization's offering and the environment that enable the breakthroughs to be made that will beat the competition;

- wanting to focus investment on the successful products that the firm is engaged in producing and selling, while recognizing that investment in new ventures is the only way that the firm can survive in the longer-term.

We could go on listing potential candidates for our paradoxical statements. The point that we are making is that only by framing these as paradoxes and using them as opportunities to develop ways of capitalizing on the new understanding that arises can the organization truly develop. The purpose is not to resolve these paradoxes, but to capitalize on the tensions that they create. To use them to concentrate on the key elements where new knowledge can be created and used.

## THE USE OF TENSION

Paradoxical statements suggest opposites, and our natural response is to take sides and make choices. When such statements are raised in a group setting, then it is likely that the process of making choices will create tension. For most of us this tension will be at what Peter Senge describes as the emotional, as distinct from the creative level. As we are promoting the use of paradox as a way of creating new knowledge and understanding, it is this creative tension that we want to capture. If we focus on the emotional tension, then the tendency will be to either reduce the opposites that we see in the paradox and seek to fudge the differences. Alternatively, we will argue to support one or other of the apparent opposites. Organizational life, and conversation, is full of such emotional responses, at times to do with views that we have about the worth of others in the group and at times about our own worth. Many managers become so disillusioned with their organizational life that irony may well be their only recourse to maintaining a sense of self-worth.

This constant matching of our personal reality with a vision of what we would wish to be happening is both a source of creative strength and one of potential weakness, as we are tempted to lower our vision in order to remove the tension. This can lead to a lowering of aspirations and standards with an eventual failure of the firm, as we balance our relationships and vision with that of our own perceived realities. What we are advocating is a way of using paradox, in organizational conversation, to harness the creative power in individuals while recognizing that emotional tension will be the natural response.

This creative tension that a paradox can produce is described by Peters (1994) in his book *Crazy Times Call for Crazy Organizations*. He also points out some potential drawbacks. In his book, Peters presents an example from Asea Brown Boveri, and in particular the views of Percy Barnevik on his strategy for breaking the company down into smaller units: a strategy aimed at promoting entrepreneurial management behaviour in markets that were suffering from a surplus of supply and hence highly competitive.

> Has the paradox at ABB struck you as it struck me? On the one hand, Barnevik radically decentralized the company, torched the fat, and awarded unusual autonomy to the several thousand 90% entrepreneurs operating profit and loss centres close to the front line. For them, it's perform or else. Yet Barnevik and Karlsson are betting the company's ability to get these busier than the devil (no central staff support, remember), do or die units to co-operate in sharing their knowledge.
>
> *Crazy Times Call for Crazy Organizations*, Tom Peters

Here the paradox is *control with autonomy*. The formulation was apparently straightforward and driven by a business need to generate more profitable sales in highly competitive markets. But Peters, by presenting this strategy as a paradox, rather than a problem to be solved, captures the sense of creative tension and potential for a breakthrough in strategic and operational thinking. In his book, Peters then suggests that designing and negotiating a unique system of rewards for co-operation, and for profit-related performance were an outcome of recognizing that the paradox was a statement of organizational strength. The tension created by the paradox had to be maintained. It had become a metaphor that represented how the organization was seeking to achieve sustainable competitive advantage.

In a group situation there is a strong pressure to conform. In an ideal world this would involve individuals sharing mental models. The sharing would strengthen as the group's experience of working together increased. But in many organizations this sharing seldom takes place beyond a superficial level. Some groups deliberately submerge individual differences and others resolve conflicts by agreeing to differ. Getting people to share mental models is difficult enough. Getting them to change them is quite a different matter. We need to explore how to approach changing these models, while capturing the creative tension that this can set up and minimizing the emotional response and hence resistance. Developing the skill required to do this takes us to the heart of effective strategic thinking. It becomes more than just a question of learning a new technique.

Our explorations can be guided by Argyris and Schon who suggested that managers can change their mental models by engaging in what they called 'double-loop learning'. The conventional approach to learning is typified by experts using the mental models that they have developed through experience to make sense of deviations and anomalies in organizational events. This is known as 'single-loop learning' and involves using these models to process through the steps of: discovering the gap, analyzing the reasons, selecting options for action and taking action to correct the gap. With this approach the assumptions, theories and mental models held by the experts are rarely questioned. The effort is applied solely to improve or resolve the perceived gap. The following two examples serve to illustrate this point.

> **Effective strategic thinking is more than learning a new technique.**

*A software company received a large number of complaints about a new release of an operating system that they had developed. The complaints were over the high number of software bugs that were being experienced in the new release. The level was far greater than had ever been seen with earlier versions of the software. The response from the company was to set up a quality assurance programme and to put more people on the 'help desk.'*

In this case, we can see that there was no attempt to look for changes in the performance measurements being used in the design and testing of the software. No moves towards a review of the applications and support being offered to the customers and the potential training needs at all levels.

*The co-operation between the divisions of a major company had deteriorated to the point where major improvements in the manufacturing processes in one division were not being shared across the company. The result was a failure to meet an increase in worldwide demand for the product. The response was to introduce a communications programme*

PART III · UNDERSTANDING THE POWER OF PARADOXICAL THINKING

*across the divisions in order to accelerate the transfer of manufacturing knowledge.*

Here we see again that there is no attempt to question the strategic thinking that led to the decision to disperse manufacturing across the divisions. There is no questioning of the variation in manufacturing capabilities across the divisions and the relevance of any quality assurance programmes that are being used. In both of these examples, the initial response demonstrated single-loop learning. Questions were asked at the policy and rules levels and were based on attempts to improve the existing systems and ways of working.

This can often be an effective way to proceed. But asking questions that challenge the mental models and assumptions behind the setting up of systems and standards, getting to the heart of the values and beliefs that are being used to drive the thinking, will help managers move into the mode of double-loop learning. Figure 9.1 illustrates how these assumptions are challenged.

**Figure 9.1**
**CHALLENGING ASSUMPTIONS**

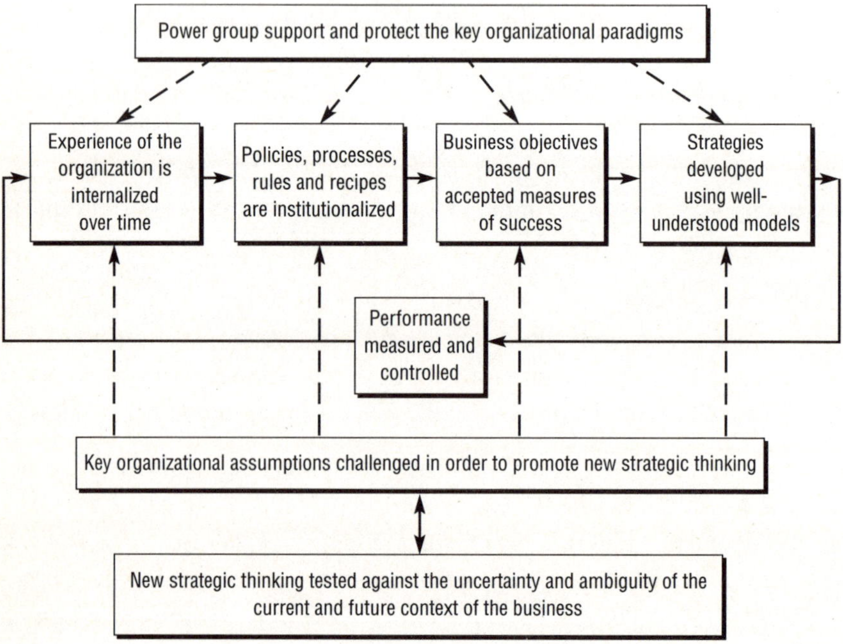

- Power group support and protect the key organizational paradigms
- Experience of the organization is internalized over time
- Policies, processes, rules and recipes are institutionalized
- Business objectives based on accepted measures of success
- Strategies developed using well-understood models
- Performance measured and controlled
- Key organizational assumptions challenged in order to promote new strategic thinking
- New strategic thinking tested against the uncertainty and ambiguity of the current and future context of the business

156

In double-loop learning managers are asked to question the assumptions that surround the use of these mental models and this allows the problem to be reframed and analyzed in new ways. This approach increases the number of perspectives that can be brought to bear on the problem. The policies, rules and processes that are being used are looked at with a view to questioning why they were set up and if they still fit the particular circumstances and context in which the firm operates.

Single-loop learning is likely to be less contentious as the norms and models in use are not questioned. In double-loop learning, conflict and friction between individuals and departments is likely to lead to increased tension. The greater the investment that individuals have made into creating their insights and mental models, the greater the temptation to avoid any questioning or to actively attack those posing the questions. The positional power that experts and those in authority can wield over others is often used to silence what they perceive as criticism. Those with less power can easily avoid questioning that leads to change by agreeing to take action, when in reality their efforts are minimal. This we would suggest is an organizational reality that we can represent as a paradox in order to generate the creative tension that will achieve the breakthrough in thinking that the strategist will need. The paradox is presented as follows:

*Organizations need to institutionalize best practice, which means that expertise is continually questioned and updated.*

Here we see two apparently sensible ideas that on closer inspection appear to be mutually exclusive, with the result that attempts to apply both at the same time would lead to the types of tensions and organizational conflict that we have outlined above. Grasping this paradox as opposed to trying to rationalize as to why both cannot exist and that one is more appropriate than the other is the way to proceed. But before we explore how best to do this, we need to see how the opportunity to

**The use of rhetoric can destroy efforts to create a dialogue.**

seize this creative tension is often destroyed by those wishing to maintain the *status quo* or achieve a winning position. The destruction can be seen to start with the use of a premise. At times very appropriate, but at others putting a block on organizational learning and progress.

PART III · UNDERSTANDING THE POWER OF PARADOXICAL THINKING

## THE USE OF PREMISE

In earlier chapters, we saw how the use of logic provides a powerful approach to developing an argument or promoting a point of view. But the true skill of the strategist relies on being able to deal with the ambiguity and uncertainty that surrounds complex situations, while knowing when to use logic and deduction to reach a state of conviction. We have also seen how the use of rhetoric contrasts with that of logical and deductive reasoning. Attempts to make a point, or persuade an audience to take action, are often based on the use of the rhetorical style. With this approach, a major premise is presented that often masks the ambiguities and uncertainties in a situation. Once the premise has been accepted, then further presentations of minor premises will quickly lead to a conclusion. The premises are presented in a way that is difficult to refute, particularly when the presenter is likely to be both powerful and eloquent.

We are not arguing here that the use of rhetoric and the promotion of premise, to make a point, is wrong or unacceptable. But we are alerting our strategist to the destructive effect that rhetoric can have when trying to establish conversations or dialogue that aims to encourage people to question deeply held mental models and to create new knowledge and understanding. We would support the use of rhetoric, but knowing when to harness its strengths and when to avoid its persuasiveness is a key skill for those involved in the strategy development process. Once again, we are asking the strategist to deal with a complex set of organizational behaviours:

- first, the challenge of being a change agent and trying to surface the mindsets of colleagues involved in the strategy development process;
- second, the question of deciding where the power lies in the group and how best to harness this power;
- third, recognizing and being able to utilize the strengths of the conversational and persuasive skills in the group;
- fourth, being concerned to emphasize the creative opportunities in the strategy development process.

Being able to understand the arguments and presenting styles, that colleagues are using, is obviously a key skill that the strategist needs to develop. But it is also necessary to understand how the approaches used to identify problems, and their solution, underpins these presenting styles.

As we have seen the drivers of strategy development are usually based on a perception of gaps in performance and the desire to pursue new opportunities for the business. These perceptions lead to the strategists identifying and tackling problems that can be classified as structured, semi-structured or unstructured. But it is important to note that one person's conviction as to the degree of structure, in a situation, may appear quite different to someone else. As the classification of the problem moves from structured to unstructured, the degree of creativity required to make sense of the situation increases and it is likely that the information required to make sense of the situation will be generated as part of the process.

Where the problem has been identified as familiar and of a routine nature however, then the response of the managers will be to apply algorithmic and well-understood techniques. For example, where the perceived return from capital investments is considered inadequate, the use of analytical techniques will be much in evidence, and the framing and resolution of the problem is likely to involve the use of rhetoric and premise.

For problems that are seen as routine, but not easily fitted into an algorithmic model, then managers will rely much more on intuition, and what are seen by the group as tried and tested methods of reaching agreement. These 'rules of thumb' approaches will represent the mental models that the managers have developed and are likely to be accepted at the tacit level. Any attempt to question the values or analytical judgements that are being used will be seen as against the culture and norms of the group. The use of rhetoric and premise will quickly surface as managers try to reconfirm that these 'rules of thumb,' or heuristics, represent the best way to proceed.

> **The paramount skill is to harness the power of paradox.**

Finally where the group have no precedent or heuristic, that helps them to make sense of a situation, then they will have to rely on the use of more creative approaches. This requires a level of personal risk-taking if the new ideas are to be surfaced and discussed. It is at this stage that the use of rhetoric can do the most damage. The aim, where creative approaches are being used, is to open up the options for interpretation rather than to close them down. It is here that the perception of the problem and the context by those involved will have a major impact on the styles that are used to present ideas and arguments. Managing these styles and getting others to recognize where style interferes with the creative process is a key skill that our strategist needs to develop. Harnessing the power of paradox in strategic thinking is the paramount skill that we are promoting in this book. But in order to do this, there are a lot of subsidiary skills that have to be learned and mastered. Having created the groundwork for this learning, we can now begin to practise constructing and using the notion of paradox before tackling the task of how to develop the skills of colleagues.

## *References*
Naisbitt, J. (1994) *The Global Paradox*, London, Nicholas Brealey Publishing Ltd.

Peters, T. (1994) *The Tom Peters Seminar: Crazy Times Call for Crazy Organizations*, New York, Vintage.

# Chapter 10

# CONSTRUCTING AND DECONSTRUCTING PARADOXES

Mastering the skills of organizational dialogue and debate  *164*

Using paradox in organizational settings: some guides and exercises  *208*

In this chapter, we will begin the preparation that will make you a champion of the paradox in your organization. To become a champion or master of any organizational activity requires two things. First, a recognition that the problems or issues being faced demand a new or breakthrough approach, and second, that you can identify a clear pay-off for the effort and risks involved. Having decided that this is the case, then you need to determine what knowledge and skills have to be acquired and what level of proficiency is required in their use.

Our experience of using newly gained knowledge and skills in organizational settings tells us that the learning curve is very steep. Some of us will have had some painful experiences of trying out a new approach or challenging the conventional organizational wisdom and have lived to tell the tale. What we learn from these experiences is that 'change' is probably the most talked about notion in management literature and the most difficult to achieve. Alternatively, many of us will have had some good experiences of introducing a change to a way of thinking or taking action in our organizations. Perhaps, if we reflect on the differences between our successes and failures, we will conclude that they were a mixture of preparation, our own skills, timing, who was involved and of course that perennial issue of luck. We might also admit that our determination to succeed and the criteria that we used to judge our success or failure were all part of the equation.

In this chapter, we can tackle some of these issues. We will help you to become a master of constructing and deconstructing organizational paradoxes. We also need to make sure that you are able to recognize how paradoxes can be used to represent thinking around the strategic issues facing the firm. Finally, we will provide you with some guides and exercises that will build up your confidence in using paradox as part of your organizational conversation. The first step to becoming a master of paradox begins here. Make sure that you have convinced yourself of the need to learn a radical approach to strategic thinking and that the pay-off is worth the effort that will be involved.

Sadly, but perhaps obviously, we are not offering a miracle cure to all those firms that are failing to capitalize on the use of strategic thinking to grow the business. But what we are offering is an approach that if used with skill and sensitivity can transform the strategic thinking activity from what for most has become a routine game that is played to one that becomes a breakthrough activity. At the individual level the strategic development process takes on a new vitality and at the level of the business the rewards become tangible.

## MASTERING THE SKILLS OF ORGANIZATIONAL DIALOGUE AND DEBATE

All managers have learned to argue and present arguments and viewpoints in a logical and rational manner. This skill is supported by an ability to persuade audiences through the use of what is known as a rhetorical style, presenting justifications through the use of statements that appear factual, and are intended to be persuasive. The reality is that the statements and arguments are often illogical and also contain inaccuracies of fact and evidence. This is the way that we carry out our organizational conversations. The approach is one of justification and argument that reflects the way that we think and our underlying attitudes and beliefs. We see an end goal or objective, and then set out to persuade others that the goal is worth achieving and that other options are less attractive. We anticipate criticism to our attitude or proposition, and are also prepared to offer criticism of the attitudes expressed by our colleagues. The skilled and successful are seen as those who can win arguments and persuade others to follow and give their support. The traditional debating society, public interviews and the topical debates that are continually presented by the media all re-inforce this approach. We intuitively recognize those that are truly skilled by the way they set out to discover what it is that their counterpart is trying to deflect or cover up in their counter-argument and then attack that point.

This all sounds plausible and most of us would support the notion that organizational dialogue and debate are based on attempting to capture and agree what might be called a 'common sense.' If this were the case, then persuasion and argument would appear to be the wrong way to proceed. What we are suggesting here is that 'common sense' appears to be the last thing that we are attempting to arrive at through the organizational processes that we have struggled so hard to master. We instead set out to construct an agreed version of the way in which the organization and its activities must be viewed, determined to clear up the contradictions represented by the conflicting ideas and arguments so that we can arrive at an agreed truth.

## Deconstructing paradoxes

When we analyze or deconstruct a paradoxical statement we see that the contrary views being presented constitute the very elements of thinking that we want to develop and use. Attempting to eliminate the contrary elements, in the common sense thinking that people demonstrate, would appear to be totally inappropriate. For those who strive for order and discipline, in organizational life, any open-ended discourse that leads to divergence rather than convergence would seem to be threatening. This presents us with a top level organizational paradox that we will use to develop the skill of deconstruction. By analyzing and deconstructing the series of paradoxical statements that follow, your journey to becoming a master of organizational dialogue and debate will have begun. The summaries that follow will help you to reflect on your new learning.

PART III · UNDERSTANDING THE POWER OF PARADOXICAL THINKING

## 1. Strategic focus and competitive advantage

*By encouraging the differences in perception and experiences that our managers have about what makes for success, we can create a unique and unified strategic focus. This focus will establish, for us, a source of sustainable competitive advantage.*

Use the above statement to complete the following activities.

1. In your own words, describe the underlying sentiments or beliefs that this statement is trying to express.

   _____
   _____
   _____
   _____
   _____

2. Pick out the two ideas that are contained in this statement that are mutually exclusive.

   _____
   _____
   _____
   _____
   _____

3. Describe in your own words some of the difficulties that would arise if these two ideas were pursued at the same time.

   _____
   _____
   _____
   _____
   _____

4. If you were asked to argue for one or the other of the two ideas that you identified in 2 above how would you do this?

_____
_____
_____
_____
_____
_____
_____
_____

5. If you were asked to argue that the ideas were not mutually exclusive and that the company should proceed on this basis, what arguments would you put up?

_____
_____
_____
_____
_____
_____
_____
_____
_____

PART III · UNDERSTANDING THE POWER OF PARADOXICAL THINKING

## 2. Creating a new vision

*In order to avoid the trap of groupthink and the continuing dependence on old and proven industry recipes, it is essential that the strategic thinking process ignores the accepted barriers and constraints that surround the organization. The aim is to produce a vision and a set of strategies that are unique, but capable of recognition and implementation by our business managers.*

Use the above statement to complete the following activities.

1. If you were asked to deconstruct the above statement, what would you identify as the two key mutually exclusive ideas?

   _____
   _____
   _____
   _____
   _____

2. In your own words say why these are mutually exclusive.

   _____
   _____
   _____
   _____
   _____

3. Select the idea that you would find it easier to support, and list the three key points that you would use to sway a group who were charged with developing strategy.

   _____
   _____
   _____
   _____
   _____

4. Now force yourself to list the three key points that you would expect someone who was arguing for the other idea to present.

5. If you were faced with having to act as a facilitator in the above group, and wanted to reach a consensus on how to proceed, what approach would you take?

6. If you were faced with having to act as a facilitator and your objective was to maintain the tension that these two apparently mutually exclusive ideas presented, how would you proceed?

PART III · UNDERSTANDING THE POWER OF PARADOXICAL THINKING

## 3. Leveraging global knowledge

*The survival of our product divisions as part of a large and globally stretched organization depends on each one being able to beat both the local and international competition on price and product innovations. Our overall success lies in being able to use the combined knowledge and expertise within the product divisions to create the synergies that will give us that unique edge over the competition.*

Use the above statement to complete the following activities.

1. List the mutually exclusive ideas that are contained in the above statement. You may find that there are more than two.

   _____
   _____
   _____
   _____
   _____

2. Which are the two that you feel are potentially the most diametrically opposed?

   _____
   _____
   _____
   _____

3. Assume that you are one of the divisional managers. List the arguments that you would raise as to why it was not possible to deliver on the competitiveness of your division, and at the same time support the group ambitions for seeking synergies through divisional co-operation.

   _____
   _____
   _____
   _____
   _____

4. Assuming that you were a member of the groups strategy department, what key arguments would you prepare if you were planning to meet with the divisional managers and convince them that without co-operation, the long-term competitive position of the firm was not sustainable.

_____
_____
_____
_____
_____
_____
_____

5. Assuming that you were the newly appointed chief executive of this organization, what four key arguments would you use to encourage the divisional managers and the group strategy team to accept the apparent contradictions and learn how to deal with them?

_____
_____
_____
_____
_____
_____
_____

## 4. Determining generic competitive strategies

*We need to standardize our procedures and working practices in order to maximize our efficiency and hence minimize our costs. In this way we will be able to meet our customers' ever-increasing needs for a high quality product that keeps ahead of the competition in terms of new and innovative features.*

Use the above statement to complete the following activities.

1. Assume that you are the director of marketing and sales in this organization. What would you identify as the elements of paradox in this statement that are likely to have the biggest impact on your being able to meet your annual sales targets?

   _____
   _____
   _____
   _____
   _____

2. As marketing and sales director, what arguments would you produce to ensure that your performance targets for this year and in the longer-term were not threatened?

   _____
   _____
   _____
   _____
   _____

3. As director of manufacturing and logistics, what two ideas would you identify as forming the paradox in the original statement?

   _____
   _____
   _____
   _____

4. What arguments would you prepare in order to ensure that you can meet both the short-term manufacturing delivery schedules and the longer-term performance of your team?

5. As director of research and development, what two ideas would you identify as forming the paradox in the original statement?

6. What arguments would you prepare to ensure that your department could perform in a way that would support the longer-term aims of the firm in a competitive market?

PART III · UNDERSTANDING THE POWER OF PARADOXICAL THINKING

7. As the chief executive, what main arguments would you prepare, based on the arguments raised by your marketing, operations and development managers, to persuade them that the paradox was real and that they would have to learn how to manage the tensions that this created?

## 5. Promoting corporate entrepreneurship

*We have become a large and complex organization, and we rely on the bureaucracy that we have developed to help keep track of things and overall control. But as the competition seeks out our weak spots, we must ensure that while pursuing efficiency we think and act like entrepreneurs at all levels of the business.*

Use the above statement to complete the following activities.

1. Identify the two apparently mutually exclusive ideas in the above statement.

   _____
   _____
   _____
   _____
   _____

2. Assume that the statement has been made by the chief executive of a large diverse corporation, and was being used to start a strategic development meeting. Identify a metaphor or analogy that could be employed to emphasize the perspective being presented.

   _____
   _____
   _____
   _____
   _____

3. If the meeting was wrestling with the paradox, what points would you expect the chief executive to make to emphasize the need for efficiency and control? What points would you expect to be made to illustrate the need to act in an entrepreneurial mode?

   _____
   _____
   _____
   _____
   _____

4. If you were at such a meeting and acting in the role of a consultant, what points would you make in order to illustrate the benefits from harnessing the tension that can be generated by grasping the paradoxical ideas?

## 6. Integrating marketing and operations strategies

*In our new high growth markets we need to satisfy our customers' concerns for functionality at reasonable prices in order to capture market share. As the marketplace becomes more sophisticated, then we can raise prices as long as we give them obvious added value. We need to build a marketing and operations facility capable of implementing such a strategy.*

Use the above statement to complete the following activities.

1. Identify, in your own words, the central paradox that underpins the above statement in terms of two apparently mutually exclusive ideas.

2. What other lower level paradoxes can you identify within this statement?

3. In such an organization, what would you identify as the main concerns that the marketing director would have about the central paradox that you have identified?

PART III · UNDERSTANDING THE POWER OF PARADOXICAL THINKING

4. What concerns would your central paradox present to the operations director?

_____
_____
_____
_____
_____
_____
_____
_____

5. If you were asked to prepare a list of points to be used at a meeting where the value of holding the central paradox was to be supported, what would the list contain?

_____
_____
_____
_____
_____
_____
_____
_____

# 7. Competitive advantage through positioning and capabilities

*Sustainable competitive advantage can be achieved by focusing on effective positioning of our products in the marketplace. Our strategy for achieving this is to ensure that our information systems help us to understand how our competitors, suppliers and customers are behaving in response to the changing industry environment. Our internal competencies and capabilities must also be identified and used as the basis for generating a unique competitive advantage.*

Use the above statement to complete the following activities.

1. What is the central paradox, in terms of two high level and apparently mutually exclusive ideas, that underpins the above statement?

2. What conflicts would you identify as likely to arise from an attempt to emphasize the importance of both product positioning in the external market and internal competence as a source of sustainable competitive advantage?

3. List the approaches to controlling the organizational activities if the argument emphasizing product positioning dominated discussions about the above statement.

PART III · UNDERSTANDING THE POWER OF PARADOXICAL THINKING

4. List the approaches to control that would be used if the internal competence approach dominated discussions about the above statement.

5. In which areas do you consider that these two approaches to control are incompatible?

6. Do you consider that these incompatibilities, in control approaches, demonstrate that the paradox has presented two mutually exclusive ideas?

CONSTRUCTING AND DECONSTRUCTING PARADOXES

## 8. The strategic intent is flexibility with focus

*Our strategic intent is to create a dynamic and flexible operation that can respond to our environment in support of our global efforts to achieve economies of scale and scope. In this way we will achieve sustainable competitive advantage in a rapidly changing world market.*

Use the above statement to complete the following activities.

1. What are the two apparently mutually exclusive ideas in the above statement?

2. What arguments would you use to support the notion of creating a flexible and dynamic organization as a way of achieving sustainable competitive advantage?

3. What arguments would you use to support the notion of using economies of scale and scope as a means of achieving sustainable competitive advantage?

181

4. Assume that you are the chief executive of this organization and that you had made the original statement. List the areas of tension that you would anticipate creating by your statement.

5. State how each of the tensions listed above would contribute to the long-term growth of the firm.

## Summary of the analyses and deconstructions

Grappling with the above statements and questions will have tested and developed your ability to appreciate the elements that make up a paradoxical statement. You will have seen how easy it is to fall into the trap of arguing that the central ideas are in conflict as they often represent a situation where entrenched views about functional priorities exist. Organizational statements about how to frame a complex set of circumstances and how to capture the feelings about alternative ways of tackling strategic issues are quite common. They are often made without too much prior analysis and often represent a mixture of experience and a declaration of strategic intent.

If this was all that was intended, then most such statements would be relegated to the after-dinner speeches and the eulogizing that managers often employ in order to create a feeling of being in control. But we are looking at such statements as representing an intention that precedes action. At the very least we are seeing these statements as a declaration of a mindset or mental model that underpins the thinking and decision making of the speaker. If we are to make use of this form of organizational conversation and expression of thinking, then we must be able to quickly deconstruct them in such a way that we can see the validity of the ideas being expressed.

What we are trying to do, by taking this deconstructionalist approach, is to capture the apparent contradictions, between the ideas, and anticipate the arguments and defences that will be made by those who favour one or the other. Our intention is to be able to recognize and promote holding in our minds, and those of our colleagues, these two opposing ideas. In this way we will create a tension that will move the conversation into new areas of thinking and learning. It is being able to hold these contradictions that is at the root of the power of the paradox in organizational conversation.

In the next section, we will practise constructing paradoxes and learning how to find the balance between apparently contradictory ideas. But first let us look at some of the ideas that have been unearthed by your analysis of the above statements. This will enable you to reflect on your new skill.

### Summary 1: Strategic focus and competitive advantage

This statement presents two views about how to achieve strategic focus in a diverse organization. It suggests that on the one hand organizations need to encourage autonomy, but on the other there is a great benefit from everyone recognizing the focus of the strategies being pursued. Organizations are constantly bedeviled by this apparent paradox. Giving people the freedom to react and respond to their own unique interpretation of events appears to be a similar mode of working that the owner or entrepreneur enjoys.

By encouraging this autonomy, the organization would appear to be gaining the flexibility of thinking that the small firm enjoys while having the leverage over resources of the big firm. But as most of us know, there are no easy ways of determining how much autonomy to allow managers and how much control is required over investment decisions, product strategies, pricing strategies, market segmentation and promotional activity – to name but a few.

As organizations develop, then there is a tendency to move from autonomy to control and then attempt to find ways of giving managers more freedom. Although this is a fairly common paradox, it enables us to see how the arguments can quickly develop in support of one or other of the ideas. Balancing the paradox so that the tensions are used to benefit the organization, rather than dissipating management effort and emotion in argument and the defence of entrenched positions, has obvious benefits. It also allows a dialogue to develop in the areas of strategic thinking. By recognizing the need to have both ideas working in the organization at the same time, the strategist can explore the extent to which the experiences and perceptions of the managers are being captured and where new processes need to be established.

Also there might be a need to run parallel organizations, with one focused on the development of the new thinking required to create innovative products and services, the other on pursuing a set of strategies that, at least for a set time, are clear and need to have the concerted support of key areas of the business. There are of course many other ways in which this paradox could be used, and no doubt you managed to identify some of these.

**Summary 2: Creating a new vision**

This raises the questions of how easy it is, or when it is appropriate to encourage the strategic thinkers to challenge the very features and thinking that have made the organization successful. We are assuming here that the organization is not in crisis, because if it were, then such radical changes are more easily accepted, even though this may lead to more disaster. In this paradox we are getting back to one of our gurus, Tom Peters, with his famous advice about 'sticking to the knitting' as a way to ensure excellence. No doubt those that favour continuing with tried and tested industry recipes will argue the Peters slogan. The firm is likely to have gathered an enormous amount of experience of the marketplace and how to do business and is comfortable in executing or recognizing in retrospect the strategies that pay off. To change is a threat.

On the other hand, one might expect the strategic thinking process to be the very place where new ideas are surfaced and explored. One way of doing this is to remove or at least suspend the barriers and constraints that the firm recognizes are limiting or framing performance. A new vision may result from this reframing and boundary removal, but we are faced with the problem of getting the new ideas accepted by business managers who have a vested interest in continuing in the old and proven ways.

In your workout you will no doubt have mined down to some of these issues and were able to see where the tensions would build up. But if we take a look at the benefits, from holding both ideas in the mind at the same time, we can quickly see the pay-off to our thinking and the firm. It is possible that the groupthink and industry recipe approach has worked to set the firm in a clear market position and the competitors will no doubt have learned to imitate and match the strategies being followed. It is the twin threats of changes to the strategic issues and context and the emergence of new and more challenging competitors that set the scene for a search for a new or revised vision.

We will see in later sections how to gain the attention and support of entrenched and experienced managers for new ideas. But at this point it is sufficient to see that the tensions that can be created by this paradox, are the key to the continuing success and growth of the firm. The main trap to avoid is that of allowing senior managers to drive through the search for a new vision while alienating and demotivating managers on whose experience and skills the firm depends.

**Summary 3: Leveraging global knowledge**
This is a much more complex statement, although at first glance it sounds like good advice and fairly easy to support. But within the statement there are five areas where a paradox is waiting to surface. Identifying and creating a dialogue around these paradoxes would be a way of opening up the strategic thinking process in this organization.

First, there is the tension that would result from the drive for competition between the product divisions for performance and the desire of the corporate group to seek synergies that would arise from sharing resources and knowledge. Organizations go to enormous lengths to find ways of achieving a balance between these two apparently mutually exclusive ideas. In an earlier chapter, where we introduced the work of Goold, Campbell and

Alexander on corporate parenting, we saw how the group has to find ways of adding to the overall performance of the firm while encouraging the individual businesses to make internal linkages that will create such synergies, but at a local level. It is this notion of striking a balance between the ideas of internal competition aimed at motivating managers and at the same time achieving co-operation that is at the heart of managing this particular paradox.

Second, we see, within the original statement, the paradox of needing to tailor the product to local country and market needs while seeking the benefits that come from the use of global branding. Global branding requires a high investment in advertising and promotion plus standardization in product features that would recoup the expenditure through the benefits of economies of scale.

This could lead to a third paradox where the benefits of using local manufacturing and distribution, in order to gain low costs and hence competitive prices, would conflict with the drives to gain worldwide volume orders that attract the benefits from economies of scale.

A fourth paradox would be where the drive for low prices at a local level would be achieved through attempts to reduce the number of changes to the product. Whereas product innovations, while keeping ahead of the competition and adding value, would mean increased costs and complexity in selling and promotion.

The fifth paradox is where local product managers want to generate changes to the product at a local level using the knowhow and networks of business relationships that they have developed, whereas the global focus requires that knowledge is shared and policy decisions on changes are then managed on a global basis.

It is clear that all of these paradoxes are sources of tension and potential conflict when managers see them as alternative positions that have to be defended and fought over. We can see that by accepting the notion in this central paradox of 'global versus local' as a chance to create new ways of seeing opportunities within the business we have a winning approach. Most organizations dissipate energy on trying to organize and control around these paradoxical issues rather than to use them as a means to create breakthroughs in how to run a complex international business. This was not an easy analysis to deal with, but hopefully you managed to see the benefits from the deconstruction of what had at first appeared to be a straightforward statement.

### Summary 4: Determining generic competitive strategies

The central paradox here was that of wanting efficiency, and hence low-cost products, in order to gain market share, while at the same time aiming for high quality and responsiveness to the changing requirements of the customers as a route to ensuring customer loyalty in the longer-term.

The approach demanded by the questions was slightly different in this case. We wanted you to envisage how the different functional directors in a firm – marketing and sales, manufacturing and logistics and research and development – are likely to identify different paradoxes within a high level statement of strategic intent.

What we are highlighting here is that the paradoxes that individuals identify are likely to reflect a high level of vested interest. For the strategic thinker, exposing the different paradoxes is the first step to understanding the mental models that are being used. Identifying the position of vested interest is of concern only where the entrenched position is blocking new learning by the team. A manager without vested interest is likely to be a poor performer. The arguments that would be raised by the functional specialists in the workout are likely to include:

- **Manufacturing and logistics**: we need to increase our investment in automation and distribution systems with additional training for all our workforce. In this way we will be able to produce a standardized high quality product at a lower cost than our competitors.
- **Marketing and sales**: we need a product that can be priced lower than our competitors and has built into it the latest features and functions that our competitors provide and that our customers demand.
- **Research and development**: we need to build customer loyalty by guaranteeing them longer-term value if they stick with our product rather than swapping to our competitors every time a new feature is on offer. Our research drive should be to create a product that meets their fundamental needs, requires low skills in manufacture and removes the requirement for innovation and change.

The final question in the analysis put you in the role of the chief executive who wanted to establish the reality of the paradox presented in the original statement and then harness the tensions that this created. You will have seen from the viewpoints raised by the various functional directors that the arguments and tensions will arise without much prompting. The managers will be quite skilled at avoiding any head-on conflicts other than those surrounding well-established personality clashes. The skill will be in how the chief executive can maintain this tension and develop a dialogue from which a new understanding of what is desirable in both the short- and longer-term can be reached. From there to agree where decisions have to be made as to how the strategy should unfold.

### Summary 5: Promoting corporate entrepreneurship

This raises the central paradox of autonomy and control that underpins most organizational conflicts: wanting the efficiency benefits that come from central control, with the effectiveness benefits that come from front-line sense making and action. A military analogy might be appropriate here where the front-line troops are expected to make local decisions depending on the circumstances, while feeding back information to HQ who can determine new objectives and strategies.

Once again too much control is just as bad as too little. As firms gain larger market share and expand their portfolio and ownership, it is likely that bureaucracy will flourish as efficiencies are pursued. Attempts at overcoming the stifling effect that this can have, on creativity and innovation, range from creating centres of innovation to setting up what Tom Peters has called 'skunk works' and corporate venturing. This is where new product ideas are developed and tested out in order to provide new directions for the corporation. Some might argue that the last thing that many organizations want is for its managers to act in an uncontrolled manner. They expect the managers to execute plans, be guided by policies and to follow procedures. Relying on the evaluation and control procedures to inform senior managers and strategists when and how the policies need to be changed.

We can see here that many well-practised arguments will arise around this paradox. Once again the identification of two, apparently mutually exclusive, ideas within the paradox will enable the true tensions to be surfaced. The on-going dialogue will ensure that the strategic thinking that follows will be shared rather than polarized by lobbyist groups.

### Summary 6: Integrating marketing and operations strategies

The central paradox here is that of short-term urgency versus longer-term vision. In the statement the managers are being asked to create an operations and a marketing facility that is able to produce, and deliver to the customer at low cost, a product that gives reasonable value to meet an unsophisticated user market. The strategy is aimed at capturing new high growth markets. A possible analogy here would be that of producing early versions of domestic white goods, home computers, television and entertainment equipment. The statement is also expressing a longer-term strategy that will require these facilities to be able to produce sophisticated products which have the ability to incorporate changes in functionality. The longer-term intention is to retain the market share, that has been won, by providing added value. The higher costs that this creates being recovered by charging higher prices.

The main arguments around this paradox are as follows.

- By being first into the market and investing in facilities in order to reduce product costs, we will not be able to create the expertise required for a high added value operation.
- Our competitors will wait until we have developed the market and then produce a substitute product that provides the added value and we will not be able to respond.
- By being the low cost producer in the marketplace we will attract an image of being cheap but ordinary that we will not be able to shake off.

You can see how the paradox can easily polarize the arguments, and how important some of the points being made are to the growth of the firm. Once again the power of the paradox acts as a stimulant to the strategic thinking process, capturing the new knowledge that such a rich organizational dialogue produces is the key to harnessing the latent power of the paradox. In later sections of the book, we will see how the ideas in the paradox also need to be balanced in order that decisions can be made on how to proceed in the face of massive apparent conflict and contradiction.

### Summary 7: Competitive advantage through positioning and capabilities

Here we have a paradox that presents a contemporary view of strategy making. It is suggesting that the strategy to be followed by the firm is to focus on arranging a fit between the resources of the firm, realized in the form of a set of products, and the external environment, while at the same time promoting the view that the strategic focus should be on identifying the internal competencies in order to create new capabilities and hence value added for customers. In the first case, competitive advantage is sought by positioning in the external market, whereas in the second case, advantage is seen as stemming from unique internal competencies with respect to the competition.

Typically, the sources of this uniqueness would include having:

- developed or acquired a set of knowledge, that is protected from the competition through patents
- evolved a superior set of internal processes of operation that deliver on the industry and market critical success factors

- invested in a unique distribution system that competitors would find difficult to copy.

We have implied by the questions posed that the two approaches are not mutually exclusive. It is always easy, when faced with two apparently opposing choices, to say, 'Well, why don't we do both?' Unfortunately managers then have to take action, and the choices are often surrounded by issues that are almost impossible to surmount. What we have suggested is that with this paradox, the way to generate a productive debate is to focus on the evaluation criteria and control processes that would have to be set up if either the positioning or the competencies routes were followed.

Taking this approach to analysis and debate will highlight the need to continue to follow the organizational paradigm that argues for positioning as a way to generate margin and growth in product markets, while searching for ways to harness the knowledge and experience in the firm that will generate new knowledge and competitiveness. The evaluation and controls required for both approaches may establish the common ground on which the strategists can build the future.

**Summary 8: The strategic intent is flexibility with focus**

This last analysis takes us full circle. Here we have a drive to become a flexible and responsive organization, while pursuing growth through economies of scale and scope on a world scale. The arguments that tell us that responsiveness requires an attention to local needs and autonomy of decision making are now well-understood. We also know that economies of scale depend on having large throughput of standardized products and an ability to move material sourcing, production, manufacturing and distribution channels as the economies of countries and exchange rates fluctuate. This could be seen as responding to the environment, but many would rather try to control the environment for a sufficient time so that economies of scale can be achieved.

Others would argue that seeking economies of scale is no longer a viable strategy in a world where new competition can emerge overnight with better and cheaper substitutes, and that distribution channels, markets and customers are capable of changing at an alarming rate. Some argue for economies of scope as the way forward for worldwide organizations. Being able to move products between manufacturing facilities and to different channels of distribution is now seen as a key competence. The paradox has again enabled us to engage in a wide debate.

The tension that these debates can create is of enormous value as it helps us to unearth the use of old recipes that have probably passed their 'sell by date'. It will also help to discover champions of the new ideas that are needed to take the firm forward. Having become masters of deconstructing paradoxes, we now need to practise how to construct the paradoxes. These paradoxes will be the ones that form the basis of effective organizational dialogue, and debate, around strategic issues.

## Constructing paradoxes

To help you to develop your skills at constructing paradoxes, we have provided a series of case studies that focus on strategic issues. You are invited to study these and to use them to construct paradoxical statements that are to be aimed at stimulating organizational dialogue. In each case we have cast you in the role of a member of a strategy making group whose aim is to promote new and critical strategic thinking. The summaries provided at the end of this section will help you to reflect on your mastery of the paradoxical approach.

## 1. Integrating design and production strategies

*Nike, the sports shoe producer, has historically adopted a production strategy that focuses on producing the highest quality shoe in order to create a worldwide image and demand. The company makes a wide range of sports shoes, and has over 800 models for use in 25 different sports in its catalogue. Each shoe is updated every six months in order to keep ahead of the competition. This is done by generating new ideas at their R&D centre where engineers and psychologists work with fashion stylists to produce the latest models. These designs are then manufactured by foreign factories around the world. This strategy has been in place for many years.*

The strategy group, of which you are a member, has been asked to review the design and production strategy at Nike. Compile two paradoxical statements that you would prepare in order to stimulate tension in the group that would lead to some critical strategic thinking.

**Paradox A:**

**Paradox B:**

## 2. Strategy as stretch in business growth

Assume that you are the leader of a team charged with producing a long-term product development strategy for the firm. You have received the following report from the chief executive and want to generate a dialogue within your team to determine how to proceed. Identify two paradoxical statements that you would prepare in order to stimulate the tension in the group that would lead to some critical strategic thinking.

*Two companies seem to me to offer us a view of how to grow our business. At Motorola, creating new products and technologies is part of their culture. Employees are very well aware of the opportunities that are associated with employing their entrepreneurial talent. Engineers, at operational levels, are developing initiatives that result in products that are not related to the products in their division. If the initiative is sufficiently promising, then the company establishes a spin-off. If a division does not want to use scarce resources to develop the idea, then the technology can be separated to another division. I also note that Jack Welch, at GE, is promoting a new principle called 'stretch.' There he is talking about setting people seemingly unobtainable goals. He has quoted an example of what they are calling 'bullet train thinking.' If you want to increase the speed of the bullet train by 10 mph, you add a little bit more horsepower. But if you want to take it from 150 mph to 300 mph, you have got to think about whether or not you want to widen the track, change the suspension system. It's not the same train with a little tweak. It's a whole new thought. That's what 'stretch' is.*

(Adapted from an article by Charles Day and Polly LaBarre in *Industry Week*, May 1994)

**Paradox A:**

_____
_____
_____
_____

**Paradox B:**

_____
_____
_____
_____

## 3. Challenging the organizational paradigm

Assume that you are the leader of a strategic development team of a major transport and logistics firm. The following report has been received from a business consultant and you are planning to use this at the next meeting of the team. What two paradoxical statements would you prepare in order to stimulate a change to the conventional planned approach that has been used for strategic development? Your intention is to move the group towards rethinking the existing organizational paradigm.

*The success of the firm has, in the past, been based on an ability to provide warehousing and distribution services to blue-chip retailers on a national basis. The firm has, over the years, been able to attract high margins through a mixture of skilful contract negotiation and control and expertise in the design and management of dedicated warehousing facilities. The business planning and control processes and procedures are very well-defined and it would be difficult to find a firm, in the industry, that could improve on the financial planning and control methods that are in use. The major blue-chip clients are locked into five- to ten-year contracts, but many of these are due to expire within 12 months. The marketplace has changed and the firm is now facing clients who want lower prices and flexible contracts. The competition is very active in this area and are willing to negotiate new contract conditions with any interested client. The competitors are showing all the entrepreneurial skills that your firm apparently had 20 years ago when it was formed. Our observation is that the business managers and operational staff in your firm are wedded to the old methods of contracting and working and will be very reluctant or even unable to change their approaches. It could be that the future of the firm depends on being able to introduce some radical changes to business practices, while recognizing that there is a large asset base and workforce to be serviced that is currently keeping you as Number 1 in the industry.*

**Paradox A:**

**Paradox B:**

## 4. The value of innovation in business growth

Assume that you are a consultant who has been asked to lead a strategic development workshop at 3M. The delegates will be a mixture of technical, marketing and finance managers. Your brief is to stimulate their ability to engage in dialogue around strategic issues facing the company. You have been given the following guide to help you focus on key issues. Your intention is to identify and use a series of paradoxical statements in order to create a dialogue. The tensions that this will create will then be used to promote critical thinking around key strategic issues. You have been able to glean the following information about the company from the CEO.

*The company has an incredible record for innovation. There is an extensive portfolio of products and businesses contributing around $16 billion in sales from some 40 divisions. The central competence at 3M is technical ability. Products have been built on the ability to coat substrates with materials and an expertise in working with polymers. New business ventures and products are aimed at achieving 25% return on sales, relying on technical advantage to create added value. A key feature of the success, of the Company, has been the use of a new product policy that requires 30% of sales to be based on new products that have been launched in the past four years. The divisions are highly decentralized and although there is a strong central technical function they are all able to build and develop their own research and technology expertise. The ability to innovate is obviously at the heart of the success of 3M, and although selling into the office products, automobile and metalworking markets is still providing niche markets, the effort to stay ahead through constant innovation is enormous. Although the company has always focused on getting to market early, and then moving out as the product becomes a commodity, this may not be the only way to proceed. If the company is going to sustain current growth levels, then it will have to take on competitors in mature markets and be able to compete on manufacturing and volume as well as technology. This is likely to require a major change in strategic thinking for the company.*

**Paradox A:**

_____
_____
_____
_____
_____
_____
_____
_____

**Paradox B:**

_____
_____
_____
_____
_____
_____
_____
_____

**Paradox C:**

_____
_____
_____
_____
_____
_____
_____
_____

PART III · UNDERSTANDING THE POWER OF PARADOXICAL THINKING

## 5. Developing marketing and sales strategies

Assume that you are the team leader of a strategy development group at Avon Products Inc. in mid-1994. You want to your team to bring some new thinking to the strategic issue of how to manage sales and distribution of the products. You have prepared and circulated, to your team, the report shown below. Your intention is to prepare three paradoxical statements about the business that can be used to generate a dialogue that will result in some tensions and new learning for the team and the company.

*Avon has historically been successful in linking centralized production to decentralized selling. Our products were sold by a sales force consisting of thousands of Avon ladies, who worked part time creating an effective cottage industry. We built this sales force at a time when many housewives were looking for part time work and many more were at home when the Avon lady came calling. Foreign sales still continue to grow but our home market collapsed when women became more fully employed outside of the home. We have attempted to change our sales approach through multi-level selling which involved our ladies both selling and recruiting others. This gave us a harder-nosed reputation and we abandoned that quite quickly. We have also invested many millions in direct sales catalogue selling and advertising. This has been unsuccessful also. My feeling is that it was the personal relationships between the ladies and their customers, who felt a loyalty to an individual and hence saved money up for her visit, that gave us our edge. Now that the demographics have changed, we need to develop some new thinking and a winning strategy.*

**Paradox A:**

**Paradox B:**

**Paradox C:**

PART III · UNDERSTANDING THE POWER OF PARADOXICAL THINKING

## *Summary of the analyses and constructions*

Tackling these case studies will have challenged your ability to be creative in the way that you interpreted the various situations and contexts. In these exercises, it is not possible to give you the depth of knowledge and intuitive feel that would exist if you were working in the particular firm. You would also be much more aware of the interpersonal relationships and power plays that would take place around contentious strategic issues. Notwithstanding these drawbacks you will no doubt have been able to come up with some paradoxical statements and perhaps much more importantly have established the power of the paradox. By bringing these paradoxes to an explicit level, the participants, in a dialogue, are given a solid base against which to test their perceptions and feelings.

Handling the power politics and the group dynamics, that follow from this contrasting of views, is something that we will cover in later sections of the book. But first we should look at some of the paradoxes that you will have identified and used to set your discussions in motion, remembering that resolution of the apparently mutually exclusive ideas in these paradoxes is not the objective. We are always trying to use the paradox that is presented to create a tension out of which we can evolve new knowledge and understanding. It is taking action based on this new understanding that creates the pay-off. Remember that the paradoxes identified below may differ from those that you created. This is quite normal as the richness of the many interpretations and perspectives is at the heart of developing new strategic thinking.

**Summary 1: Integrating design and production strategies**

There are two key issues here. First, producing standard lines would be attractive in that this means lower production costs and lower inventory levels. But on the other hand, the industry growth has been based on the notion of fashion and companies keeping ahead of the competition. This presents the paradox of pursuing market share, through price and availability, while wanting to build customer loyalty through brand image and responsiveness.

The second issue is that of conducting the manufacturing in house where costs and the links to design are more easily controlled, while foreign or outsourced manufacturing gives lower total production costs and an ability to reduce investment in fixed assets. This can be presented as the paradox where the desire for central control conflicts with the advantages to be gained from allowing flexibility for those involved on the supply side. You may also have identified the paradox that presents the desirability of economies of scale while wanting the flexibility that comes from outsourcing to a number of independent suppliers.

The framing of these ideas in the form of paradoxes will generate an extensive dialogue among the strategy group. The more conventional approach where delegates are expected to present position papers and develop their arguments is a lot less effective. If these issues were raised in this more conventional manner, then individuals would take up defensive positions, and the opportunity for a breakthrough in thinking would be lost.

**Summary 2: Strategy as stretch in business growth**
The Motorola statement places innovation and entrepreneurial thinking and action firmly on to the agenda. It also raises the question of central control and the importance attached to moving learning and knowledge across autonomous divisions. The GE example presents an analogy with the development of a high speed train to argue for staff being able to think outside of the box and break the conventional organizational paradigm.

The most obvious paradox is that of wanting a focused strategy, within the company, and at the same time wanting business managers to have a breadth of vision. The focus helps to refine the product manufacturing processes achieving cost reductions and a rapid move down the learning curve. But at the same time, the firm relies on managers being able to learn from the activities in other divisions, from competitors and other industries. This all takes place against a longer-term vision of where the firm is going in terms of technology, markets and product developments.

The second paradox is closely linked to the first and is that of wanting to encourage incremental innovation, in product development and the whole design and delivery process, while recognizing and encouraging the need for radical paradigm shifts: a strategy where both incremental and revolutionary innovation are taking place at the same time. Faced with this set of apparently mutually exclusive ideas, the conventional approach would be to argue for a separate R&D unit to be set up, for 'skunk works' to be instituted, for new product development to be outsourced, and for boundary crossers and product change champions to be appointed.

All of these are attempts to resolve or solve the paradox by pursuing the apparently exclusive ideas in totally separate ways. While we are not suggesting that these approaches will fail, we are suggesting that the more fundamental problem that needs to be tackled is for managers to learn to hold these conflicting ideas in their minds at the same time. Only by doing this will sufficient learning take place and both incremental and exploratory actions identified. This will stretch the interpretations and perspectives of the managers. The power of the paradox approach resides in this learning process.

**Summary 3: Challenging the organizational paradigm**
The consultants' report sounds very convincing. On the one hand, it is congratulating the firm on being very strong on traditional management planning and control and confirming that this has enabled the firm to become the market leader. On the other hand it warns that this very strength may become a weakness as the market has changed and the competition have responded by being adaptive to the new demands of the clients. It is likely that the managers, at the business and operational levels, have become wedded to what could soon become a strategy that is out of tune with the times.

The first paradox that this presents is that of wanting to maintain the existing paradigm, which in this case is around contract negotiation, warehousing expertise and control procedures aimed at blue-chip clients, and at the same time wanting managers to demonstrate originality in strategic thinking and break the paradigm. Many firms, faced with this situation, would attempt to solve the paradox by setting in place a new organizational structure, aimed at focusing on entrepreneurial activity in order to match the competition. Others would focus on cost-cutting and putting more effort into holding on to the existing clients. By framing the situation as a paradox, rather than as a problem to be solved, the strategic development team have an opportunity to create a much wider understanding of the situation facing the firm. The temptation to seek solutions, where the future is uncertain and surrounded by ambiguity, can thus be avoided.

Another paradox that can be used is where the firm want to continue with an approach to strategic planning, that values certainty and the ability to set clear objectives and controls, while recognizing that winning strategies will, in the future, depend on being able to be flexible and manage chaos. Here we see the managers recognizing the need for change, but being reluctant to move away from a winning formula. Some managers would see this as a time to introduce a long-term culture change programme and others would want to introduce incentive and performance-related bonus schemes in order to motivate managers towards a more entrepreneurial approach.

A third paradox is that where a firm focuses on market positioning, using all of the conventional approaches to competitive strategy formulation, while recognizing that a focus on the internal dynamics of the firm will provide industry and market leadership. Many managers are wedded to the market positioning approach and are supported in this by a myriad of analytical approaches. The market research industry has been built up on this idea of positioning. But there is an emerging recognition of the value of building on the knowledge base and intellectual capital within a firm as a way of achieving sustainable competitive advantage. This view is seen as being more relevant to an information-technology-driven economy. So it is likely that the use of this paradox will become increasingly popular as a focus for creating new knowledge within a firm. A close reading of some of the writings of Hamel and Prahalad will show that managing this paradox is likely to become the key area in strategic thinking and development.

**Summary 4: The value of innovation in business growth**
Being invited by 3M to help develop a change in strategic thinking would be quite a challenge. The company have a track record and culture that has been built around encouraging freedom of thinking and action that keeps the firm ahead of the competition. Here we are faced with a change in the markets, where to stay ahead is becoming increasingly expensive and difficult. The suggestion is that the firm will need to learn how to compete on the basis of manufacturing and distribution competencies and less on technological innovation. The first paradox that could be used is that of wanting to maintain large margins, through creating customer loyalty to the innovative nature of the firm's products and services, while focusing on gaining market share through economies of scale and hence price and value for money. Here are some of the tensions that this would bring to the surface.

- If customers see 3M as an innovative products company, a move to a cost-competitive product would send mixed messages to the marketplace.
- Key employees are attracted to a company that offers a leading edge technological environment for their creativity. Any moves to change this would destroy our core competence.
- Unless we stop seeing ourselves as market leaders and start to gain from the pioneering efforts of others we are always going to have a high margin on sales but a low return on assets. This will pull down our return on investment.
- Key stakeholders expect us to be leading-edge inventors, not mass producers in small and highly competitive markets.

No doubt, we could continue to build on to this list of tension-creating statements. The speed with which these arguments and defensive positions are likely to be taken up emphasizes how powerful the posing of a situation as a paradox can be. A second paradox could be presented around the notion of core competencies. This can be framed by posing two contrasting statements.

- **Statement 1**: The firm has historically built its success and reputation on scientific breakthroughs that were then rapidly turned into commercial products and services. We have to retain, in-house, the competencies that will enable us to continue to do this in order to maintain our image in the marketplace.
- **Statement 2**: We have to keep our scientific competencies in-house, but learn to become a leader in the field of outsourced activities. These activities will be in the areas of manufacturing and distribution. We need to do this by forming a network of alliances and partners. In this way we will build an image as an innovative low cost producer.

Many managers would see the drive to maintain an image for scientific innovation and for low cost production as being mutually exclusive. There are of course many firms that have managed this balancing act. But according to the brief in this fictitious exercise that we have been given for 3M then they have not managed this yet. We would expect arguments to centre around how manufacturing can be outsourced when the technical expertise built into the products is of such a leading-edge nature. Others might argue that this was an area where creativity should be applied to good effect.

In all these arguments, we will see an attack on the underlying paradigm that has been built into the organizational culture. Making changes to solve this paradox could be catastrophic in that they may well unhinge the very features that have created the companies success. The use of paradox would hopefully hold off the temptation to take drastic action and emphasize the need to learn how to manage the apparently mutually exclusive ideas that have been presented.

The third paradox is around the question of the role of the corporate group. In earlier sections of the book we looked at the work of Goold, Campbell and Alexander and their notion of corporate parenting. The parenting paradox is that the corporate group would want to decide on and control the policy of manufacturing across all divisions in order to gain from economies of scale and scope. While, at the same time, encouraging divisions to pursue research and product development that could be a direct feed into

CONSTRUCTING AND DECONSTRUCTING PARADOXES

this centrally driven activity. This drive towards central control while wanting businesses to adopt an entrepreneurial and autonomous approach to growth appears to represent two mutually exclusive ideas. Some of the tensions that framing the situation in this way might produce are as follows:

- Decisions on investment in research and development need to be taken at a local level where the needs of the particular industry and customers are known. If the decisions are made on the basis of likely cross sales and manufacturing economies then the high margin gains from sales could not be achieved.
- If divisions are encouraged to outsource manufacturing, in a way that suited their industry, then a greater flexibility in partnerships can be achieved. It would also mean a reduction in risk as it would not be necessary to build up a massive investment in manufacturing assets. It would also create a distribution network that suited local industry patterns and demands.
- A central control of manufacturing and distribution would change the way that customers perceive the firm. They would see the firm as able to innovate and then give them the benefits of a lower cost product through innovative applications in manufacturing.

Once again we can see how the tensions that this creates can be surfaced and managed when the situation is framed as a paradox. The approach helps the strategic thinkers to break out of existing mindsets and paradigms by moving the underlying thinking from the tacit to the explicit.

**Summary 5: Developing marketing and sales strategies**
Here we have a situation where the sales levels are falling and this is being attributed to a change in the demographics. Women are no longer in the home waiting for the Avon Lady to call. Various alternative ways of selling have been tried, including direct mail and increased product advertising but these do not appear to have been successful.

The first paradox here is that of pursuing a strategy that is aimed at establishing loyalty to the brands through a unique process of distribution and sales while wanting to take advantage of a much wider range of sales approaches and distribution channels. The experience of widening the sales approach appears not to have worked and the argument is that the marketplace is sensitive to the image of the firm in relation to the sales process. Unfortunately the demographics suggest that the sales process can no longer work as the customers are no longer accessible at their homes.

At first glance this could appear as a problem to be resolved whereas we are suggesting that the key is to explore the potential for balancing these two apparently mutually exclusive ideas. Arguments could be developed suggesting that alternative routes to the customers must be found, others might suggest that new thinking about how to segment the market is the way forward.

Alternatively some managers might want to look at the margins on sales by item and determine which ones benefitted from personal selling and which had become commodities. These arguments have to be exposed and linked back to the original paradox in order to check out how they are helping to find new ways of managing the paradox and not just arguing towards on or the other extremes.

A second paradox is that of recognizing the need to match the products and services of the firm to the marketplace in order to achieve profitable growth and at the same time wanting to identify and focus on the core competences of the firm as a way of creating a sustainable competitive advantage. Competing on the basis of market positioning while focused on an identification and growth of core competences. These appear at first as mutually incompatible ideas. In the case of Avon many managers would argue that an analysis of demographics and the image of Avon, that made them market leaders in sales, shows that the market positioning has to change. That the old paradigm has to be abandoned. From this position they might then argue for a change to alternative distribution channels, a change in name for the products, a move to selling to the large outlets as part of their own label. Others might want to hold on to the old paradigm of home sales and suggests that new market sectors needed to be identified, for example teenagers and those who have retired. A new product range might have to be produced but that should present few problems. The paradox will have brought out these contrasting and conflicting views and from this dialogue a way of managing rather than solving the paradox will be achieved.

A third paradox that might be appropriate for creating a dialogue is that of core competencies and outsourcing. This could be posed in the form of a statement or premise as a way of starting a dialogue.

**Statement**: *The hidden part of the Avon success story has been its ability to identify, produce and package products that the customers found better value for money than those of our competitors. The costs were managed at the factory level and the value was added by our Avon ladies. What we now need to do is to continue to focus on our expertise at product* *identification, design, packaging and manufacture, at the same time as forming alliances and partnerships with others who will provide the added value and volume from the selling and distribution activity.*

This represents quite a change to the existing paradigm, within our fictitious Avon exercise. The tensions that this will generate can be seen from the following questions.

- If we outsource our selling what will this do to our image?
- Do we now become known in the marketplace as a manufacturer or is it that our marketplace has changed from the home customer to the buyers in large distribution chains?
- If we outsource the sales how do we get feedback in sufficient depth and quality that will enable us to keep up with innovations in product design and packaging?
- We run a great danger of loosing out on the edge that we get from our intellectual property rights.
- How will we prevent buyers from putting us in a competitive position with other manufacturers and making us compete simply on price?
- How can we outsource the product design and manufacturing and rebuild our image of personal selling?

It is easy to see how the arguments would build up and defensive positions be established. It is also likely that consultants would be asked to conduct surveys and hard data be sought to confirm or otherwise some of the assertions that would be made. What we have stimulated here is a dialogue that would quickly develop into a debate and then a straight argument as deeply held values begin to surface. We will see in the following chapters what has to be done in order to learn how to manage this process – a process that involves maintaining the quality of the dialogue, as the balance in the paradox becomes more clear, and then helping to identify the required exploratory actions that will promote action and closure. In the next section we will begin to explore how paradox can be used in organizational settings. We will do this by using a mixture of guides and opportunities to practise the skill.

# USING PARADOX IN ORGANIZATIONAL SETTINGS: SOME GUIDES AND EXERCISES

In this section, we begin to focus on how to use paradoxical statements in generalized settings before tackling the question of applications in your own organization. We have seen how the experienced strategic thinker is able to tolerate a high degree of ambiguity, when faced with complex sets of issues and ideas, but certain apparent contradictions will stand out as key and thus amenable to being framed as paradoxes. The skill is being able to focus on those paradoxes that are likely to contribute to the development of the strategic thinking of the managers involved. Having captured the essence of the paradox we need to understand how the tension that is created by the ensuing dialogue can be harnessed.

We know that surfacing a paradox involves posing two apparently mutually exclusive but independently supportable ideas. We also know that individuals will then either want to accept the paradox or argue for one or other of the ideas. The following guides and exercises provide a structure or framework that can be used to address the paradox. Doing this in a way that brings out the key strategic issues and surfaces new learning. There are three ways in which we can deal with the paradox once it is surfaced and acknowledged by the team. We need to practise each of these approaches.

## 1. Accepting the paradox

Attempting to resolve a clear paradox by sheer strength of argument, where a win/lose approach is adopted will only lead to loss of an opportunity to learn, for example, where there is an incongruity between expectations and performance. This might occur where a firm in a growing market that had increased sales volume was no longer achieving the required profit performance. Framed as a paradox, it is likely that key players would argue that their approach, to its resolution, was to be favoured. Such an approach could easily cloud or hide some key learning points, for the team, that would be of enormous value when applied across a broad range of strategic issues.

What we are arguing here is that by accepting a paradox and learning to live with it, two things can be achieved. First, the team can identify any inconsistencies in their understanding of the issue that may be real and not just based on a lack of understanding. Second, they will be able to see the forces that are influencing the adoption of one or other of the apparently mutually exclusive ideas. Let us take a paradox that lies at the heart of strategic thinking in a lot of companies and see how we would approach learning to come to terms with it.

Consider the paradox of seeking to pursue both incrementalism and radical change. Here the paradox would be stated as follows:

*The business relies for its success on everyone working to institutionalize best practice and establish procedures that will improve our offering and aid focus. We also need to be able to identify and respond to opportunities in the environment that will require radical change to the way that we operate and do business.*

How would you answer the following three questions concerning this paradoxical statement?

1. What is the basic explanation behind this paradox?
2. What secondary explanation could be given?
3. If the decision was that the team accept this paradox, and decide to live with it, what would you see as some obvious consequences and benefits?

Try to answer these questions before going on to read the commentary that follows.

## *Commentary*

Accepting and deciding to live with a paradox require that the team are able to articulate and explain the underlying meaning. In the above case, the explanation is that the value added by the organizational activity is a combination of efficiency, through the effective use of resources, and by innovation at all levels. By accepting the paradox, the team acknowledges that small changes, in the way work is done need to be captured and turned into procedures and processes, at the same time encouraging people to think outside of the box. The benefit of accepting the paradox is that managerial time spent on arguing each of the apparently mutually exclusive ideas is saved. It acknowledges that inconsistencies in the mental models that managers hold about change need to be shared and that they can inform one another. The benefits from a strategic thinking standpoint are that strategies focused on the development of core competencies can be linked to the opportunities in the changing environment. Finding original ways of matching incremental improvements to breakthrough opportunities is the hallmark of the effective strategic thinker. We now need to look at the second way of dealing with a paradox. This involves attempting to resolve the paradox as opposed to accepting it.

## 2. Clarifying the levels of the paradox

Here the ideas represented in the paradox are accepted and agreed as being sound. The approach emphasizes the separation of the two ideas in order to then explore where the linkages exist. This approach, unlike that of acceptance described above, involves an attempt to change the perspectives of the managers involved. The intention is to resolve the paradox in the minds of the strategic development team. There is an inherent risk that differences in viewpoints will threaten relationships between members of the team. But once it is agreed that the paradox has to be resolved, then an investment of intellectual energy and the associated risk taking are the natural consequences.

> How would you answer the following questions if your objective was to resolve the paradox of seeking to pursue both incrementalism and radical change (page 209)?
>
> 1. How would you describe the two mental models and sets of assumptions that are likely to be held by:
>    (a) the managers who support incrementalism as a strategy?
>    (b) the managers who support radical change as a winning strategy?
>
> 2. At what level of the organizational activity, would you consider first the incrementalist approach, and second the radical approach to be most likely to be seen in operation?
>    At industry levels and competitive positioning, corporate investment, stakeholder added value, strategic thinking, strategic planning, operational management, administration and procedure definition or at the level of individual thinking and acting?
>
> 3. How would you see the motives of individuals, at the level that you determined in 2 above, impacting on their support of one or other of the ideas in the paradox?

## Commentary

Here we are attempting to clarify the levels in the organizational activity that the members of the strategic development team are using to frame the paradox. Determining these levels of distinction and their relationships is key to resolving the paradox. The notion being used here is that it is individuals and the drives that come from the mental models that they hold that create organizational action. If we are to change these models, then we need to help members of the team to surface these models and make them explicit. For example, some individuals may be using a model that sees strategic planning as requiring original thinking and that operational activity should be definable and measurable in cost-effectiveness terms. Others might see the strategic planning as having to be consistent with providing stakeholder benefits that focus on the shareholders and therefore needing to be approached incrementally, whereas they might see the operational activity being an area where radical innovations are required in order to create sustainable competitive advantage.

Alternatively, some members of the team will see the organization being driven from a strict top-down hierarchy. Hence the radical change comes from the senior management team, the job of the strategist being to convert these radical changes into a realistic set of actions, and the challenge being to adapt the organizational effort and direction to these changes in ways that allows the rest of the organization to focus on incremental change. Finally, some members of the team may view the organization as being driven by the ambitions of key individuals and feel that any concepts of change would be tempered by their views of how these ambitions were being played out in relation to innovation and change. We now need to look at the final way of resolving the paradox. This takes account of the time dimension.

## 3. Timing and sequence in a paradox

With this approach our attempts to resolve the paradox are based on the assumption that the two ideas dominate at different times. It is also likely that the two ideas are linked in a time sequence or causal manner. What we are attempting to do is to separate out the two ideas and understand how one side impacts or sets the conditions for the other to exist.

PART III · UNDERSTANDING THE POWER OF PARADOXICAL THINKING

> Again, using the paradox concerning incremental versus radical change on page 209, attempt the following questions. Assume that your objective is to resolve the paradox.
>
> 1. If you were attempting to develop strategies aimed at increasing margins, for a firm that was a market leader in a mature industry sector, would you adopt an incremental or radical innovation perspective? What justifications or arguments would you use to support your case?
>
> 2. Where a medium-sized firm, in a mature industry, decides to change the industry structure by introducing radical innovations what constraints, from within the firm, would it face?
>
> 3. As a general rule would you expect the sources of radical innovation to derive from inside the firm or from the external environment?

## *Commentary*

In using time and sequencing to resolve this paradox, we are relying on the strategic thinkers being able to understand the context in which the firm operates. Although this sounds like an obvious and simple requirement, it is often not the case. A great deal of sensitivity and personal skill is required to handle inputs from the executive group while attempting to understand the operational realities. Strategic thinkers rarely operate in a value-free world. With this particular paradox, we can see that understanding the context in which the firm is operating and balancing the interests of the various stakeholders is vital. Firms in mature industries gain market share through a focus on product and service improvements and an ability to institutionalize working practices at all levels. Organizational structures will have been developed to match the incremental changes that take place as the firm fine-tunes its activities. Major changes are likely to arise as a result of trying to respond to major external threats. The firm will see its strengths being around stability and everyone understanding how the business works. Incremental and radical innovation can thus be seen as sequential, and the time intervals between these two states being depends largely on the rate of change in the industry.

Incrementalism also sets the stage for radical innovation as firms reach a point where the margins are gradually eroded by the competition and the customers demand more value for money. Alternatively where a firm is faced with a highly volatile and competitive environment, then the demand for radical change may be predominant. The success of the firm depending on being able to be proactive or respond to such changes. In this case there will be a much shorter timescale between radical and incremental innovations. Some firms decide to manage these pressures by splitting their organizational structures into new start-up divisions and others that focus on turning the new ideas into commercial realities. Other firms focus their business entirely on radical innovations and either sell off the ideas to other firms or license out. Whichever approach is taken, we can see that it is possible to resolve the paradox by using this time frame and sequencing approach. The general model that we have developed is that organizations are dominated by existing structures and relationships, that left to their own devices, the managers would follow an incremental approach to innovation and that radical innovations are initiated only when senior management identify that a major change in performance or strategy is essential. This results in the identification of the management style and culture needed to support change. Changes to the structure follow and the management settle down to achieve effective operation by using the incremental approach. The timescales over which organizations change from radical to incremental modes of activity varies between industries. Although there are obvious advantages to be gained from both approaches the intellectual effort and management time involved in switching between these modes should not be underestimated.

These exercises have shown how capturing the apparently mutually exclusive ideas in a paradoxical statement can be a source of creative thinking. We now have three approaches to dealing with the ideas that are presented. Acceptance and learning to live with the paradox bring new understanding of the mental models being used by the members of the team, and an ability to recognize the need to be explicit about any compromises that are being made. Attempting to resolve the paradox through exploring the levels at which analysis and the mental models of the team members are focused on creates the opportunity to reach new levels of mutual understanding. Finally, clarifying the relative dominance of the ideas over time and their sequential relationships gives us the opportunity to develop new paradigms and ways of framing organizational realities. Acceptance and resolution of paradoxes are only possible if we can first identify organizational settings in which they can arise and be pursued.

## Paradox and organizational conversation

The challenge is to decide when it is appropriate to frame ideas as a paradox. In some of the earlier workouts, we saw how the chief executive or the leader of a strategic development team was in a strong position to use the paradoxical statement to start a discussion. These set pieces may not always be available and often the opportunity to use the power of a paradox approach will arise in conventional meetings.

## Using paradox in conventional meetings

Managers often find themselves in meetings that are aimed at resolving a problem that has arisen, for example, where there is a gap between expectations and performance, e.g., a breakdown in service delivery or in a process, an unexpected demand from a major customer or a failure of a major supplier. The managers faced with such a situation will adopt a rational problem-solving approach where the aim is to identify the factors that are behind the symptoms of the real problem. In these situations, the managers are aiming to restore the equilibrium and *status quo* and not looking for or likely to be sympathetic to any attempts at deep questioning.

The opportunity to use the paradox approach arises where the competing power figures in the group establish entrenched positions that are obviously defensive and can easily become combative. Surfacing a clear paradox that embraces both of the conflicting ideas will capture the attention of the meeting. Then there is an opportunity for both of the ideas to be held at the same time. The challenge then is in getting the meeting either to accept that the paradox has to be lived with or to explore the levels at which the analysis is being made or to see the time sequencing and relationships between the two conflicting but sound ideas. This will have to be done quite deliberately and with clarity in the face of attempts by the power figures to return to arguing their case. This is not an easy arena in which to practise the skill of developing paradoxical thinking, but you will be pleasantly surprised at the way in which the energy being put into the defensive arguments is moved towards a focus on the mutuality of the two ideas. The resolution of the problem will be accelerated by this clarification of perspectives among those at the meeting.

## Using paradox in agenda setting discussions

The routine day-to-day running of the organization will throw up mismatches and anomalies that challenge the existing paradigms that are held about the firm. The organization may have established management processes that enable these anomalies to be captured in a formal way. But it is more than likely that they will be discussed in informal settings and have meaning for managers at the implicit level. These anomalies need to be surfaced and captured in what some organizations call 'agenda setting discussions.' These discussions could include expanding a view on the changing nature of markets, changes in the wider environment, an imbalance in stakeholder support or a need to raise the level of capability in specific areas. Here the use of paradox is much more straightforward. The belief of the participants in the need to develop new thinking will be much stronger and more open. It is still quite normal to expect the participants to take up positions that are partly defensive of the *status quo* and partly based on deeply held values and beliefs. The selective use of the paradox will help to focus on the differences in perspectives held and to establish new ways of framing issues and reaching feasible agreements. The final setting for the use of paradox is of course that of the strategic planning and review process. We will be covering this area in Part IV.

# Part IV

# HARNESSING THE POWER OF PARADOXICAL THINKING

Chapter 11

# DEVELOPING YOUR POWER AS A STRATEGIC THINKER

Identifying your top ten paradoxes  225

Underlying perspectives that drive the key paradoxes  235

> *Everything that happens happens as it should, and if you observe carefully, you will find this to be so.*
>
> Marcus Aurelius (AD 121–180),
> Roman emperor

The earlier chapters have provided an insight into the cutting edge of developments in the field of strategic thinking. You have practised the construction, deconstruction and use of paradoxical statements in a variety of settings. In this chapter we focus on the paradoxes that you are most likely to draw on in your own strategic conversations. We will look at how the ideas in these paradoxes can be balanced, and also how the tension that this creates provides the source of power that drives the development of new strategic thinking. We begin by revisiting and confirming some of the ideas that have been raised, in earlier chapters, concerning strategic thinking. This will establish a firm base for our next steps.

We will start our review with a premise.

*The art of the strategic thinker is to be able to generate creative ideas on how to develop the business and to be able to excite other thinkers so that these ideas can be turned into competitive advantage for the firm.*

What we are talking about here is accelerating the ability of the managers to generate original and effective strategies. The fundamental problem that our premise faces is that the managers, who we might want to excite about new ideas, are already focused on the daily running of the business, tackling the myriad of problems that constitute business and operational life. Their interest is in obtaining and utilizing the resources of the business in order to remain competitive. They have learned that the best way to do this is to develop and institutionalize best practices, thus capturing the experiences and skills of the workforce that arise from running the operation. The result is that new thinking, and hence new strategies, do not fit easily into the dynamics of organizational activity. But the scene is changing. The growing interest in creating knowledge-based organizations is challenging conventional approaches to organizational development. This is evidenced by the current revival of resource-based theories of the firm, where the focus is on building core competencies as the way to achieve long-term competitive advantage. Commentators argue that the growth of the core competence approach has been accelerated by the sophistication and use of information technology.

The more traditional approach to strategic thinking, on the other hand, where a firm has to find a position in the marketplace that makes best use of its products and services in relation to the actions of the competitors, is becoming less fashionable. This market-positioning view is still very widely respected and is perpetuated by the managers who find the use of associated analytical models reassuring. But as we have seen in earlier chapters, many of the leading gurus are now suggesting that the effective strategic thinkers are those that are creating resources not only to fit tomorrow's markets but also to create those markets. We have in effect two models being used here. First, one that sees the resources of the firm being known and fitted or matched to the environment – a form of ends/means model. Second, we have a more dynamic and evolutionary model where the pathway to establishing sustainable competitive advantage has to be found on the presumption that building unique core competencies will lead to success.

The historic mistrust of the formalized strategic planning process, conducted by strategists who are remote from the realities of the business of the firm, has created a groundswell that argues for a firm adopting what has been framed as corporate entrepreneurship. Here the development of capabilities and thinking is shared by a much wider section of the management population. This approach has been extended to include suppliers and customers and even competitors in exploring the ways forward for the firm. Corporate entrepreneurship relies less on a unique dynamic leader, and more on inspiring leadership at all levels. One might be forgiven for smiling at this point, when one considers the media coverage given to industry leaders such as Bill Gates and Richard Branson. But this could be a core competence of the media that we are observing and not a demonstration of the source of the organizations' strategic thinking.

The strategic thinker is not operating in a value-free world. We have seen how the notions of stakeholders and the articles of corporate governance can be used to control or temper the excesses of imagination and action resulting from the work of the strategic thinker. The ownership and agency arguments, expounded by economists and others, have raised questions over the freedom to act and on whose behalf these actions are being taken. But there are no clear guides for the strategic thinker beyond an adoption of personal morale codes and the law to help navigate in these waters. The public adoration of the conglomerate, as a hallmark of strategic entrepreneurial activity, has now waned and corporate management is back in fashion. The notions of corporate parenting activity and the importance of adding value to the subsidiary businesses confirms this revival of the role of the corporate.

The values argument can be better understood by pausing, for a moment, to consider where the spark or trigger for creative strategic thinking stems from. Historically, we would expect the drive to come from a vision and mission statement that had been generated by a strategic group aided by a visionary and inspirational leader. In reality, the triggers arise from a perception of a performance gap, a major change in the environment, a threat of a takeover or a downturn in support from major financial backers. Such triggers have been the precursors of a revival process for many firms. But much of the research on firms that achieved revival and surprised the marketplace with their growth rate has shown a common ingredient to be present. They have all managed to generate what has been described as a collective level of excitement. The cynics might put this down to vested interest, others to luck and mysticism. But most experienced managers would agree that risk-taking, hard work and focus on the task in hand often result in mediocre performance, unless there is an element of perceived luck and a shared enthusiasm for success. The strategic thinker would be well-advised to maintain a keen eye for that enthusiasm, finding positions and processes within the firm that will enable new strategies to be recognized and embraced.

We now need to extend our earlier premise in order to position the strategist in relation to the operational activity of the firm. The conventional position is within the strategy development and planning processes. But there is also a unique position that can be sustained. Our argument, so far, has been that strategic thinking is associated with originality and framebreaking activities. But we have also seen that the business relies on local problem solving and the institutionalization of working practices. Here we have set ourselves a paradox and can use this to develop our thinking. We would suggest that both of these activities can exist in a firm, but that we need to consider their temporal relationship and the organizational levels at which we are setting our perspectives. We have decided that living with this paradox is not an option. Our premise is that in order for a firm to sustain competitive advantage, it must have a clear focus on meeting the targeted objectives, at the same time allowing the strategic thinkers to explore and find the way forward. This exploration involves using the anomalies that arise from the actions involved in running the business. The logic behind this premise is that conventional and hence incremental development of the business is based on following well-understood strategies or relies on strategies emerging. The day-to-day business activity identifies and solves many problems and does this by using organizational paradigms and the industry recipes that form the mindsets held by the managers. This process generates anomalies or signals that do not fit easily into the models held by the managers, and unless they are so large that attention has to be paid to them, then they are reduced to an informal or tacit level in the organizational conversation.

What we are suggesting is that these signals, or perceptions of things that do not fit or cannot be dealt with, be used as the inputs to a formalized strategic thinking process. They become part of an agenda setting process that is used to generate suggestions for changing the strategies being pursued and the mindsets of the managers who are running the business. The outputs from the strategic thinking group must be sufficiently persuasive and recognizable by the business managers if the ideas are to be accepted and used. Figure 11.1 illustrates how this process of using anomalies drives the strategic thinking.

The new strategies will obviously be perceived as being to some degree or other radical, but the purpose of the strategic thinking process is more that of an advisory or informing process as opposed to one of directing. The extent to which the strategic thinking group should involve the managers engaged in running the business will be explored later. Although this approach creates a unique position for the strategic thinker, it exists alongside the more conventional strategic planning approach, our reasoning for this being that the processes are related in time and that one sets the scene and context for the other. If you remember, this was our way of dealing with the paradoxical situations that were explored in previous chapters. We can now begin to identify the paradoxes in your own organization and how to set about balancing those that you are most likely to use.

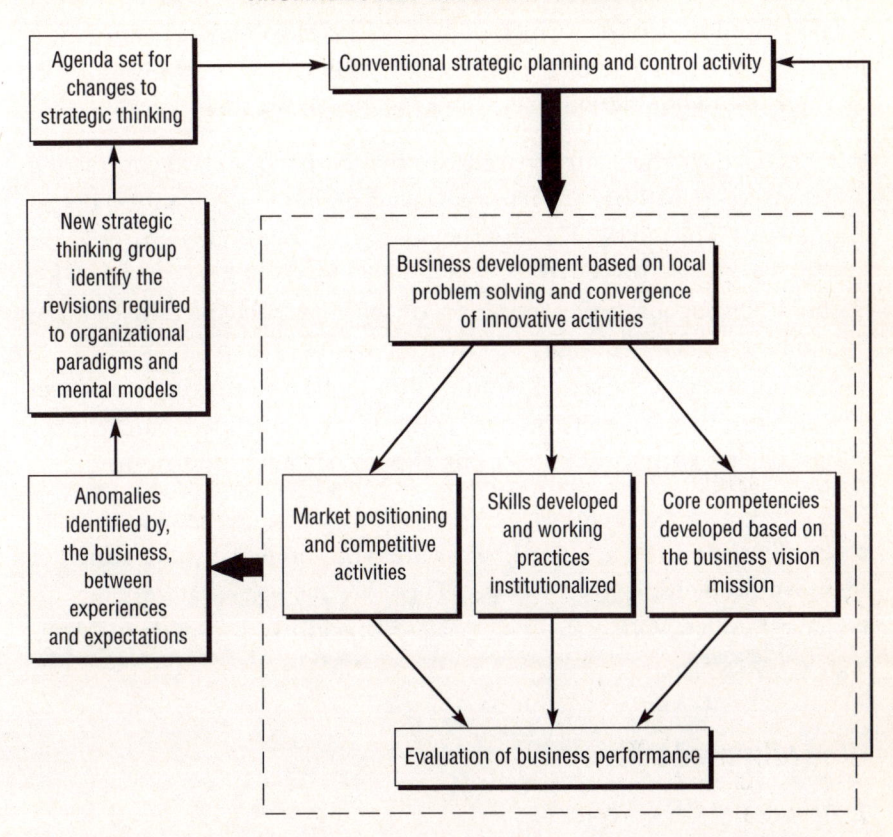

**Figure 11.1**
**ANOMALIES AND STRATEGIC THINKING**

[Flowchart showing: Agenda set for changes to strategic thinking → Conventional strategic planning and control activity → Business development based on local problem solving and convergence of innovative activities → Market positioning and competitive activities / Skills developed and working practices institutionalized / Core competencies developed based on the business vision mission → Evaluation of business performance → Anomalies identified by, the business, between experiences and expectations → New strategic thinking group identify the revisions required to organizational paradigms and mental models → back to Agenda set for changes to strategic thinking]

## IDENTIFYING YOUR TOP TEN PARADOXES

In tackling this chapter you will need to adopt a very self-centred perspective. It is likely that in most situations where you are engaged in strategic thinking that your own mental models and intuitive approaches will predominate. Only by understanding yourself, including your drives and values, will you be able to help others. Paradoxes can be seen to include values and beliefs, as the apparently mutually exclusive ideas represent the basis of argument or tension between individuals and groups within an organization. We have seen, in earlier chapters, how this tension can be used to explore mental models and lead to a reframing of understanding and the creation of new organizational knowledge. What we now need to look at is which of the paradoxes you favour or are most likely to use, and some of the values and beliefs that are involved.

There are two underlying sets of paradoxes in organizations.

- First, we have the control paradoxes that derive from two contrasting perspectives of how to determine and achieve organizational end points or objectives. The first perspective is one that is focused on achieving work objectives by pursuing a clearly defined set of tasks; the other encourages exploration of what the objectives should be and how to achieve them.
- Second, we have the set of paradoxes that reflect values that stem from differentiation. These paradoxes contrast the traditional management approaches with those supporting expediency and opportunism.

A number of examples of paradoxes that we would expect to arise within these two sets are given below and you should consider which of these would figure in your top ten. These are the ones that you need to be most familiar with and able to use to develop your power as a strategic thinker.

# Control paradoxes

## 1. Autonomy versus control

This presents the question of recognizing the need to give people the freedom to react and respond to their own interpretation of events and make local decisions while wanting to exercise central control. The thinking here can also centre around wanting control in order to gain operational efficiency, and at the same time wanting to seize opportunities that would lead to greater effectiveness. As organizations grow, there will be a tendency to focus and control, whereas for organizations that face a downturn in their fortunes, the question of control *versus* autonomy will be a lot less clear. Living with the paradox, once the implications have been confronted, is one option. Alteratively, looking at the levels at which these ideas could be seen to impact on the firm and their sequential relationships could open up new thinking and understanding.

## 2. Building a strong culture versus new learning

Here we have the conventional approach to developing a strategy that stems from the leader. Implementation relying on being able to create a supportive culture. As the strategic direction becomes clearer, then the organizational processes and structures are all directed towards maintaining this strong culture. But this can be seen to reduce the chances of new learning taking place. Organizational reward systems and the focus of the leadership on evaluating the development of the key strategies will reduce the opportunities for thinking outside of the box. Considering the paradox at different organizational levels and in terms of the sequential links between these ideas can be a very powerful source of organizational learning.

## 3. Managing clear objectives versus managing chaos

The conventional management approach is based on valuing certainty and the ability to set clear objectives and controls. Most managers are reluctant to move away from winning formula and proven industry recipes. A recognition that the future is full of ambiguity and uncertainty encourages managers to believe that it is more important to learn how to manage the ensuing chaos. Here we have two apparently mutually exclusive views which on closer inspection have relationships in time and significance at different organizational levels. To use the tension that this paradox surfaces we need to know the perceived state of the firm in relation to expected performance. Also we need to understand the ways in which different areas of the business or functions would benefit from a planned or chaos management approach. Some strategies will have longer-term horizons than others, and short-termism will probably need to be recognized and tackled with an eye to any longer-term implications.

## 4. Originality in strategic thinking versus maintaining the status quo

The issue here is that of knowing when to challenge the very thinking that has created the success of the organization. If the organization is not in crisis, then originality in ways of seeing and changing the strategies are not likely to be taken seriously. But one might expect that the strategic thinking process is the place where we would expect to find new thinking. The challenge here is to be able to identify areas where the firm could benefit from some new thinking and link this to forecasts of future environmental changes. A look at the competitors, albeit through benchmarking exercises, may also raise the expectations and abilities of managers to engage in new ways of seeing the unfolding strategies. The timing and levels at which this paradox can be explored soon become apparent.

### 5. *Entrepreneurial* versus *bureaucratic culture*

The paradox presents two ideas that are clearly sequential: firms that are either at an early growth stage and directed by an entrepreneur, and those that are large and seek to revitalize the way they engage in entrepreneurial activity – here calculated risks are taken, and the firm engages in breaking existing paradigms as a way of regaining the dynamism required for growth. In large corporations the two cultures can be seen to exist in different divisions at the same time and at different levels in the organizational activity. The need to focus in order to achieve efficiency, while at the same time being aware of the need to seize opportunities and overcome obstacles through entrepreneurial activity forms the twin pillars on which winning firms are built. This paradox crops up in many forms, and if used as the basis of a dialogue can lead to major improvements in performance and morale.

### 6. *Social responsibility* versus *commercial intent*

This paradox is based on the ideas behind corporate governance and the notion of the manager acting as agent for the shareholders. Living with the paradox is rarely an option, as the challenges and implications involved hit at the heart of the modern organization. The growing views as to the importance of adding stakeholder value and public concern over environmental and other related issues mean that this is a key to the survival and sustainability of the firm. The most likely approach to resolving this paradox is by considering the levels at which it has the most impact on the operation of the organization. Analysis at both corporate and operational levels will highlight areas in which new learning has to take place.

## 7. Divisional competition versus corporate synergies

The natural tension that is associated with competition between operating divisions and the subsidiary businesses is well-recognized. What often needs to be debated much more rigorously is the contribution that a parent or corporate group can make to the effectiveness of these businesses. The reluctance of senior and corporate managers to relinquish control over the businesses can lead to many inefficiencies and wasted management time. On the other hand, there is a major contribution that can be made by the corporate group to the way funds are managed and the businesses linked. This paradox is key to the growth of both the corporation and their businesses.

## 8. Planned versus opportunistic strategies

This paradox will be found at the heart of most strategic thinking and planning activities. Managers who have become used to setting objectives and then controlling the effort used to achieve those objectives will want to plan their way forward. Others will be looking for ways to create a more flexible capability in the way the firm is developed and operates. There will be a number of factors influencing the approach taken to formulating strategies that are aimed at developing the competitive capability of the firm. Pressures from stakeholder groups, vested interest within the team and the culture and history of the firm are likely to create the greatest influence. Remember that here we are looking at a situation where the team are arguing for one or other of two apparently mutually exclusive approaches to strategic management.

Living with the paradox would, we suggest, not be a viable option. Making the opposing points of view explicit would help in moving towards a resolution of the paradox as would looking at the levels, in the firm, at which the strategic thinking was likely to have an impact. For example, it might be more appropriate to view the corporate level strategies as amenable to a planned approach, whereas at the operational level the nature of the market dynamics might benefit from a more opportunistic approach. This might need to be supported with some training or even to the setting up of alliances with suppliers. Alternatively it could be that a better understanding of the time sequencing between the planned and opportunistic strategies would indicate ways in which the paradox could be resolved.

# Value paradoxes

## 9. Cost versus *quality*

This paradox appears, at first sight, to be fairly straightforward in that the ideas are mutually exclusive. High quality will obviously mean higher costs. But if we hold the paradox and look at the definitions and perceptions of quality, we may see ways of reaching a resolution. If, for example, quality is seen as representing a standard and a quality gap is defined as mismatch in expectations between supplier and user, then we have room for new understanding and learning. Once again, we can see that the strategic development team will be faced with some strong arguments from managers within the firm depending on their position, experiences, mental models held and of course vested interest. Looking at the paradoxical ideas at different levels will bring out the conflicts between those with a marketing perspective, those faced with a design requirement that has to be met and those looking at the financial aspects of performance.

The time sequencing and linking approach might also result in managers being able to agree on areas where quality needed to be achieved at a premium cost and others where an adequate level of quality could be provided, at an agreed cost, and a programme of staff and customer awareness introduced.

## 10. *Local* versus *global*

For some firms, the choice of whether to adopt a set of strategies that focus on tuning into local needs or of creating a global image and range of products and services may not be straightforward. The firm may already be involved in international trading or direct investment in other countries, or have formed alliances and joint ventures which impact on the way that they interpret global and local focus. For most firms, it will be a question of using the paradoxical statement to address issues and problems that have arisen from previous decisions. In this case, living with the paradox and relying on the conflicts between the various factions and power figures to develop an effective strategy may be an option. Where this does not seem to be working, then a closer look at the paradox will accelerate the tension and lead to new thinking.

By looking at the various levels, at which the paradox applies, we can see that localization strategies are appropriate where the situation is volatile and the aim is to gain market position. From a global perspective, the benefits from investment may be around image at a corporate level or around the economies of scale that come from centralized manufacturing and distribution. The range of variables and arguments that will arise from the use of this paradox are enormous as will be the associated learning.

## 11. Loyalty to brand versus loyalty to innovation

The notion of loyalty is used in this paradox to indicate the belief that is held as to why customers continue to use the products and services of the firm, in spite of apparently attractive offers from competitors. The two conflicting ideas presented by the paradox are (a) that loyalty is dependent on the features that the customers see as being attached to the benefits from the brand and (b) that innovation is the attractive element. Within the strategic development team, it is likely that there are different views held on how to secure the longer-term success and competitive capability of the firm. Living with the paradox may not be an option as the investment required to achieve the two conflicting ideas involve different areas of the firm. Investment in marketing and product delivery and support, the other on research and development and strategic alliances. Investigating sequencing, product and industry life cycles and linkages between the two ideas will lead to some new and effective ways of resolving the paradox.

## 12. Long-term vision versus short-term strategy

Strategic thinkers are often accused of worrying about tomorrow while forgetting about today, while those focused on the competition and meeting more immediate business performance needs are accused of short-term thinking. It is perhaps more about finding a balance than about fighting for corners. Short-term strategies are often aimed at retaining market share or responding to moves from a new entrant to the marketplace or those of competitors. Short-term strategies are often seen as responsive and rely on being able to gain support from all levels of the firm. But the short-term strategies are often the base on which longer-term strategies have to be built and hence the two are intrinsically linked. In looking at the linkages between these two conflicting ideas, we can use the notions of market positioning and resource based development.

Market positioning will encompass thinking about immediate and longer-term competition while the resource-based view will highlight the ways in which capabilities and core competencies need to be developed. A sequential link between the market-based and resource-based views can be readily seen as can the need to focus the timing of strategies at the various levels in the firm.

### 13. *Customer care* versus *market share*

For many firms, this paradox generates an enormous number of conflicts and uses valuable management time in dealing with them. Pursuing market share through offering higher perceived customer value at lower perceived cost than the competitors is a key strategy. Lower cost production requires both a high volume of throughput and a focus on efficiency in procurement, manufacturing and delivery. Building customer loyalty is in the short-term perhaps not a key consideration. Here we see the use of the sequence and linking between these two ideas as the way to tackle resolution of the paradox. As the market matures and customers become more discerning then the firm moves attention to building loyalty and adding value through intangible factors associated with the product or service. It is obviously important for the firm to match the image that is being promoted with the application of these two development strategies.

### 14. *Incremental* versus *radical innovation*

The focus, for many firms, is on incremental or continuous improvement at all levels of the business. But firms recognize that by focusing on this approach, they eventually become vulnerable to new developments by competitors and newcomers to the marketplace. The more volatile and turbulent the technology and the marketplace, then the greater the need to innovate. Many firms see these innovations being aimed at changing the rules of competition as well as being about product and service improvements. Living with the paradox can be approached through developing a clear understanding as to what constitutes a radical innovation and what are some of the triggers or signals to such innovations, also what timescales are involved in pursuing and benefiting from a radical innovation. For some firms, the decision will have been taken to separate out these two ideas by forming organizational structures that keep the activities isolated. The strategic thinkers need to consider the extent to which the operational activity should be the source of such triggers, and how these groups can be sensitized to watch out for indicators that the incremental improvements will not provide a long-term solution.

## 15. *Focused strategies* versus *breadth of vision*

For the strategic development team, this is a key and probably recurring paradox. The pressures from key stakeholders will be to focus and build on areas of the business that appear to be linked to growth. Searching for winning strategies in areas of low performance. On the other hand, there will be a tacit belief and a drive from the chief executive to maintain a breadth of vision in order to secure the future. Studying these alternative perspectives from the point of view of the immediacy of the operations and matching this to the longer-term trends in technology and the industry may indicate how these ideas are linked. Pursuing this paradox may result in a new way of viewing the way that the firm is evolving and where there is a need to introduce exploratory strategies. These strategies may accelerate the ability of the firm to move between a perspective that is focused on short- and medium-term performance and one that embraces a wider vision. This flexibility in thinking can be used to create a competitive edge for the firm.

## 16. *Values* versus *rules*

A great deal of management frustration can be captured and exposed through this paradox. It can be used to explore the ways in which the firm relies on a set of tacit values to direct strategic thinking and how these are supported by policies and rules. As an organization grows, then there is a natural move towards capturing experiences and learning in the form of processes, procedures and rules. The way in which these rules are interpreted and used will depend on the underlying values and beliefs of the managers. The strategic thinkers need to be aware of these values as they will have a major influence on the development of new strategies. Some would argue that the strategies have to fit the organizational values and be supported by policies and rules that are respected. Others would argue that the structure, policies, culture and rules have to be adapted to support the strategies. Resolution of this paradox can be tackled through recognizing the linkages between the two ideas and how the stages of development and the degree of turbulence in the industry determines their relative emphasis.

## 17. *Core competencies* versus *outsourcing*

Where the strategic thinkers are using a resource-based view of the firm, they will attempt to identify those competencies that are the key to the current success and those required for the future. Within this, they may see outsourcing as a way of getting rid of those activities that they see as non-core. Alternatively, they may want to use the resources of an alliance partner or joint venture arrangement to supply the core competence. Defining core competencies needs to be done with a clear view of the present and future competition and the longer-term mission of the firm. Bearing in mind that the core competencies of a firm will have resulted from the operational activity itself. The process of using resources, both expertise and finances, will have generated experience and learning from the work activity, which will have in turn created capabilities within which the core competencies can be identified. Exploring the perspectives held and the associated timing of these ideas will result in a clearer understanding on how to proceed.

Among the paradoxes that we have identified above, you will probably have found some favourites. None of these present an easy option for the strategic thinker, as each presents a very high-level abstraction of a complex set of issues. Many of the above paradoxes are interlinked, and in many cases it will be necessary to engage in a detailed dialogue in order to make your meaning clear. Remember that your own values and beliefs will be creating a bias in how you frame and argue the paradox. Organizations are dominated by conversations and arguments that can be framed as paradoxes. We have learned how to construct and deconstruct a paradox. This has lead to our being able to develop ways of living with and resolving paradoxes. We have seen how through the use of time sequencing and different levels of analysis, we can find a balance between two apparently mutually exclusive ideas. We now need to look at how the paradoxes themselves need to be brought into balance, through organizational dialogue, in order to avoid the biases that come from overemphasis.

## UNDERLYING PERSPECTIVES THAT
## DRIVE THE KEY PARADOXES

Strategic thinking takes place against a background of conflicting ideas and approaches as to the best way to develop the business. These conflicting ideas are symptomatic of the dynamics at work within the organization and can be framed as paradoxes. Our earlier chapters have argued that adopting an 'either . . . or' approach, to the conflicts and resulting tensions, will dissipate the energy of both individuals and the organization itself. Any attempt to resolve the conflicts that are framed by these paradoxes is usually driven by the desire to establish stability and order, so that goals can be agreed and actions taken that will result in their achievement.

But our experience of organizational life and the arguments and exercises in this book will have shown that paradoxes are never truly resolved. We either argue for one idea being better than the other or power our way to reaching an agreement. Recent studies of high performance companies by Walter Goldsmith and David Clutterbuck and other writers all indicate that successful firms are skilled at balancing the many pressures and demands on them. Maintaining this balance is seen by many companies as a natural outcome of having an appropriate culture and management style. This statement is probably easy to agree with, but not very helpful in terms of providing a framework for action and improvement. We need to look more closely at how strategic thinking can be helped by adopting this balancing premise.

We know that by pursuing a specific value, with single-minded dedication, will lead to short-term success, while at the same time requiring that we destroy any chance of obtaining a balance between opposing ideas. Singlemindedness for many managers is seen as a virtue, as long as the values being pursued are in tune with their own and that the actions do not threaten their own objectives. What we can see clearly is that pursuing one idea at the expense of an opposing idea will move us from a position of creating tension to one of expending all of the resources or destroying one or other of the forces required for the tension, the tension being our source of power in the strategic thinking process. But we need to explore some examples of this happening by using the paradoxes that we have so far identified.

Within our set of 'paradoxes of control' we identified eight key paradoxes that create the tension that powers our strategic thinking. Given an ideal organizational climate, where dialogue enabled us to explore and address these paradoxes, we would expect to find the balance that would move us to peak performance. By this we mean that those involved in the strategic development process would produce a set of strategies that would be recognized by the stakeholders as desirable and feasible in terms of implementation and ultimate organizational performance. We should note that these strategies may be a mixture of those that seek clear ends, those that are exploratory and those that are more radical and stimulating major change. The point of balance and the relative predominance of these paradoxes, one with another, will obviously depend on many factors. For example: the dynamics of the industry, the actions of competitors, the power figures, the abilities of the managers.

These are just some of the factors that will be influencing the key paradoxes. It is this that creates the dynamics of the organization and the way that these factors influence the individual and collective mindsets and actions of the managers that determines where the balance has to be struck. But behind these control paradoxes there are two dominant perspectives. One based on a determination to define and achieve a task and the other focused on exploration. Figure 11.2 illustrates the influence of these underlying perspectives.

The following ideas stem from a task perspective:

- central control
- strong culture
- managing to plans
- *status quo*
- bureaucratic culture
- commercial intent
- divisional competition
- planned strategies.

If the balance moves too far towards this task perspective, then we would expect an organization to be characterized, in the extreme case, by obdurate and oppressive behaviours at all levels. The effect of this, except in some industries, would lead to a lack of responsiveness and an eventual failure of organizational performance. Alternatively, the opposing ideas to the above are being driven by a perspective that supports exploration:

## Figure 11.2
## CONTROL PARADOXES AND UNDERLYING PERSPECTIVES

**Task perspective** ↔ **Exploration perspective**

- Central control ↔ Local autonomy
- Strong culture ↔ New learning
- Managing to plans ↔ Managing chaos
- Maintaining the *status quo* ↔ Originality in strategic thinking
- Bureaucratic culture ↔ Entrepreneurial culture
- Commercial intent ↔ Social responsibilty
- Divisional competition ↔ Corporate synergies
- Planned strategies ↔ Opportunistic strategies

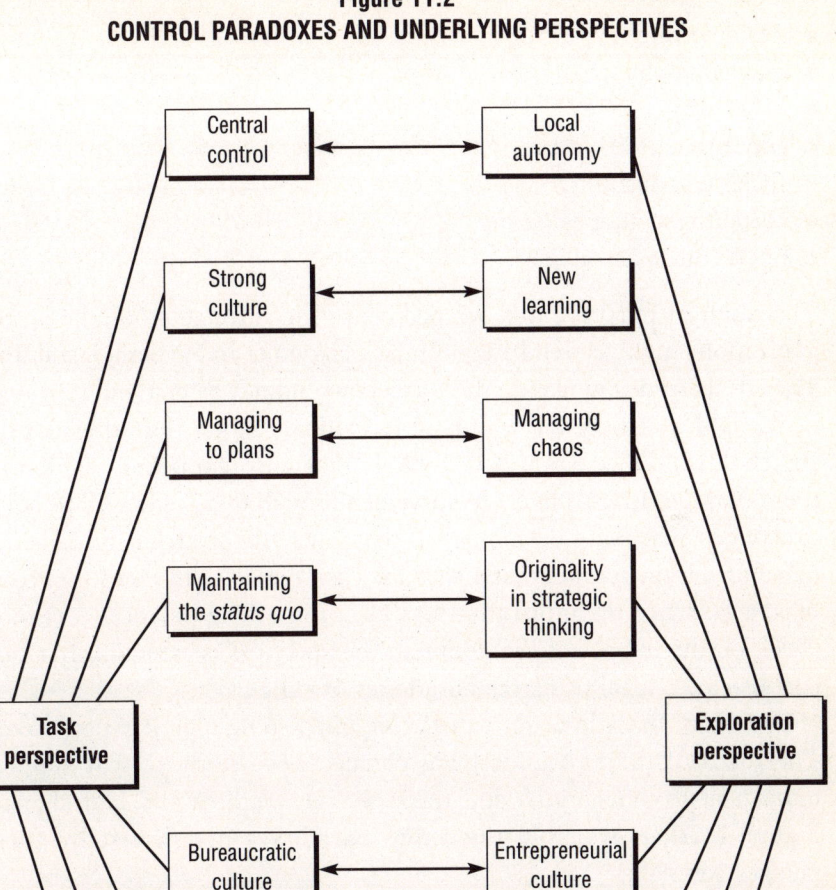

- local autonomy
- new learning
- managing chaos
- originality
- entrepreneurial culture
- social responsibility
- corporate synergies
- opportunistic strategies.

The result of pursuing this perspective to the extreme would be an organization characterized by egocentric behaviour and general instability. The effects of this would be that targets would not be met and resources being used to satisfy the whims of individuals rather than those of the stakeholders. Once again it is unlikely that an organization exhibiting these characteristics is likely to survive, although there may well be some exceptions. The point being made is that where the strategic thinking can benefit from the tension that a paradox can create, it can also suffer from bias, even when the motivation has been to strike a balance. A regular check on the impact of the dominant perspectives is essential. But bias can also arise from using the paradoxes of value.

The set of 'paradoxes of value' contained some nine key paradoxes. The focus of the two underlying perspectives are those that support management conventions and those seeking opportunity and change. Figure 11.3 shows how the value paradoxes are driven by these perspectives.

The following ideas stem from the management conventions perspective:

- cost
- local focus
- brand loyalty
- long-term vision
- market share
- incremental innovation
- focused strategies
- rules
- core competencies.

Here an over-zealous focus on this management conventions perspective would result in an organization that was characterized by its

DEVELOPING YOUR POWER AS A STRATEGIC THINKER

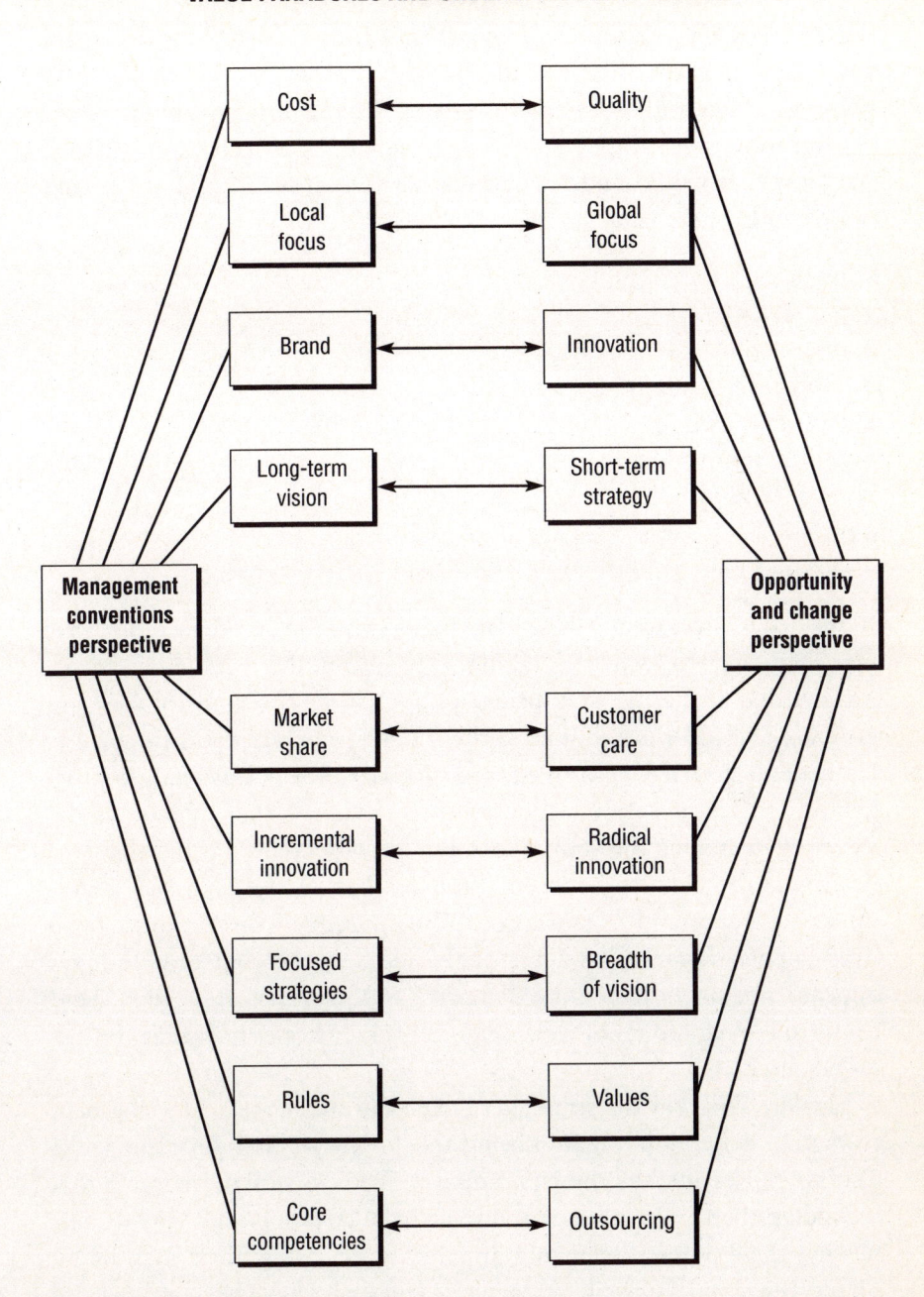

**Figure 11.3
VALUE PARADOXES AND UNDERLYING PERSPECTIVES**

| Management conventions perspective | | Opportunity and change perspective |
|---|---|---|
| Cost | ↔ | Quality |
| Local focus | ↔ | Global focus |
| Brand | ↔ | Innovation |
| Long-term vision | ↔ | Short-term strategy |
| Market share | ↔ | Customer care |
| Incremental innovation | ↔ | Radical innovation |
| Focused strategies | ↔ | Breadth of vision |
| Rules | ↔ | Values |
| Core competencies | ↔ | Outsourcing |

239

determination to avoid risk. We are using the notion of risk here in the sense of the extent to which managers are prepared to make decisions where a high level of uncertainty and ambiguity exists. Many organizations tend towards this type of characterization. But in the business world it is likely that competitors would soon take advantage of an organization that exhibited this risk avoidance approach. Alternatively, the ideas that would underpin a perspective that was based on seeking opportunity and change are listed below:

- quality
- global focus
- innovation
- short-term strategy
- customer care
- radical innovation
- breadth of vision
- values
- outsourcing.

If pursued to an extreme, these ideas would result in an organization that was characterized by its risk taking. Once again, there are many organizations that are perceived as being at this extreme and many of these are growing at rates that are above the industry averages. Gurus such as Hamel and Prahalad, Tom Peters, and many others, advocate that organizations should attract and reward individuals that operate at the extremes in arguing the above ideas. But as in all things it is the ability to determine the balance between extremes that, in the long run, determines the successful organization. The consequences that arise from over-emphasis on one or other of the ideas in the control paradoxes appear to be potentially more damaging to the organization than those found in the paradoxes of value. Figure 11.4 illustrates how these frameworks interact.

The key skill that the strategic thinker and the strategic development team need to develop is that of being able to use the multiple frameworks that are represented by these paradoxes. The next skill to master is that of finding the key paradoxes and their balance points as a way of harnessing their power. Balancing apparently opposing ideas may be an undervalued and rare skill among colleagues who have been trained and constantly exposed to the 'either . . . or' frame of reference. Some

DEVELOPING YOUR POWER AS A STRATEGIC THINKER

steadfast efforts will be required to help the strategic development team and then the wider group of managers change these traditional ways of thinking. The results may take time to appear, but will result in personal and organizational rewards. In the next chapter, we will look at how to approach this task in your own organization.

**Figure 11.4**
**PARADOXES FORM MULTIPLE FRAMEWORKS**

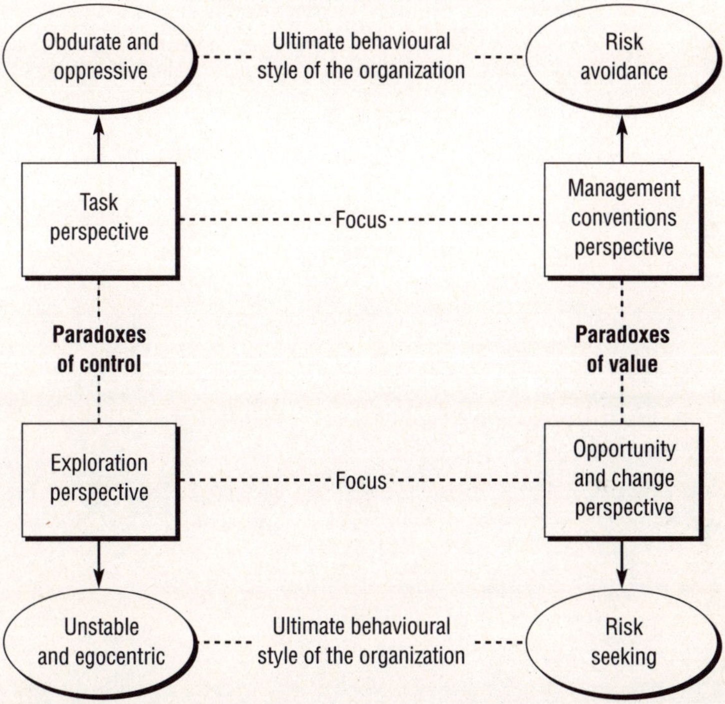

- Obdurate and oppressive —— Ultimate behavioural style of the organization —— Risk avoidance
- Task perspective —— Focus —— Management conventions perspective
- **Paradoxes of control** / **Paradoxes of value**
- Exploration perspective —— Focus —— Opportunity and change perspective
- Unstable and egocentric —— Ultimate behavioural style of the organization —— Risk seeking

# Part V

# APPLYING PARADOXICAL THINKING IN YOUR ORGANIZATION

# Chapter 12

# IMPLEMENTING A DEVELOPMENT PROGRAMME

An audit of organizational paradoxes  *248*

Workshop 1: Creating sustainable competitive advantage  *254*

Workshop 2: Implementation of strategies  *260*

Workshop 3: The scenario approach to creating new thinking  *267*

Summary  *273*

> *If a man will begin with certainties, he shall end in doubts, but if he will be content to begin with doubts, he shall end in certainties.*
>
> Francis Bacon (1561–1626)

In earlier chapters we looked at how paradoxical statements can be used in organizational conversation and in the strategy development process. The next step is to share this skill with colleagues and reap the benefits from this new way of working and thinking. You now begin to demonstrate your mastery of the power of the paradox. This will involve taking your strategy development team, or the key players in your group, through a series of developmental programmes as shown in Figure 12.1.

**Figure 12.1
THE WORKSHOP PROGRAMMES**

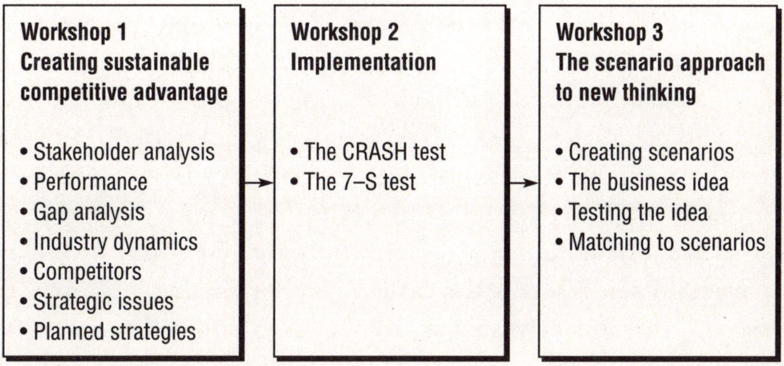

| Workshop 1<br>Creating sustainable<br>competitive advantage | Workshop 2<br>Implementation | Workshop 3<br>The scenario approach<br>to new thinking |
|---|---|---|
| • Stakeholder analysis<br>• Performance<br>• Gap analysis<br>• Industry dynamics<br>• Competitors<br>• Strategic issues<br>• Planned strategies | • The CRASH test<br>• The 7–S test | • Creating scenarios<br>• The business idea<br>• Testing the idea<br>• Matching to scenarios |

The first step is to get the team to conduct individual audits of where they would locate the balance in key organizational paradoxes. These audits will provide the underpinning for three developmental strategic workshops. The first uses conventional approaches to developing strategies that will create sustainable competitive advantage. This provides an opportunity to look at how the balances within the paradoxes impact on the thinking and outcomes. The second workshop looks at the implementation of strategies that have been identified in the first programme. Conventional approaches to doing this are again used so that the influence of the balances in the paradoxes can be identified. So far the team will have been working with existing knowledge and perspectives. The third workshop introduces the concepts behind the creation of new thinking and new knowledge. Here the scenario approach to strategic thinking will be used to extend the time horizons used by the team. The focus here will be on the longer-term strategies and perspectives required to achieve a sustainable competitive advantage. During these three workshops, the team will be developing their strategic thinking by adjusting their view of the balance points in the paradoxes. They will also be making collective decisions as to whether to:

- accept and thus live with the paradoxes;
- clarify and relocate the level at which they conceive the paradoxes to be working;
- revisit the timing, sequencing and relationships between the paradoxical ideas.

The timing of the personal audits, workshop durations and how the process is to be managed will vary according to work pressures and interest. As with all change programmes, it is important that enthusiasm and support are achieved from the start. A suggestion is that the programme sequence be introduced in the period prior to the annual strategy review. This can then be seen as preparing the ground for a review or as a new way of conducting the process. Alternatively, if the climate is right and the team are in need of a rethink of the way that they approach their work, then the programme is a natural progression. Your own experience, gained from some of the earlier exercises in the book, will have given you the confidence to introduce the programmes that are outlined below. We have therefore presented the steps and contents of the programmes which you may want to modify in the light of the particular pressures under which you are working. These programmes can be run without the aid of an external facilitator as long as you are confident about your understanding of the use of paradox that has been covered in the earlier chapters.

## AN AUDIT OF ORGANIZATIONAL PARADOXES

Members of the strategic development team are invited to complete an audit of a set of organizational paradoxes. A paradox is a statement that contains two apparently mutually exclusive ideas. Each of the ideas are in themselves perfectly viable when considered alone and would attract support. But supporting one of the ideas appears to challenge any support given to the other. An example of a paradoxical statement would be:

> *We have become a large and complex organization and we rely on the bureaucracy that we have developed to help keep track of things and overall control. But as the competition seeks out our weak spots, we must ensure that while pursuing efficiency we think and act like entrepreneurs at all levels of the business.*

The paradox hidden in this statement is that of autonomy and control. It suggests that the organization wants the benefits that come from central control and conformity, while at the same time requiring that line managers act in independent ways, as though they were entrepreneurs. Most of us would take this paradoxical statement at face value and try to live with it, some would argue that it was impractical or inappropriate, others might just see it as wishful thinking and ignore it. What you are being asked to do here is to study the list of paradoxical statements given below, then for each one to consider where you would strike a balance between the contrasting ideas. The perspective or mindset that we would like you to adopt, when doing this, is where you are considering the strategic position of the company or your division. We want you to locate the position that you would adopt when faced with having to argue for the ideas in the paradox. We will then share our findings from the audit and use this as the basis for a series of strategy development workshops.

## AUDIT

Indicate where you would strike a balance between the following paradoxical ideas, i.e., giving an indication of where you would stand if this paradox was used to frame an argument concerning the strategic emphasis in our own organization. Use the audit grid shown in Figure 12.2 to record your decisions.

1. We need to ensure greater local autonomy while ensuring that we maintain central control over key areas and decisions.

2. Our effort should be in building a strong culture and sets of processes that match our strategic direction and intent. At the same time we must recognize that our success depends on being flexible and open to new ideas and learning.

3. Setting clear goals and identifying the means of achieving them, in a controlled manner, is the key to our success. But we also need to recognize that our environment is dynamic and it is vital that we develop the skills and attitudes that thrive on managing chaos.

4. Strategic developments need to be focused on ensuring that we maintain the capabilities that we have built up over the years and continue to promote a consistent image in the marketplace. At the same time we should ensure that our strategic thinking breaks out of the tramlines and creates new ways of seeing and developing our business.

5. Institutionalizing our experiences and knowledge through procedures and processes is the key to our success. We must continue to promote this way of managing as it leads to both efficiency and effectiveness. But to ensure that we stay ahead of the competitors we need to establish a culture that rewards the entrepreneur who is able to bring in new thinking.

6. Survival and growth of the organization depend on our having a total focus on achieving our commercial goals. We need to do this within a framework of socially responsible behaviour which will satisfy all of our stakeholders.

7. The separate business divisions are required to act as independent businesses and meet their commercial targets. But at the same time we are operating as an integrated company and divisions need to support each other and seek the synergies that come from co-operation with the corporate group services.

8. The satisfaction of our major stakeholders is a paramount concern for the organization. Our strategic thinking and developments must therefore be undertaken in a planned and controlled manner. Opportunities will arise to improve our performance in the marketplace and we must ensure that our thinking and procedures are flexible enough to let us seize the advantage.

IMPLEMENTING A DEVELOPMENT PROGRAMME

## Figure 12.2
## GRID: THE PARADOX BALANCE AUDIT

| | | 3 | 2 | 1 | 0 | 1 | 2 | 3 | |
|---|---|---|---|---|---|---|---|---|---|
| 1 | Local autonomy | | | | X | | | | Central control |
| 2 | New learning | | | X | | | | | Strong culture |
| 3 | Managing chaos | | | | | X | | | Managing to plans |
| 4 | New strategic thinking | X | | | | | | | Maintaining the *status quo* |
| 5 | Entrepreneurial culture | X | | | | | | | Bureaucratic culture |
| 6 | Social responsibility | | X | | | | | | Commercial intent |
| 7 | Divisional competition | | | | X | | | | Corporate synergies |
| 8 | Opportunistic strategies | | X | | | | | | Planned strategies |
| 9 | Quality improvements | | | | | X | | | Cost reductions |
| 10 | Local focus | | | X | | | | | Global focus |
| 11 | Innovations in product and service | | | | | | X | | Intangible brand loyalty |
| 12 | Long-term vision | | | X | | | | | Short-term strategy |
| 13 | Customer care | X | | | | | | | Market share |
| 14 | Radical innovation | | | | X | | | | Incremental innovation |
| 15 | Breadth of vision | | | | | | X | | Focused strategies |
| 16 | Values | X | | | | | | | Rules |
| 17 | In-house competencies | X | | | | | | | Outsourcing core competencies |

251

9. Getting our costs down below that of our competitors is vital to our survival and growth. At the same time we need to provide our customers with a set of products and services of a quality that makes us the supplier of first choice.

10. It is imperative that we supply local markets with goods and services that meet their needs more effectively and at a lower price than those of our competitors. We can only do this if we have a global focus and seek the economies of scale and scope that can arise if we establish universal products and services.

11. Loyalty from our customers to our brand depends on their believing that we provide a consistent and reliable set of benefits. Many of these benefits are intangible and therefore difficult for our competitors to imitate. But we also need to ensure that our products and services incorporate a continuing stream of improvements and innovative features. In this way we will outperform our strongest competitors.

12. Short-term strategies are vital to our continuing success. Achieving profitability targets, cash flow requirements and sales forecasts are just a few of the measures that our strategies are aimed at supporting. Longer-term thinking is the area where our strategic thinkers make their contribution and we need to ensure that they have an influence over our current business direction.

13. Our initial demand for market growth depends on being able to offer customers higher perceived value at a cost that is lower than that of the competitors. To do this we need volume and a set of strategies that focus on efficiency in all parts of our value chain. This includes procurement through to after sales service. We also need to introduce strategies that will help us to retain our market share by noting and responding to the particular and changing requirements of our customers.

14. Business success depends on everyone in the organization looking for ways of improving the way things are done. Our strategies need to support this incremental improvement approach as this will maximize our operational efficiency. But we must all be aware of the need to think in radical ways in order to avoid becoming trapped in our own success. Our strategic planners and managers should therefore set up ways of capturing radical ideas and introducing them into the business.

15. Strategic development must be focused on supporting those areas of the business that are growing while helping those that are performing badly. At the same time the strategies should incorporate a breadth of vision that will create the future for the business.

16. Every organization is driven by the values, held by the power figures and influential stakeholders at one level and by the managers and workers at another. It is the combination of these values that creates the uniqueness of the business and the competitive edge. An organization depends on encapsulating these beliefs in sets of policies, procedures and rules while recognizing the need to challenge the rules with new strategic thinking.

17. The development of core competencies within the business is a key strategy for achieving sustainable competitive advantage. As the business grows, there will be a drive to outsource some of our activities and form joint ventures and alliances. Strategic developments will need to ensure that core competencies are extended to include those of our joint venture and alliance partners.

# Workshop 1
# CREATING SUSTAINABLE COMPETITIVE ADVANTAGE

This workshop will enable the strategic development team to work through the stages involved in reviewing how the organization sets about creating sustainable competitive advantage. It will highlight the sources of strategic thinking in the team.

Each stage in the programme provides an opportunity to use the power of paradoxical thinking. By framing organizational ideas as a paradox and establishing a dialogue as to where the balance has been struck new, strategic thinking will result. The stages are described here in outline only as it is not the intention that you should adopt a new way of approaching strategic development. But the reader can be confident that the outline programme can be used to run the workshop. The purpose of the workshop is therefore to:

- help the strategic development team to review their strategic thinking on how the organization creates sustainable competitive advantage.
- provide an opportunity to experiment with ways of dealing with the organizational paradoxes.
- highlight any new thinking that results from the process of framing ideas as paradoxes and engaging in dialogue.

## Stage 1: Stakeholder analysis

The team should be invited to consider which groups they consider to be the main influencers and beneficiaries from the activities of the business. This process will involve identifying:

- the key stakeholder groups
- their financial and tangible input to the business
- their intangible contribution
- their ability to co-operate, operate or act independently from the rest of the stakeholders
- how they judge or measure the performance and outcomes of the business
- their relative importance to the business in terms of their ability to influence outcomes
- their key values and beliefs.

Use the stakeholder analysis grid shown in Figure 12.3 to capture the data and impressions gained from this analysis.

IMPLEMENTING A DEVELOPMENT PROGRAMME

## Figure 12.3
## GRID: THE STAKEHOLDER ANALYSIS

|  | Stakeholder group 1 | Stakeholder group 2 | Stakeholder group 3 | Stakeholder group 4 |
|---|---|---|---|---|
| Financial and tangible inputs to the business | us | customers projects | suppliers c/supplies premises | |
| Intangible contributions | skills knowledge expertise | reputation WISPA (contact) | support | |
| Ability to co-operate and operate independently of the other stakeholders | ✓ | ✓ | ✓ | |
| How the stakeholder group judges business outcomes and overall performance | Profit | Increased revenue (and added costs) perceptions problems | Revenue from us | |
| The relative importance of the stakeholder group in terms of their ability to influence business outcomes | high | very high | medium | |
| The key values and beliefs of the stakeholder group | fun creativity problem-like | Value for money | rural smaller stores | |

255

PART V · APPLYING PARADOXICAL THINKING IN YOUR ORGANIZATION

Some of the paradoxes that have been highlighted in the audit can be used to help frame and engage in a dialogue around the stakeholder analysis. These will include:

No. 6 – Social responsibility *versus* commercial intent
No. 7 – Divisional competition *versus* corporate synergies
No. 12 – Long-term vision *versus* short-term strategies
No. 15 – Breadth of vision *versus* focused strategies
No. 16 – Values *versus* rules

Where the team decide to use one of the above paradoxes to frame the dialogue, then the following steps should be taken:

1. Capture the relevance of the paradox and agree that its use is helpful.
2. Share the individual audit information on this paradox so that the differences in where the balance was struck can be seen.
3. Engage in the dialogue.
4. Conclude as to whether the team are able to live with the paradox now that their relative positions are understood, resolve it by considering the level at which the paradox is to be applied, resolve it by seeing the ideas as being sequential and linked.
5. Capture any new learning that the team agree has resulted from the dialogue and the analysis of the stakeholders.

## Stage 2: Current performance against plan

Here the team will be using conventional accounting metrics and financial ratios plus a mixture of other industry sector, operational and market based metrics.

They will probably make use of gap analysis techniques to find out where the business is and where it needs to get to. It is also helpful to identify the critical success factors for the business as a way of reflecting on performance measures. This work will also link back to the stakeholder analysis to confirm that satisfaction is being achieved, or otherwise.

The paradoxes that can be used to frame some of the perspectives, of the team, that are being used include:

No. 1 – Autonomy *versus* central control
No. 7 – Divisional competition *versus* corporate synergies
No. 9 – Quality improvements *versus* cost reduction
No. 10 – Local focus *versus* global focus
No. 12 – Long-term vision *versus* short-term strategies

Where the team decide to use the above paradoxes then they should follow the Steps 1 through 5 as shown in the section above. As the team become more familiar with the using these paradoxes, the power that this gives to the strategic thinking process will become increasingly obvious.

## Stage 3: Industry dynamics

This can be approached by using Porter's PEST analysis technique, remembering to focus on those aspects of the far environment that are likely to impact on the firm or that provide a business opportunity. This will also include a consideration of who the major competitors are in the market sector and how both they and overseas competitors will be influenced by these environmental factors. In analyzing these factors, it is helpful to identify the degree to which the environment is likely to change in terms of either added complexity or novel and original opportunities. Also to consider the rate at which the key factors, that will impact on the business, are changing and if the available information sources provide adequate visibility.

The paradoxes that will help frame the ideas that will arise include:

No. 2 – New learning *versus* strong culture
No. 3 – Managing chaos *versus* managing to plans
No. 4 – New strategic thinking *versus* maintaining the *status quo*
No. 7 – Divisional competition *versus* corporate synergies
No. 10 – Local focus *versus* global focus
No. 12 – Long-term vision *versus* short-term strategies
No. 14 – Radical innovation *versus* incremental innovation
No. 15 – Breadth of vision *versus* focused strategies

Once again the process that should be followed in using these paradoxes is that spelled out in Steps 1 through 5 above.

## Stage 4: Competitor strategies

The conventional technique for considering competitors is Porter's Five Force model. Most managers are familiar with this model and the need to consider the generic strategies that competitors are using, i.e., cost, focus and differentiation. Major competitors can also be profiled in terms of their objectives, resources, performance, current products and services and strategies being followed. A benchmarking study, comparing performance against competitors on factors that are critical to success in the industry, will often highlight areas where new strategic thinking is required. The use of portfolio analysis has been discredited over the past years as presenting a simplistic view of how firms formulate market-related strategies. But many managers find this helpful in highlighting the way in which the perception of competition between internal divisions as well as competitors can be captured. Forward and backward integration by competitors is also a key part of the analysis required in this area. The paradoxes that are likely to arise are:

- No. 6 — Social responsibility *versus* commercial intent
- No. 7 — Divisional competition *versus* corporate synergies
- No. 8 — Opportunistic strategies *versus* planned strategies
- No. 9 — Quality improvements *versus* cost reduction
- No. 10 — Local focus *versus* global focus
- No. 11 — Innovations in product and service *versus* intangible brand loyalty
- No. 12 — Long-term vision *versus* short-term strategies
- No. 13 — Customer care *versus* market share
- No. 14 — Radical innovation *versus* incremental innovation

Once again the process for using these paradoxes is as outlined above.

## Stage 5: Strategic issues facing the company

This stage pulls together the issues that have been identified from the previous stages. There will be issues arising from the:

- expectations and interactions of the key stakeholders;
- performance against plans and the wide range of metrics being used;
- industry dynamics and the impact from the wider environment;
- competitors' strategies and trends.

It is conventional to align these issues against a time frame and comment on their relative priority in terms of requiring attention at the corporate or operational levels. The paradoxes that are likely to arise in this summarizing activity will include:

- No. 3 — Managing chaos *versus* managing to plans
- No. 4 — New strategic thinking *versus* maintaining the *status quo*
- No. 10 — Local focus *versus* global focus
- No. 12 — Long-term vision *versus* short-term strategies
- No. 15 — Breadth of vision *versus* focused strategies

## Stage 6: Current and planned strategies

The earlier stages will have identified the key issues facing the organization and against these it is possible to evaluate current and planned strategies. Two conventional perspectives are used to conduct this evaluation. The market-positioning perspective is the more familiar approach. Here the firm is seen as having to be positioned in the marketplace to obtain a best fit of its strengths and capabilities with respect to competitors. The other perspective is described as being resource-based. Here the firm is seen as possessing a set of capabilities that have been determined by experience and the creation of tangible assets such as plant, machinery and patents. These capabilities are complemented by the expertise and skills of the workforce, and those of external alliances partners. Within these capabilities, the firm is seen as having a set of core competencies that have to be protected and renewed if the firm is to remain competitive over the longer-term. The team can use these two perspectives to determine first whether the current strategies are producing a competitive advantage, and second where new strategies are required.

The paradoxes that are likely to arise during this stage include:

- No. 2  – New learning *versus* strong culture
- No. 4  – New strategic thinking *versus* maintaining the *status quo*
- No. 7  – Divisional competition *versus* corporate synergies
- No. 8  – Opportunistic strategies *versus* planned strategies
- No. 10 – Local focus *versus* global focus
- No. 12 – Long-term vision *versus* short-term strategies
- No. 14 – Radical innovation *versus* incremental innovation
- No. 15 – Breadth of vision *versus* focused strategies
- No. 17 – In-house core competencies *versus* outsourcing core competencies

This first workshop will have achieved all of the original objectives and set the scene for the second workshop that focuses on how the implementation of the strategies should be managed.

# Workshop 2
# IMPLEMENTATION OF STRATEGIES

Implementation is often the weakest link in the strategic management process. The sense of purpose and excitement that comes from the analytical and thinking stages has passed and how to make it happen is the next challenge. Obviously any strategies that reach the implementation stage will have been tested for both feasibility and potential pay-off. But as we have seen from earlier chapters there will always be an element of uncertainty and ambiguity about the environment in which the strategies will operate. There is also the question of overlap and the relationship between strategies and the way in which they will be interpreted both within and outside of the organization.

There are two techniques that most managers are familiar with and can be used to explore these implementation issues. The first involves a review of the criteria surrounding the decision to implement a particular strategy. This requires an analysis of each strategy in terms of its clarity, risk, advantage, skills demand and help required. This is known as the 'strategy CRASH test.' The second technique or approach is the 7–S model developed at McKinsey and Company to help managers address the difficulties in implementing change. This highlights the many interconnections between the elements in an organization that have to be addressed simultaneously during the implementation process. Here the use of paradox will be paramount as many of the changes that managers are expected to embrace will present counter-intuitive propositions. Dealing with these apparently irreconcilable and intractable problems will be a major challenge. As we approach the workshop, remember that the purpose is to provide the strategic development team with an opportunity to experience the tension that framing ideas as paradoxes can create. This tension then becomes the force that will enable new thinking to take place about how to implement the strategies and to manage the on-going development of the business. The purpose of the workshop is to improve the strategic thinking capability of the team.

This workshop will enable the strategic development team to review the feasibility of implementing the strategies that were developed in Workshop 1. It will highlight potential barriers to implementation that will have to be overcome, and where attention has to be paid to the various elements involved in the translation of the strategies into policies. It is important to remember that the implementation of strategies needs to be seen as an on-going activity rather than one event with a finite outcome. The implementation process needs to incorporate this flexibility and dynamism, as events both within and outside of the organization will be changing. The degree of flexibility will depend on the structure and maturity of the industry and the vision and strategic intent of the power group.

## Stage 1: The strategy CRASH test

The team are invited to review each of the strategies that emerged from Workshop 1 in terms of their feasibility of implementation. This should be tackled by allocating a simple percentage score against each of the criteria listed in the grid shown in Figure 12.4. The objective is to draw out the perspectives, on implementation, held by the team members.

The paradoxes highlighted in the audit should be used to frame the arguments and promote a dialogue. The process used in Workshop 1 to do this is repeated here for convenience.

1. Capture the relevance of the paradox and agree that its use is helpful.
2. Share the individual audit information on this paradox so that the differences in where the balance was struck can be seen. Note that Workshop 1 may have resulted in individuals changing the point at which their balance was struck. Also the resolution of the paradox that the team agreed may need to be revisited as the context and level at which the paradox is being applied may have changed.
3. Engage in the dialogue.
4. Conclude whether the team are able to live with the paradox now that their relative positions are understood, resolve it by considering the level at which the paradox is to be applied, and by seeing the ideas as being sequential and linked.
5. Capture any new learning that the team agree has resulted from the dialogue and the analysis.

### Criterion 1: Clarity

Is the strategy coherent in that it follows from a proposition and analysis that can be readily communicated and understood? It should be consistent with the purpose of the organization and be easily seen as being directed at meeting the requirements of the key stakeholders. The strategy should be based on addressing key issues in the environment that have a longer-term influence on the business and not simply tactical. The strategy should be easily linked to the vision and strategic intent of the organization and likely to be supported over sufficient time to realize tangible results in spite of setbacks and barriers – in effect a clear, supportable and robust strategy. The dialogue that will arise from the attempt to agree a percentage score against this criterion can be helped by using all of the paradoxes highlighted in the audit. This is to be expected and makes the point that we have argued earlier that the ideas captured in these paradoxes represent the dynamics of the organization. The team may wish to decide which of the paradoxes to use, in framing their ideas, or to use the following as a guide.

## Figure 12.4
## GRID: EVALUATING IMPLEMENTATION STRATEGIES

| Criterion | Percentage score for each strategy identified in Workshop 1 | Commentary |
|---|---|---|
| Clarity | | |
| Risk | | |
| Advantage | | |
| Skills | | |
| Help | | |

# IMPLEMENTING A DEVELOPMENT PROGRAMME

    No. 1   – Autonomy *versus* central control
    No. 2   – New learning *versus* strong culture
    No. 7   – Divisional competition *versus* corporate synergies
    No. 12 – Long-term vision *versus* short-term strategies
    No. 14 – Radical innovation *versus* incremental innovation
    No. 15 – Breadth of vision *versus* focused strategies
    No. 17 – In-house competencies *versus* outsourcing core competencies

**Criterion 2: Risk**

Risk is an over-used word in business, and we are using it here strictly in the sense of the timing of the strategy. In particular the extent to which other competing events, both within and outside of the organization, are likely to influence the success of the launch, initial survival and outcome of the strategy. We are assuming that the strategy is aimed at a longer time horizon than the immediate budget year. But the reality is that it will be interpreted and therefore influenced and managed against a range of current activities. The question therefore is the extent to which the team feel that the strategy is at risk due to these short-term pressures. The following paradoxes can be used to frame the team dialogue.

    No. 3   – Managing chaos *versus* managing to plans
    No. 4   – New strategic thinking *versus* maintaining the *status quo*
    No. 7   – Divisional competition *versus* corporate synergies
    No. 8   – Opportunistic *versus* planned strategies
    No. 10 – Local focus *versus* global focus
    No. 12 – Long-term vision *versus* short-term strategies
    No. 13 – Customer care *versus* market share
    No. 14 – Radical innovation *versus* incremental innovation

**Criterion 3: Advantage**

Here we are considering the contribution that the strategy is likely to make to the sustainable competitive advantage of the business. The work in the first workshop will have resulted in strategies that are aimed at achieving advantage, but their success will depend on many factors. What we are evaluating here is the degree to which the team feel that external and internal factors will be overcome or can be leveraged to advantage. For example, competitors will react more vigorously to some strategies than others. Also the vested interests and the competing targets that managers are working to within the organization will have an impact on the direction and success of each strategy. Once again all of the paradoxes highlighted in the audit can be used to frame the dialogue. As a guide the following may be used as a focus.

No. 1  – Autonomy *versus* central control
No. 5  – Entrepreneurial culture *versus* bureaucratic culture
No. 7  – Divisional competition *versus* corporate synergies
No. 12 – Long-term vision *versus* short-term strategies
No. 14 – Radical innovation *versus* incremental innovation
No. 17 – In-house core competencies *versus* outsourcing core competencies

## Criterion 4: Skills

This will involve the team in an evaluation of the skills which the organization needs in order to implement the strategy. The word 'skills' is being used in its widest sense and embraces the total capability required for success. This would include the management expertise, the knowledge base, the resources both human, financial and physical, the skills and expertise and, if appropriate, the network of outside alliances and partners. The paradoxes that can be used here include:

No. 2  – New learning *versus* strong culture
No. 7  – Divisional competition *versus* corporate synergies
No. 10 – Local focus *versus* global focus
No. 14 – Radical innovation *versus* incremental innovation
No. 16 – Values *versus* rules
No. 17 – In-house core competencies *versus* outsourcing core competencies

## Criterion 5: Help

This final evaluation concerns the extent to which the success of the implementation depends on gaining help from within the organization and from outside. The help can take the form of internal groups sharing knowledge and resources, the corporate group protecting the implementation activity from any short-term demands and set backs. The outside help would take the form of stakeholders, regulators and network partners. What the team are evaluating is the degree to which this help will be available when required. Paradoxes that would help frame the dialogue include:

No. 1  – Autonomy *versus* central control
No. 5  – Entrepreneurial culture *versus* bureaucratic culture
No. 6  – Social responsibility *versus* commercial intent
No. 10 – Local focus *versus* global focus
No. 12 – Long-term vision *versus* short-term strategies
No. 14 – Radical innovation *versus* incremental innovation

During the workshop it is important to check the extent to which the underlying perspectives of the team, are influencing the thinking. Also any new learning that has arisen from reviewing the balance points and resolution of the paradoxes should be captured explicitly.

## Stage 2: Using the 7-S model

(Adapted from the basic model attributable to R.H.Waterman, Jr.)

Here the team are invited to consider the strategies that were generated from Workshop 1, using those that are still seen as viable following the evaluation process. These strategies will contain a mix of requirements and resources at the implementation stage and an environment that is supportive. There are six key features of the internal organization that need to be considered. The team may consider that these areas need management attention in order to reflect the strategic intention. Alternatively the team may decide that it is more appropriate to modify the strategies. At this stage in the development programme, the team will be very familiar with the use of the paradoxes identified in the original audits. Hence no explicit references are made to them in the following programme. Here are the six key features.

- **Structure**: The team should explore the extent to which the organizational structure and the way in which tasks are allocated and divided support the strategies. Potential barriers need to be identified and change requirements highlighted.
- **Systems**: Here the team consider the formal and informal systems used to direct and control the business. Focusing on areas where these systems will be expected to provide the information flows, evaluation and control points that are required to support the implementation of the strategies.
- **Style**: The way that the management is perceived as currently behaving needs to be explored. Strategies that call for a change to the behavioural style have to be identified. The team then need to consider the extent and feasibility of the changes that are required.
- **Staff**: The team need to understand the mechanisms that are in place to reward, motivate and train staff. The strategies may demand different skill sets to be brought together and ways of working changed.
- **Skills**: This has been considered in earlier workshops, but it is worth revisiting. The aim here is for the team to understand the range of skills required for implementation of the strategies and the extent to which these are available. An audit of how skills and expertise are applied to existing strategies may give an indication of where these allocation systems need to be changed. Outsourcing those skills which are not seen as core to the business can be considered only once this audit has been completed.
- **Shared values**: This is a key area for the team to understand. There will already exist an underlying set of shared values within different sectors of the organization. These values will drive the response and support to any planned changes. Where the strategies being considered represent a major change, then it is likely that attention has to be paid to the values that exist and how far they can be expected to change.

## PART V · APPLYING PARADOXICAL THINKING IN YOUR ORGANIZATION

Obviously many of the ideas that will arise from the dialogue around these issues will have been framed as paradoxes. This will have helped the strategic development team arrive at a shared understanding of the relative importance of these organizational factors. The skill required is then to be able to use this new understanding to either change the strategies or to influence the perceptions of others.

## Workshop 3
## THE SCENARIO APPROACH TO CREATING NEW THINKING

In earlier chapters we saw how the gurus and the practitioners within leading companies have focused on improving the strategic thinking capability of senior managers. One approach that has been used by companies such as the Royal Dutch Shell is that of scenario planning. The approach can be used by the strategic development team to enhance the richness of their strategic conversation. It will also provide an additional opportunity to harness the power of paradox in developing new strategic thinking.

The concept behind scenario planning is quite straightforward. It involves the identification of areas in the future environment of the business where the managers feel a high level of uncertainty exists. This uncertainty arises because the nature, form and extent of impact of the detailed elements that make up these areas are unknown. The relationships and time sequencing of the items in these areas is also uncertain. For those teams where the identification of the future is already deeply ingrained, and understood, then this can become the starting point for thinking about alternatives and the potential impact on the business. This identification process results in the agreement of a number of future scenarios in which the business will have to operate. Each scenario is represented in the form of a plausible story that can be defended in terms of the linkages and dependencies of its elements. The stories will result from the historic understandings the managers have of the business environmental dynamics.

The three or four scenarios that are to be used should contain new and original perspectives on the business concerns and issues. The team confirm their definition of the main business idea, or ideas in a multiple business. This involves identifying how the business idea adds customer value, how competitive advantage is being pursued and how the organizational capability is configured and supported by core competencies. The business idea is then tested for robustness against the different scenarios. A robust business idea will continue to add customer value by using the planned capability and core competencies, while producing a satisfactory financial return in spite of competitors' actions. Outcomes will include a possible rethink of the business idea, a redefinition of competitive strategies, a rearrangement of capabilities and resources, a change in the ways that core competencies are managed, a change to the environmental monitoring processes and a change to the strategic thinking within the team. The team can also identify creative ways of influencing the industry and marketplace so that the scenario that most fits the business idea is eventually realized. Figure 12.5 illustrates how the scenario approach operates.

PART V · APPLYING PARADOXICAL THINKING IN YOUR ORGANIZATION

## Figure 12.5
## THE SCENARIO APPROACH

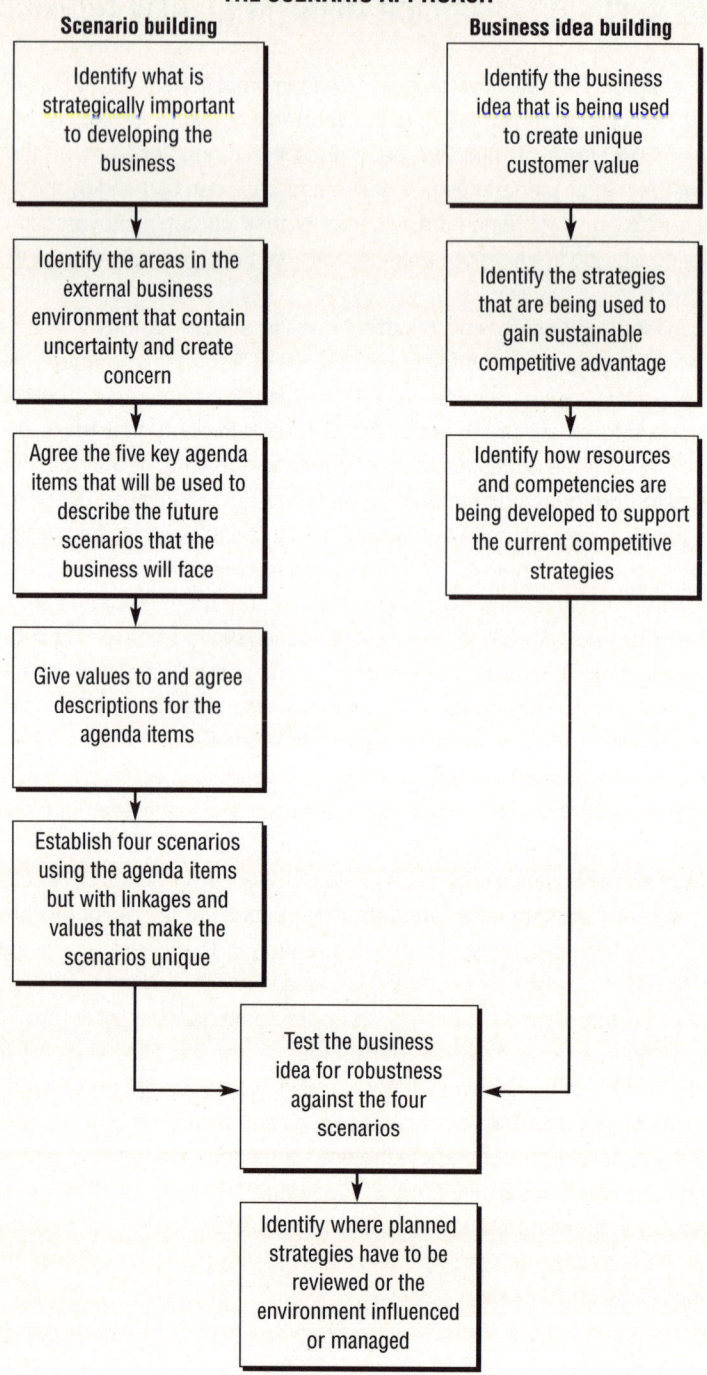

**Scenario building**

- Identify what is strategically important to developing the business
- Identify the areas in the external business environment that contain uncertainty and create concern
- Agree the five key agenda items that will be used to describe the future scenarios that the business will face
- Give values to and agree descriptions for the agenda items
- Establish four scenarios using the agenda items but with linkages and values that make the scenarios unique

**Business idea building**

- Identify the business idea that is being used to create unique customer value
- Identify the strategies that are being used to gain sustainable competitive advantage
- Identify how resources and competencies are being developed to support the current competitive strategies

- Test the business idea for robustness against the four scenarios
- Identify where planned strategies have to be reviewed or the environment influenced or managed

This workshop will provide the strategic development team with an opportunity to stretch their ability as strategic thinkers. It will focus on the definition of environmental futures, which become scenarios in which the business will have to operate. The business idea or proposition that drives the business will be defined and then tested for robustness against these scenarios, and the outcome will be an enhanced way of thinking about the strategic imperatives for the business. Throughout the workshop the team will continue to make use of the shared understanding that has been reached over the balancing of ideas within the organizational paradoxes.

## Stage 1: Describing the future scenarios

The team should be invited to complete the following tasks:

1. What are the key areas in the current external business environment that you feel most uncertain about in terms of their nature, form and likely impact on the success of the present business?

2. Using the list produced, decide which of these areas are of strategic importance to the future development of the business.

3. Define, to a level of detail that you can be confident with, the items or features that make up these areas. For example, if the area is 'the way in which the technology is developing,' then you may need to collect industry reports on technological trends or on how the technology will be usable in emerging nations, etc. The precision of your definitions will depend how important you consider it is to offer a description that would justify a consultant's report in the area. Conventional techniques of analysis such as PEST and Porter's Five Force Model may help to focus the investigation. You may also need to collect opinions and viewpoints from outside of the organization.

4. Decide on a future time horizon that will make sense to the business concerns being considered.

5. Identify four scenarios in which the business will be expected to operate in the time horizon that you have selected. This will involve taking items from the areas that you investigated, in **3** above, and arranging them into four separate sequences of linked events and dependencies. What you will be doing is building four distinct, but plausible, stories. Each of these will explain how the future will be created and can be understood. They will contain new and original perspectives and thinking. The temptation to see these as 'good' or 'bad' should be resisted. They must all be possible and likely. The differences will lie in how the story is constructed in terms of dependencies and the relative emphasis or

measures attributed to the items. This is a creative activity and should be supported by the appropriate facilities and environment.

6. Having clustered the items into the four scenarios they should be given a distinctive name so that their contents can be quickly recalled to mind. Creating a shorthand identification within the development team. This may help to institutionalize these scenarios so that they can be communicated to a wider audience at a later date.

## Stage 2: Identifying the business idea

The team should be invited to describe the basic notion that underlies the idea that the organization is pursuing in its attempt to create sustainable competitive advantage. Where the organization is a multibusiness, then the team should identify one of the businesses to explore in this workshop.

The following questions should be tackled:

1. Why should customers want to do business with us as opposed to our competitors?
2. What do we have to be good at in order to continue to attract these customers?
3. How do we set out to create customer added value?
4. What competitive advantage do we use and are we effectively exploiting that advantage?
5. What distinctive competence do we have over our competitors, and how are we exploiting, developing and protecting this competence?
6. What are the key strategies being used to develop and grow the business?

## Stage 3: Testing the business idea

Here the team are invited to test the business idea against the four scenarios that have been described in Stage 1 above. The following questions should be used.

1. Will the added value that the business is providing for the customer be sustainable in each of the scenarios?
2. Which of the scenarios most fits our added value approach and why is this so?
3. Will our current capability and core competence be relevant in each of the four scenarios?
4. Which of the scenarios most fits our capability arrangements and core competencies and why is this so?
5. Are our growth strategies sustainable and appropriate in each of the four scenarios?
6. Which of the scenarios most fits our strategic mix and why is this so?

7. Which of the four scenarios seems to be the most likely one to form a fit with our business idea and the strategies being pursued?
8. Which are the most influential items in those scenarios and what has to be done to ensure that we monitor developments and ensure that these items take the form that suits the organization?
9. How can this be achieved?

The evaluation grid can be used to match the business idea to the scenarios (see Figure 12.6).

## Stage 4: New thinking and the use of paradox

In using the scenario approach, the team will have revised their view of the strategies being used to fit the business to the future. These views need to be raised to the explicit level and used to influence others in the organization. It is also important to communicate these new ways of seeing the business using the scenarios that have been developed. Other managers in the organization should be invited to share these through the use of stories and anecdotes, building scenario thinking into the organizational conversation. The ways in which the paradoxes were used to frame the discussion also need to be captured. The team will have become very adept at using the strength of the paradox and striking new balance points within the ones they offer. The team should now be using this approach in their wider dealings within the organization as a first step at transferring the skills.

## Figure 12.6
## GRID: MATCHING THE BUSINESS TO SCENARIOS

| Sustainability of: | Scenario 1 | Scenario 2 | Scenario 3 | Scenario 4 | Reasons |
|---|---|---|---|---|---|
| Added value | | | | | |
| Capability and competence | | | | | |
| Growth strategies | | | | | |
| Strategy mix | | | | | |
| Best fit | | | | | |
| Key items | | | | | |

# SUMMARY

In this section we have taken an initial look at how to apply paradoxical thinking in your organization. Organizational conversations problem solving and decision making are areas where it can be effectively applied. But more particularly we have looked at where it can accelerate the ability of teams to think strategically and create new and original thinking. Earlier work on constructing and finding the balance points within the paradox created the base for this section. The organizational audit of paradoxes used by the strategic development team began to highlight differences in perception and emphasis. The importance of raising these differences above the tacit level so that an open dialogue could take place was highlighted. The paradox audit made this possible.

It was also important to take the team into a situation where the power of the paradoxical approach could be harnessed to the business. Workshop 1, that looked at how the organization approaches the creation of sustainable competitive advantage, gave such an opportunity. Following a conventional strategic analysis and evaluation process provided a familiar environment for this to happen in. Emphasis was placed on getting the team to explore the application of specific paradoxes to each stage in the process in order to highlight their use, the aim being to implant a discipline rather than suggesting a formula type of approach to using paradoxes. The difficulty of turning strategies into implementable programmes was addressed, and outlined in Workshop 2. The CRASH test and the standard McKinsey 7–S model were used to allow the members of the strategic development team to have free rein over the use of the paradox approach. Finally an opportunity to harness the power that comes from the tension in paradox was provided in Workshop 3. The scenario approach was used to help the team create views of likely futures for the business and how the current and planned strategies would define these futures. This is a key area for the strategic thinker where new and original ways of seeing the future in relation to the emerging business provide opportunities for the creation of new knowledge. The team will by now have become quite sophisticated in the way that they use paradoxical approaches in both formal and informal settings. The power of paradox in strategic thinking has now been secured.

# EPILOGUE

The central theme of this book is that successful organizations are becoming increasingly reliant on being able to create new knowledge – at the same time it is imperative that they make best use of the old. Living with that paradox represents an enormous challenge for all organizations and cultures. But it is the capacity and spirit to clarify and manage the inherent tension that this creates in our lives that differentiates the winners from the rest. The struggle to be the best depends on the way in which success is counted and who is evaluating the benefits. External stakeholder satisfaction, as always, will be a key measure of this success, whereas when we look inside the organization, the measurement and evaluation becomes much more complex. The tensions quickly become apparent even to the most intrepid manager.

By focusing on the way paradoxical statements are used, in organizational conversation and debate, we gain an insight into how these internal tensions can be harnessed. The contemporary, and seductive, style that highlights opposites, and then argues for one or the other is deeply ingrained in the management psyche. But uncertainty and ambiguity in situations represent the new pay-offs that are ahead rather than the harbingers of disaster. They indicate the new Klondike for those organizations that are seeking fame and fortune. Tapping into conflicting ideas that are presented in the form of paradoxical statements will provide the enquiring strategic thinker with a breakthrough approach that will revitalize and inspire existing approaches to developing strategies.

Perhaps we can be accused of underestimating the challenge and difficulties that this approach represents. Not everyone is able to articulate and deconstruct paradoxical statements. Discovering which ideas are stemming from deeply held values and knowledge, when facing managers in a discussion, requires skill, stamina and persistence. The natural process is reversed. Rather than trying to win the argument, we are faced with opening up and exploring positions that are held, using our new understanding as a source of strength and power rather than seeing it as a threat. Managers all operate from positions of vested interest. No-one approaches their work from a value free or neutral position.

Managers are at best seen as territorial, at worst paranoiac, and the tensions that abound are often dissipated in attempting to win what are essentially internal battles. Our contention is that this naturally occurring tension must be harnessed to promote the new thinking that will result in sustainable competitive advantage for the organization.

Given the increasing dynamism in the business and social environment, the role of the leader and the strategic thinkers becomes even more critical to survival. Managers are increasingly being exhorted not only to manage the opposition but to construct and influence the future itself. Managing the future and living on the edge have become almost a management credo for the new millennium. The strategist no longer has the luxury of simply relying on amassing research data and performance figures, based on historic deeds, to forecast the future and how to get there. The game is much too complex and important to leave it to this soothsayer mentality. Repackaging old knowledge or getting new knowledge from the outside consultants will be an option whose half-life will soon be counted in months rather than years. We have to utilize the tensions that dialogue and debate create and harness this to our ability to create new organizational and hence strategic thinking. The use of the paradox gives us the key to this treasure chest of organizational wealth. It will take nerve and perseverance for the strategic thinker who wants to challenge the organizational management paradigm that worships opposites. Winning will, in the future, be about harnessing these tensions, calling on the skills of the ancient mariners who utilized the forces of nature and harnessed these to the skills of the crew and the purpose of the ship. The metaphors for understanding organizations are the paradoxes that are used and the benefits come from harnessing their latent power – not arguing over which idea should win. The voyage becomes the purpose, rather than the purpose determining the voyage.

# INDEX

Adding value 33, 126
Alexander, Marcus 34, 132
Ambiguity in information 64
Ansoff, Igor 16, 125
Argyris, Christopher 155
Asea Brown Boveri 134, 154
Auditing paradoxes 248
Avon 198, 205

Banc One 68, 134
Bartlett, Christopher 50
Bounded rationality 76
Breakpoint effect 25, 100
British Airways 108
British Petroleum 134
BTR 134
Business
   Developing new 19
   The lexicon of 103
Business growth
   Directions for 16, 96
   Innovations in 203
   Venturing as a form of 19
Business idea 270

Cadbury Schweppes 134
Campbell, Andrew 34, 132
Canon 134
Capabilities 110, 189
Chaos 59, 128
Coca-Cola 45, 129
Competitive advantage 77, 117, 166, 189, 254
Competition
   Analyzing the 16
   Market and resource based views of 9
   National and global 26
   Recipes for beating the 99

Conglomerates 33
Core competencies 10, 95, 110
Corporate group
   Entrepreneurship within the 175, 188, 222
   Governance by the 31
Corporate strategy
   Determining generic 172, 187
   Renewal as 70
   Social consciousness through 40
Courtaulds 134
CRASH test 261
Creativity and unstructured problems 159
Critical success factors 111

Dialogue in organizations 83, 164
Double-loop learning 155

Economies of scale and scope 52
Economic integration 46
Empowerment in organizations 66, 68
Entrepreneurs 20, 98
Entrepreneurship at corporate level 19, 175, 188
Evaluation of strategies 262

Ford Motor Company 97

GEC 134
General Motors 32, 151
Geus Arie 137
Ghoshal, Sumantra 50
Global paradox 151
Goold, Michael 34, 132

Hamel, Gary 67, 109, 130, 131
Hanson 134

Heijden, Kees 137
Honda 140

IBM 88, 151

ICI 134
Industry
  Foresight within an 109
  Dynamics within 257
Innovation
  Continuous and incremental 24
  Focus on 23
  Implementation of strategies and 69
  Radical 71, 99
Intuition
  Reliance on 11
  Linking analysis and 54

Knowledge
  Explicit and tacit 79, 139
  Leveraging 16
  Using dialogue to create new 83

Learning
  Short-term adaptability in 83
  Single- and double-loop 91, 155
  Styles of corporate 132
Leveraging
  Building global knowledge through 170, 185
  Resource 48
Levi 45
Levicki, Cyril 108
Logic as a source of power 64, 158

Market positioning 94, 113
Matsushita 36, 109
McKinsey 7–S 265
Mental images held by managers 79
Metaphors used in organizations 14, 140
Mintzberg, Henry 127
Mission 108
Models
  Cascading of 18

Generalization of 11
Hard and soft data used in 11
Process based 15
Use of meta 14
Motorola 70
Multiple frameworks used in organizations 241

Naisbitt, John 151
Nike 192
Nonaka, Ikujiro 139

Ohmae, Kenichi 131
Organization
  Audit of paradoxes in an 248
  Development of an 69
  Development of the mind of an 91
  Dialogue in 164
  Dynamic aspects of 81, 101
  Language as 105
Ownership 31, 38, 47

Paradigms in organizations 195, 202
Paradox
  Accepting the 208
  Clarifying the levels of a 210
  Consensus and differences in 153
  Constructing and deconstructing a 165, 191
  Definition of a 150
  Dilemma as a contrast to 42
  Global 151
  Harnessing the tension in a 153
  Timing and sequence in a 211
  Underlying perspectives of a 235
  Use in argument of the 151
Paradoxes
  Auditing organizational 248
  Autonomy *versus* control 226
  Building a strong culture *versus* new learning 227
  Core competencies *versus* outsourcing 234
  Cost *versus* quality 230

# INDEX

Customer care *versus* market share 232
Divisional competition *versus* corporate synergies 229
Empowerment *versus* control 66
Entrepreneurial *versus* bureaucratic culture 228
Focused strategies *versus* breadth of vision 233
Incremental *versus* radical innovation 232
Local focus *versus* global focus 230
Long-term vision *versus* short-term strategy 231
Loyalty to the brand *versus* loyalty to innovation 231
Managing clear objectives *versus* managing chaos 227
Originality in strategic thinking *versus* maintaining the status quo 80, 227
Planned strategy *versus* opportunistic strategy 229
Social responsibility *versus* commercial intent 228
Thinking *versus* planning 56
Values *versus* rules 233
Parenting advantage 34, 132
Pepsi Cola 10
Peters, Thomas 128, 154
Philips 151
Planning
  Strategy as 75
  Thinking as 56
Porter's Diamond 49
Porter, Michael 126
Portfolio management 113
Positional power 157
Positioning as a strategy 179, 189
Prahalad, C.K. 67, 109, 130, 131
Premise
  Dealing with the 64
  Use of a 158
Pursuit of excellence 76

Quinn, James 127

Rational choices in strategy making 124
Revolution as organizational change 96
Rhetoric in argument 64
Risk in managing investment 46
RTZ 134

Satisficing behaviour 124
Schön, D.A. 155
Scenario planning 55, 137, 267
Semler, Ricardo 68, 98
Senge, Peter 135
Shell International Petroleum Co Ltd 134, 137
Simon, Herbert 123
Sloan, Alfred 97
Stakeholders
  Analysis of 38, 254
  Power of 39
  Pressure from 76
Strategy making
  Large corporation 33
  Opportunism in 13
  The impact of international perspectives on 45, 48
  Planning as 75
Strategy as stretch 193, 201
Strategies
  Characteristics of successful 66
  Competitor driven 257
  Corporate driven 19
  Focused 166, 183
  Globalization of 45
  Implementation of 260
  Intent of 78, 109, 130, 181, 190
  Resource based 94
  The leader as an initiator of 99
Strategic thinking
  Anomalies and 224
  Developing your powers of 219
  Flexibility in the styles of top team 134

279

    Hard data in 56
    Innovation in 23
    Impact of language on 114
    Management activity as 78

Takeuchi, Hirotaka 139
Tarmac 134
Tension
    Paradox and 149
    Use of 153
Thinking
    Learning from strategic 23
    Levels of 19, 78, 139

    New organizational 271
    Paradoxical 248
    Planning as 56
    Sources of 114

Uncertainty in planning 64, 82
Unilever 36, 134

Value chains 51, 111
Vision building 108, 129, 168, 184

Wack, Pierre 137
Wal Mart 129